Stop the Merry-Go-Round
Stories of Women Who Broke the Cycle of Abusive Relationships

Stop
the
Merry-Go-Round
Stories of Women Who Broke the Cycle of Abusive Relationships

Milton S. Trachtenburg
ACSW, CAC

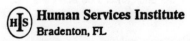

Human Services Institute
Bradenton, FL

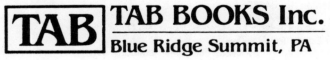 TAB BOOKS Inc.

Blue Ridge Summit, PA

Library of Congress Cataloging-in-Publication Data

Trachtenburg, Milton.
    Stop the merry-go-round : stories of women who broke the
cycle of abusive relationships / by Milton S. Trachtenburg.
        p.   cm.
    1. Adult child abuse victims—Case studies. 2. Women—
Mental health—Case studies. I. Title.
    RC569.5.C55T73   1989
    616.85′822—dc20   89-20288
    ISBN 0-8306-8007-1 (pbk.)   CIP

TAB BOOKS Inc. offers software for sale. For information and a catalog, please
contact TAB Software Department, Blue Ridge Summit, PA 17294-0850.

Questions regarding the content of this book should be addressed to:

Human Services Institute, Inc.
P.O. Box 14610
Bradenton, FL 34280

Development Editor: Lee Marvin Joiner, Ph.D.
Copy Editor: Pat Holliday
Cover photograph by Susan Riley, Harrisonburg, VA.

Contents

PRELUDE

I'm in great shape, aren't I?
I hate men and I don't trust women.

Sometimes I Hear Voices

Sometimes I hear voices. I'm a therapist, and the voices I hear haunt my nights—and sometimes even my days. The voices I hear contain a litany of pain and anguish. Sometimes they rip through me and need to be set free. So, I write. I speak in the voices I have heard—the voices of those who have shared their pain and anguish with me. In this book, I will share some of the voices with you. I have fictionalized the names of the participants to protect their privacy, but the facts are altered only enough to ensure anonymity.

By presenting a self-help book in the form of a dialogue, between therapist and patient, I hope to help the reader identify with the women who have overcome the problems created in their dysfunctional homes. I believe that this presentation will enable the reader to get in touch with her own feelings—a necessary component of change.

I have chosen to use the pseudonym Robert Sand when referring to the therapist in these stories. I found it more comfortable writing about him as though he were someone else. The stories of these women need to be told. They remained silent long enough. I will speak for some of them, and others will speak for themselves. All of the voices are those of abused women. Perhaps in the sharing, someone may come to care, or develop a desire to change something. Listen! Perhaps their courage will allow you to tell the things you cannot tell . . .

I was abused by my mother when I was a child. I was abused by my husband as an adult. I abused myself with drugs and alcohol. I abused myself by having sex for money, or with men who had no love for me. It felt right at the time because I had no love for myself—I still don't. I feel unworthy. I want to hurt somebody. I hate myself. I take my anger out on my children. I destroy friendships through my anger and insecurity. I run to sick men to seek comfort. I don't know who I am. I cover it all up with jokes and smiles and assurances that—hey, I'm okay today—I didn't pick up a drink or a drug. I can't stop the pain. I'm thirty-three years old and still suck my thumb and play with a piece of satin to try to make myself feel better. I'm in great shape, aren't I? I hate men and I don't trust women. Sometimes, I even resent my kids just because they are there and I want to be alone, or I want to go out and have fun.

I have this friend. He tells me I'm special and I have all kinds of good qualities. When he says those things to me, sometimes I just want to rip his face off. Doesn't he know how much I want to believe those words, but inside I know it's a crock and he's gonna be just like the others and want something back from me? Maybe if I shut my eyes, he will disappear.

I think I'm gonna be okay soon. See, there's this guy I met. He makes me feel great. He really turns me on. Maybe if we get it on, I can forget my pain and feel good for a little while. I have to keep it my secret though. Too much to lose if I open my mouth because everybody will tell me I'm not ready for a relationship. What do they know, anyway?

I have heard those words so many times, words of pain, bitterness, distrust, rage, fear, hopelessness and, most devastating of all, denial. The previous paragraphs are but an excerpt from one of the stories in this book, the story of Leslie. I chose to tell stories which portray successful therapeutic encounters because this is a book about hope and change, not about the agony which preceded them. Change begins by adopting a belief that things can be different——and better. The rest is hard work. Sometimes, I use simple formulas to demonstrate a philosophy of change to clients. One such formula is $R = GI/PE$. Translated, the formula means that: *Recovery equals Good Intentions over Painful Efforts*. The key elements are desire for a positive outcome and acceptance that change is a painful process which is, nonetheless, worth the effort.

The most difficult thing to write about is something that you despise. Hate blinds you to reality and objectivity. I am totally intolerant of the abuse of women. I have decided to write about abused women, not because it is something from which I might derive some satisfaction in the telling, but because the abuse of women is so pervasive in our society. If I can, through this telling, enable one woman to take some positive action in her own behalf, then I shall have performed a service which I consider valuable. In writing about abused women, I am not denying that men are also abused. I am restricting this writing to the abuse of women because the consequences of the abuse, which are shaped by society's attitudes and remedies, are vastly different for men and women. When men are abused as children, they often become abusers. Women abused as children tend to remain victims in their adult relationships.

It is not my purpose to write a textbook with theories and numbers. Instead, I hope that the stories about abused women which I am sharing will enable the reader to gain a better understanding of how an abusive family pattern develops, and how it affects the later life of the child who was the primary victim. The storytelling method allows the reader to gain insight into both the feelings of the victims of abuse as well as some of the changes they underwent in their journeys to recovery. I have learned that there are few total villains in the real world. Often, the perpetrators of abuse were themselves abused as children, or are still being abused as adults. This is not to make excuses for them. I only want to shed light upon the reasons behind their behaviors. There is no excuse that would stand up to a test of reason. The perpetrators have choices, too.

I'm a therapist, a male therapist, who works predominantly with abused women. I try to accept that there are some things which my gender may prevent me from understanding. At the same time, I know enough not to say things like, "I'm here to help you." That is condescending and demeaning. If I accept that no one can help *me*—I do not enjoy feeling like the recipient of help—I can also accept that any individual, male or female, wants to feel empowered and independent. This is especially true of abused women who have had all or part of their power over their own minds and bodies forcibly taken from them.

The stories I will share with you are all true. The women about whom I write are all now part of me through our connectedness during their therapeutic journeys. Some of their pain has become my pain. Perhaps through this telling, I can relieve it to some degree. Sometimes, I want to shout out in the rage which they could not express. However, they are the ones who must learn to express their rage and hurt so that they can invoke their own process of change. I'm lucky. I was never abused within the context of my family. Perhaps that is why I have been able to serve as a conduit for the pain of others. I have room to store it—temporarily.

The dialogue in the stories is from my memory rather than a verbatim recording of the actual words spoken in the treatment. The details of the women's lives are altered somewhat so that they cannot be identified by others.

Many of my former clients have chosen to maintain contact with me over the years and I have had the privilege of seeing them grow into healthy, productive, self-directed human beings. Some have entered new and positive relationships. Others have maintained independence and feel that their needs are best met without a life partner, at least for the present.

I write in the hope that some of the insights, which were developed by each of us through pain and tears, might help the reader examine his or her life to determine if he or she might be the victim or perpetrator of abuse in a relationship with another person. The title, *Stop the Merry-Go-Round*, was chosen because abuse, like a contagious disease, can be passed on from individual to individual and from generation to generation. Like a merry-go-round, abuse ends only when you stop the cycle by getting off.

Each story presents a different aspect of abuse. Through the progress of each woman, we can examine how each developed the values and attitudes which ensured she would remain in an abusive relationship as an adult. Through the insights gained, both in therapy and in new life situations, we can also look at some of the steps taken to invoke permanent, stable change. Three of the women were abused emotionally and physically in their childhood. The fourth was abused sexually as well. The fifth was more neglected than abused, but through her parents' failure to see her as a person, she, too grew to adulthood without the necessary tools to pick a healthy mate or to see herself in a positive light. Each went on to either pick abusive partners or subject themselves to abuse through self-destructive behaviors. Each finally made remarkable progress toward developing a balanced life.

If I can make one conclusion before I begin . . . It occurs to me that conclusions are usually reserved for the end, but in this case, I feel that it is so important that it should be stated right at the beginning. I want to advise the reader that the most powerful ally of abusive people is the silence of their victim. If you are the victim of abuse, you need to know:

Help is available.
  No one can do it alone.
    First you have to believe that you are worthy of
    better than this!
    Become indignant.
      Tell and tell and tell . . .

LESLIE

I'm afraid to share my story with you.
I don't want you to hate me for what I've done.

Inner Truths

I Don't Need Help to Feel Bad

"How did it happen? Sometimes, I have trouble remembering the events of my life. Robert, my therapist, helps me open up lost regions of my past. It hurts so much. I want to get better, but sometimes I'm more afraid of the pain of the past than of the pain I create for myself today. I'm afraid to share my story with you. I don't want you to hate me for what I've done."

When I asked Leslie if she would share her life with you, I knew there would still be pain. I told her many months ago that coming from a dysfunctional family is like swallowing fish hooks. Sometimes, fish hooks hurt even more coming out than going in. Leslie has worked in therapy and in her life to remove many of the "barbs" which made her life so chaotic and so painful. After a particularly difficult encounter in her therapy, she and I sometimes joke that maybe the hook that just came out was a harpoon and it will get easier after this. Her life is becoming increasingly full and whole, but a lifetime of rejection, abuse, self-abuse, negative self-concepts, and lack of real nurturance, takes a long time to overcome. Maybe it really isn't that long a time, but when you are in pain, it sure seems to be.

Leslie didn't portray a very pretty picture of herself the first day in individual therapy. Her words expressed some of the negative feelings which eight months earlier had brought her into my group for abused women. I sometimes wish that she had been able to see herself through my eyes back then. As Leslie's therapist, I felt from the beginning that she had the potential to become a remarkably special woman—if she was willing to deal with the issues which shaped her life into the chaos it had become.

It is difficult to convey to you what I saw when I sat with her at the start of our therapeutic journey. She would show her dark side first, because after thirty-three years of pain—inflicted first by others, and later by herself—she feared that everything that happened would be negative. Instead of waiting for what she saw as inevitable pain, or rejection, she acted to ensure that every incident in her life would end painfully, and in rejection. Despite her middle-class upbringing and college education, Leslie spoke in the harsh slang of the street, emulating a toughness to cover her vulnerability. From the day I met her, I encouraged Leslie to enter individual therapy, but her trust level was so low, she knew she would simply lie about herself and didn't want to waste her time—or mine. She was equally uncomfortable in the group, but was able to hide behind several different created personalities. At first this endeared her to the group but later frustrated the other members completely. They began to see that she lived behind a series of masks she never removed.

Trust built slowly between us. She dropped out of group for a couple of months, but returned when she found she was getting sicker. One night after group, when I had known Leslie for about seven months, I noticed that after the group had left, she remained in the room.

After a few minutes, she asked, "Will you be my best friend in the whole world?"

I looked at her. She was dead serious and the pleading look in her eyes told me that this just might be the most important moment in her entire life.

"Leslie, I couldn't be more flattered or honored by anything that has ever been offered to me. But for now, at least, don't you think that it might be better if you settle for a relationship with me, as the best therapist I can be for you?"

"Yeah," she said, in that slow, drawn-out way she had of speaking when she wanted to keep attention on herself. "I guess what I'm really saying, Robert, is that I trust you —a little, anyway." She smiled, but I knew she was speaking deep conflicting inner truths. "I gotta talk to somebody or I'm not gonna make it. I've been thinking real seriously about picking up drugs—and I don't want to. Is it gonna hurt to talk about it?"

Leslie's life consisted of avoiding pain, but she avoided old pain by creating new pain. She was now seeing that she was in a no-way-out situation. To run now was to run back to complete self-destruction. To fight meant confronting all of the demons which tore at the fabric of her existence— past and present.

"Come on into individual therapy, Leslie. We'll move only as fast as you are ready to. I won't say it's going to be a painless process, but you have to get things out of you. Hey! Life is about tigers. If you don't eat them, they eat you!"

"But if I don't like it, I quit—just like that."

"You got a deal." I smiled and she relaxed for the first time.

"That wasn't easy, you know. I've kept my secrets for a long, long, long, long time. And maybe I'll keep on keepin' some of them. Who knows?"

Yeah, who knows? In any case, Leslie began her journey to herself with that remarkable encounter seven months ago. Through therapy, Leslie began exploring her negative feelings, her self-doubts, and as she grew, she also began to accept her many positive aspects. She presented insights which helped others, and which may help you understand her journey toward recovery. She and I will provide our impressions of that journey. I do not presume to speak for Leslie. Each of us can genuinely feel only our own pain and pleasure. I will simply react to what she is

Leslie

saying, except where we are recreating a conversation between us.

Change is not a simple, definable process. Neither can this story be told in a simple progression by beginning with Leslie's childhood and bringing you up to the present in sequence. We need to look at what she is and was, and how her past created the inevitability of her adult reactions to the world. Leslie's initial presentation of who she was, in her first session of individual therapy, remains indelibly fixed in my mind:

"Leslie," I began, "why don't you give me a brief sketch of yourself as you view what your life is like today. I'm not here to judge you, but I need to know who you are in your own mind to help you decide what you want to work on."

Leslie cut to the chase with no formalities. "I was abused by my mother when I was a child. I was abused by my husband as an adult. I abused myself with drugs and alcohol. I abused myself by having sex for money, or with men who had no love for me. It felt right at the time because I had no love for myself—I still don't. I feel unworthy. I want to hurt somebody. I hate myself. I take my anger out on my children. I destroy friendships through my anger and insecurity. I run to sick men to seek comfort. I don't know who I am. I cover it all up with jokes and smiles and assurances that—hey, I'm okay today—I didn't pick up a drink or a drug. I can't stop the fuckin' pain! I haven't had a drink or a drug in almost nine months, but I feel like I'm no more than one step away from the next one. I'm thirty-three years old and still suck my thumb and play with a piece of satin to try to make myself feel better. I'm in great shape, aren't I? I hate men and I don't trust women. Sometimes, I even resent my kids just because they are there and I want to be alone, or I want to go out and have fun. To be honest, it's not sometimes, it's all the time!

Stop the Merry-Go-Round

"I have this friend. He tells me I'm special and I have all kinds of good qualities. When he says those things to me, sometimes I just want to rip his face off. Doesn't he know how much I want to believe those words, but inside I believe it's a crock and he's gonna be just like the others and want something back from me? Maybe if I shut my eyes, he'll disappear.

"I been thinking all week since we talked after group about what I was gonna say. Now that you know my whole story, am I fixed?" The look on her face begged me to say yes, but she knew. She knew.

"I wish it was that easy, Leslie." At moments like that I wished I had chosen some other profession, one that didn't require me to bring pain to attain healing. "It's not the telling that gets it out, it's dealing with the feelings, and that's going to take a lot of time and courage.

"Let me try to help you focus in a bit to look at some of the pieces of what you just told me—which, by the way was a beautiful portrait of your whole life in a few sentences. Okay? When you think of your life, what stands out most in your mind?" I tried to remain neutral about where she should begin.

"The pain, always the pain," she said, trying to avoid looking directly at me.

"Tell me where it began," I asked.

"I don't remember my childhood."

I hear this statement so often from abused people. "Well, maybe if you recall a particular incident, it will bring back other memories and you can fill in the gaps from what you know might have been so." I waited patiently as Leslie sat and pondered for a few moments. "For instance," "How about your first day of school? Can you remember that?"

Her face lit up in recognition. "Yeah, I remember. I couldn't wait to get there. It was a place to be happy." She

Leslie

15

smiled brightly for the first time. "I remember I panicked when my mom dropped me off and I was afraid and crying, but once I found out that it was going to be fun, I felt safe for the first time in my life.

"Before, I said that pain was the first thing I remember. It was the fear. My home was a dark place—dark." Leslie paused and looked up. Her eyes were hollow, and for the first time, she dropped the pleasant mask she wore when she arrived.

"Leslie, do you recall any specific incidents from when you were little?" I asked, now feeling that she had opened a door and was ready to proceed through it. When a person begins with a presentation that is as strong as Leslie's I feel that she is giving a message that she wants to get to something quickly because the pain of carrying it around has become intolerable. Also, because Leslie had been involved in the women's group for a number of months, we had already established a level of trust. She felt she could share some of her life with someone for the first time.

Leslie curled up in the chair, and I could picture a five year old child sitting across from me. She pursed her lips and looked down at her hands and remained silent for several minutes. She looked up at me several times and then looked away. "I never trusted anybody before. Not anybody! How do I know I can trust you? No, that's not fair. I wouldn't be here if I didn't trust you—at least enough to give you a chance—a little chance, mind you! Why did I say that? It's like I'm trying my best to hurt you or reject you and you never did anything to make me do that."

"It's okay, Leslie. Let me earn your trust. Don't just give it to me because I say I am trustworthy. I'll bet you heard that 'you can trust me' line from a lot of guys, didn't you?"

"Ho! Didn't I ever. Yeah, you'll earn my trust. I like that."

"Do you remember any incidents from your childhood you know—something that you can identify that made you feel bad?" I watched as she tried to remember. Her mask was off and her face was distorted by pain. Her mouth was twisted and her eyes were clouding with tears. "You look like you're about to cry."

"You don't know how long it's been since I really cried," her tough mask now in place. "I learned as a kid that you don't cry. You know, 'come on, cry, and I'll really give you somethin' to cry about!' Leslie sat silently, her face a mask of frozen anger.

"I remember something from when I was real, real little. Me an' my brothers and sister were playing in the house. My mom had this rule—we weren't allowed to make any noise. But how can five kids play and not make any noise? We were just having fun and she came storming into the room and threw us out of the house. I mean threw us out—down the concrete steps. I was so tiny, tiny, I remember I couldn't even reach the doorknob. For the first fifteen minutes, we just sat there nursing each other's wounds. We were so scared.

"Then we begged to come back in but the door was locked. My mom told us that if we tried to get back in, we'd be sorry. Finally, after what seemed like forever, my mom said, 'Ok, you can come back in.' We thought that it was going to be safe now. This was our home.

"As each of us came through the door, mom began hitting us and throwing us up against the wall. Right then, there was more shock than pain. The pain didn't come until later. This was our mother doing this to us! None of us even tried to defend ourselves. This was the person who loved us and was doing this to us. Where were the neighbors? Why didn't anybody try to stop her? I learned that you can't trust anyone who says they love you."

Leslie cried then. I encouraged her to just let her feelings pour out until they were gone. "I told you never to wear mascara when you are in therapy with me," I said to her softly after she had exhausted her tears.

"Gimme some Kleenex! I think there's a lot more crying where that came from. Y'know, Robert, it's like my tears are a fire extinguisher. Afterwards, the pain is less. But you have to find somebody you can trust and you don't know how hard that is." Leslie leaned her head back and closed her eyes. I saw her face in repose for the first time.

I watched her for a few minutes and allowed her the luxury of having a private space in the world where the fear and the pain were outside the door. I thought to myself that there are a lot of people who need a safe place where the fear cannot enter, and where there are enough secure doors.

The following week, Leslie continued talking about her early life.

"I learned real early that I was better off never telling the truth to my mother. She only wanted to hear good things, so when I would tell her about school, it was always how much the teacher praised me for helping clean the blackboard. 'Good!' she would say. The more she would compliment me, the more stories I would make up. I spent all of my time making up stories so she would hug me and kiss me and say nice things to me. And, if I did anything bad, I would tell her about this other kid who did bad things. 'What a rotten child,' she would say, 'not like my good girl.' I guess that's how I learned to lie about everything. It became so natural that I didn't even know when I was doing it." Leslie paused and looked at me for reassurance. I knew what she was about to say.

"It's been eight months now since I told a lie. After that first night in group, I learned how much my lies can hurt another person." Leslie needed to talk about this incident because it was a critical moment in her life.

"I remember after hearing Lisa talk about being sexually abused, and how the group was so tender to her when she was crying, that I wanted some of that tenderness, too. So without even thinking, I made up that story about how my brother had raped me and I fought him and he overpowered me. And how the group reacted and gave me all that positive attention! Now I see where it came from. I've been getting attention that way all my life.

"I'll never forget what happened after that. I got home and I was going out of my head. It hit me that women in this group were really abused sexually when they were kids and had to live with that and here I was, lying about it happening to me just to get attention. I was shaking so hard I couldn't sleep and I was seriously thinking about going to my cop man and getting just a few sleeping pills to get me through the night. Then I remembered what you said at the end of the group. 'If you're hurting, don't be afraid to pick up a phone and call somebody.' I was so wrapped up in myself that I didn't bother to get anyone's number. I didn't even remember any of their names! So, two in the morning, I asked information for your number and called you. I bet you still love me for that, don't you?"

"Leslie, do you remember the other half of what I said about calling somebody?"

"Yeah, I do. 'It's better for two people to lose half a night's sleep each than for one person to lose her life.' I also remember what you told me after I confessed what I did to you. Man, I thought confessing it to you would be the end of it. Then you said, 'Leslie, what do you think you ought to do about it?' I was expecting you would scream at me and call me a stupid jerk-off or something. That's what I was used to hearing from my mom—and even worse from my husband. You were telling me that I had to decide how to handle the worst thing I ever did. I knew I had to be honest with the group, or I could never go back. I knew that this group was my last chance to survive, and I wasn't makin' it before I got here.

"That next week, when I had to tell the group I lied about being raped, I wanted to throw up. I knew I was sitting in a room with women who had been abused, raped, molested, and I used their pain to get sympathy. And then, on top of that, they all forgave me, even Caitlin, who was having the toughest time with incest in her life. It helped me change the way I saw people, but not right away. Every time I want to believe that you can't trust anybody, I remember that night. It helps."

"So, what you learned as a child about lying isn't working out here in the adult world? When you were a kid, lying protected you from punishment, and now, it only creates pain. Is that what you are saying?" Leslie was sitting with her hands covering her face like a small child who has been discovered doing something illicit. "You can look at me, Leslie. You have nothing to be ashamed of."

Leslie kept her face covered and talked through her hands. "Yeah, I do. I have a lot to be ashamed of. A lot of things I can't even tell you about—yet."

"Sometimes the things you don't want to talk about are the things you most need to get out. We have all the time in the world." Leslie lowered her hands and looked at me. I smiled encouragement to her.

"All the time in the world." Leslie leaned forward in the chair, and continued. "Y'know, when I'm in this room, I almost believe that, but out there, it's so hard. It's like it's closing in on me all the time. The kids, no money, responsibilities. When is there time just for me? I need some fun, too, y'know?"

Stop the Merry-Go-Round

"I hate to disillusion you, but when is there time for any of us? Do you think that recovering from a troubled life gives you special privileges? Sometimes, when I hear things like what you're saying—and I understand the needs are real—I'm tempted to flat-out challenge the person saying it to trade problems with me even up. It's okay to want what you want, but don't give up if you can't have it. Sorry, I'm on my soapbox today. I know you haven't had many breaks in your life, but they come when they come, not when you want them." I shook my head and smiled, realizing that I was doing the same thing she was doing.

"Maybe someday we can talk about your problems, Robert. I know you're human, too." Leslie's appearance changed, and a softer, more nurturing version appeared for a moment.

"Tell you what," I answered with a smile. "As soon as you're safe and feeling like the most special human being on the face of the earth, then we can talk about me, okay? In the meantime, I'm able to handle whatever problems I have. You are still close to the edge where you're in danger of falling off."

"That's the difference. It's not whether you have problems. We all have them. It's having the—whatever—to deal with them. Maybe when I know what 'whatever' is, I'll be on my way, huh?" We laughed at her ability to turn her pain into humor.

"And, in the meantime, to be able to laugh—even a little—at yourself, and with someone else, is the best medicine in the whole world. Leslie, thank you for bringing a moment of laughter into my day."

Leslie began crying. "I'm the one who should be thanking you. I'm not used to getting compliments. They still hurt so much."

"We still have so far to travel," I thought to myself as we ended the session.

Leslie

"Let's talk about jealousy," Leslie said, as we began another session. Leslie had been working with me for about a month in individual therapy when she opened her session with this comment. She had opened almost every individual session and group by saying, "I was thinking about not coming tonight," but this opening line was new for her. I waited for her to continue.

"I didn't forget, Robert. I wasn't planning to come tonight." We both smiled. I knew she needed this element of control in the relationship and felt that if I accepted her right to decide whether or not she was going to participate, it might help her gain mastery over her life.

"Anyway," she continued, "why am I always so jealous of other women—when it comes to guys, especially? You know, I'm jealous of the women I think are prettier than me or built nicer, or taller, things like that." Leslie squirmed uncomfortably in her chair. I knew that this was a subject about which she really didn't want to talk.

"Did something in particular happen to bring this up?" I asked. She sat quietly for a few minutes.

"I never told you much about my relationships with men, did I?"

"Just that your relationships were not really satisfying your needs for intimacy." I felt it was best not to lead Leslie, but rather, see where she wanted to go with this.

"Yeah, that's putting it diplomatically. Sometimes, I feel like a little whore. I don't know. I can't ever find somebody who loves me whom I love. When I love somebody, he doesn't love me. When somebody loves me, I have to reject him—and bad—if you know what I mean. I always had this thing. I'd do anything to get a man to love me and as soon as he did, I'd blow him off. And I'd stick like glue to a guy who didn't love me to try to get him to. Am I making any sense at all?" Leslie looked to me for help or advice.

I was fairly certain that Leslie's inability to develop healthy relationships as an adult could be traced back to her relationship with her parents. She had been open about her mother's treatment of her, but had failed to mention her father. Sometimes, what a person doesn't say is most significant. In this instance, Leslie's failure to mention her father indicated to me that there was a significant amount of feelings with which she chose not to deal.

"Leslie," in my best if—I—can't—find—a—front—door—a—back—door—will—do manner, "tell me about your father. You haven't said much about him."

"What's he got to do with what I do with men? My father's dead, and you don't talk bad about the dead!" she almost yelled, trying to avoid the question. She stared at me angrily, and for a few moments, I thought she was going to get up and walk out.

"You look like you're about ready to cut and run."

"Yeah, well, it's not your father we're talking about, is it?" Her mouth was fixed in a grimace.

"How do you feel about your dad, Leslie?"

"I love him. He was the only good person in my whole life!"

Leslie squirmed in her chair, and, without thinking, reached into her pocketbook and withdrew a long strip of white satin and began rubbing it. I noticed how discolored it was. "So, this is the satin security blanket she mentioned," I thought to myself. "Playing with a strip of satin is healthier than taking drugs to relieve anxiety and pain." I was very careful about not reacting to what she was doing. "Tell me about your father. You never talk about how he fit into your life."

Leslie

"W— well," she stammered, "he wasn't really home that much. My mom and him never got along. He worked all the time."

"What kind of work did he do?" I asked, trying to keep the conversation going.

"Uh, a little of everything, I guess. He never really made much money. He was a schemer and a dreamer, but he was always trying something. Mom was always complaining about how she had to work or we would've starved. I guess she was right. But I know she really wanted to work. When he did come home, he would always give me a big, wet kiss. My mom would yell at him and tell him it was sloppy an he should stop it.

"Mom told us that dad never wanted children. She hated him and tried to get us on her side. Sometimes I'm so confused I don't know what to think. Once, she even told me that I wasn't his child, but I don't want to believe that. Maybe she just did that to get back at him. I don't know. It wasn't right to tell me that."

I chose not to deal with the issue of whose child she was. It would have been conjecture and in no way productive. "Sometimes, do you feel that in order to love one of your parents, you have to hate the other—you know—choose sides? Is that what you were made to feel?" Leslie looked at me and for a few moments, didn't answer.

"I mean, what was I supposed to believe? Mom would beat the hell out of us and then she would turn around and hug us and tell us she loved us. And, she said she didn't remember beating us. To this day, she denies it ever happened! Once, when I was about nine or ten, she beat me so bad that I was black and blue all over—including bruises on my face. When she came in to wake us up the next morning, she was all over me with, 'Oh! My baby had a terrible accident. What happened to you, darling?' I wanted to scream at her, 'You did it! Can't you even remember beating your own child?'"

"Didn't your father ever try to stop her?"

"It wouldn't happen when he was home. Dad would come home every once in a while but was never really there when we needed him, y' know? Maybe mom was takin' her anger at him out on us. And there was what mom was always feeding us about him—how irresponsible he was, how he never really cared about us kids. It was almost like she was blamin' him for the beatings.

"She told us that he was always sayin' that his life was ruined by having kids. But when she would be screaming at us, she would be the one sayin' that her life was ruined by having us. 'If it hadn't been for all of you, I could have been a great actress,' she'd say. I mean, it's hard not to believe your mom. And she told it both ways!"

Leslie was caught in a trap which was worse than any faced by many others with whom I have worked. Like Jaime, about whom you will read later in the book, Leslie was confronted not only with her own anger, but with ambivalence as well. Ambivalence tends to leave a person in a perplexing dilemma. There are reasons to both love and hate the person who gives you mixed signals. At least, when someone is a clear threat, defenses can be set up against being further hurt. But when they tell you they love you and they hate you, they want you and they reject you, it is impossible to know how to react. Whatever choice you make will prove incorrect. "It's as if there was nothing real you could hold on to."

"How did you survive?"

"I made up a life in my head. I had the world convinced that I was a princess and everybody loved me. I always had a smile on my face and I was everybody's friend in the neighborhood." Leslie rubbed the strip of satin frantically as she talked.

Leslie

"But, at what price to you?" She stared at the satin and continued rubbing it as tears poured from her eyes.

"I'm gonna be punished for talking about the dead," she muttered.

"Leslie, you have to make choices. If you want, you can continue living the life you are living. You are the one who came here because you don't want to live in pain and chaos any longer. You can't have it both ways. You need to accept that anything you say here isn't meant to hurt your father. He is dead and beyond hurting."

"It's something I was taught and it's not easy to get rid of," she said, looking genuinely frightened.

At this point, Leslie needed to be confronted with a laundry list of those behaviors, attitudes and values with which she had to deal if she was going to make any real changes in her life. It was clear to me that in presenting them to her, I was not going to invoke instant change, but I felt she had to be made aware of the contract between us as therapist and client. I have rarely used direct confrontation, but Leslie was so good at avoiding dealing with her issues, that I felt it was appropriate at that moment.

"You need to look honestly at the facts of your life to try to find out why you are so totally self-destructive. I'm not saying these things to hurt you, but I think you need to choose between living in your fantasies and coming into reality. If I ask you questions, it is because, if I am going to be able to help you sort out your life so you can set new goals and find more comfortable ways of living, we need to talk openly and honestly about your life. You run from the pain of the moment back to the eternal pain of your life. You indicate that your relationships with men are less than positive, but if we are to try to help you change that—if you want to, that is—we need to look at where you developed the attitudes which keep you repeating the negative patterns.

"Sometimes, I have to just lay it on the line. This is your life. You can choose to walk out of here, but if you choose to stay, I have to ask you questions which may be painful. You have to work on developing enough trust so that you can allow yourself to look at your life."

"Damnit," Leslie snarled, "all I ever wanted was to be happy. Is that too much to ask?"

"No, it isn't. The problem is that you are going about getting what you want in ways that assure that you won't get it!"

"Yeah, how's that?" Leslie was becoming very belligerent.

Leslie needed to be made aware of the fact that her negative self-concept strongly contributed to her making negative choices in the conduct of her life. I then attempted to help her look at this possibility, as well as the fact that she used her anger to protect her present pattern of behavior. In order to accomplish this, I decided to create a situation in which she would draw her own negative conclusions. "How do you feel about yourself?"

"I told you, I hate myself."

"How do you feel about your life?"

"It sucks."

"Do you have a man in your life right now?"

"Yeah, so what?"

"What's he doing for your life?"

"He's giving me all the happiness I have right now, that's what." Leslie was squirming in her chair now.

"I'm confused. You say that your life sucks, you hate yourself and in the next breath, there's a man that gives you all the happiness you have. How much happiness do you have?"

Leslie

"Well, for the few hours I get to spend with him, I forget about my pain." She was beginning to calm down slightly.

"Are you saying that he's like the drugs you took for all those years? Something to take away the pain?" I looked at her and saw that she was not really responding to anything I was attempting to convey.

Leslie sat frantically rubbing the piece of satin, her eyes glazed and dull. "In the most important way, he's like all the others," she began, speaking more to herself than to me. "He won't even make a date with me. If I see him at an NA meeting, we get together, but he won't make plans. I told him I love him; he says he likes me but doesn't feel love for me. But I can't get enough of him. I just want to hold him all the time and weld myself to him. I know he's not right for me and I'd never marry him, but he takes away the loneliness when I'm with him. I get jealous when he even talks to another woman. I just cling to him and let her know that she better keep her hands off him. I feel like a teen-ager when I get like that.

"I know that someday, I have to give him up and just be with nobody for a while, but I'm not ready yet."

"Leslie, how many times did you say those exact words about drugs?"

"Yeah, I know, but you can't ask me to give everything up at once." She appeared on the edge of desperation.

"I'm not asking you to give up anything. All I'm asking you to do is look at what you are doing and judge whether it's something that adds to your life."

"All I'm sayin' is I can't do anything until I'm ready—really ready. Robert, I'm gettin' really tired now and I have to stop."

Leslie had some inner mechanism which wasn't allowing her to move on to new ways of living her life. She had been able to share some of her pain. Even that was new for her, but she was unable to let go of old behaviors. They gave her what little pleasure she had in life, but at the same time, kept her from experiencing more rewarding relationships.

Leslie called to cancel the following session, but she returned a week later with no mention of the previous week. "I been thinkin' about what we were talkin' about last time and I want to go into it some more," she began.

"I thought about how I used men all my life, and I'm still doin' it. Hey, they use me too—especially sexually—but I get what I want out of them."

"How do you mean, 'Get what you want?'"

"This part's embarrassing. You're not gonna like me very much when you hear some of the things I've done." She sat like a small child, anticipating punishment.

"Leslie, there's nothing I haven't heard, and if you don't know by now that I am not here to judge you, you may never learn it."

"I did a lot of things I'm ashamed of," she mumbled.

"Everybody has a list of things they are ashamed of. Sometimes it helps to tell them to one person you trust."

"This is so hard to do," she said.

"I know you need to be liked and respected, but you need to like and respect yourself, too, and in order to like and respect yourself, you are going to have to get rid of the things in your past that are haunting you. The way to really be liked and respected is to live a positive life today, not to lie about what you've done in the past."

"I've slept with men for money," she said.

"That's an almost necessary part of an addiction, if you stay in it long enough and don't have some kind of permanent enabler, like a husband or boyfriend," I answered.

"I slept with men for money after I got sober—the last time was last week."

Leslie

29

"Just talk about it. Let it go. It must really hurt."

"Aren't you gonna ask me why?," she asked, desperately.

"Talk about your hurt. That's more important than 'why.' Why? Because! Okay? Come on, let it go." I sat back and waited while she absorbed this new way of looking at her life. For a great many years, Leslie had done what she wanted, and lied about it, or rationalized it away afterward. She was paying a price of constant inner pain which she mollified by having sex or by playing with a satin ribbon.

"When I got sober, everybody told me to stay away from men for a long time because I can't handle relationships. I didn't listen. There's this one guy, I call him my service man. He's married, but he and I get together—you know. He sometimes buys me things. The sex is good and it don't really hurt anybody, does it?"

"You know what they say, if you have to ask . . ."

"I know this guy in the NA program. He's just a friend. He makes me laugh. I don't like him as a boyfriend. Anyway, he's always askin' me to sleep with him and I always refused. Until last week . . ." Leslie held herself as if she would explode. "I was broke—as usual—and he offered to buy groceries for me 'n' the kids if I would fuck him. I didn't want to, but I gave in. I figured what was the difference. I just lay there like a corpse. It was over fast. After he left, I freaked out. I went runnin' out of the house and I almost went to get drugs. I don't know what stopped me.

"The last three years of my addiction, after I left my husband, I just picked up men and used them. It just kept gettin' sicker and sicker. One guy I was sleepin' with, I told him I was pregnant and had to get an abortion and that he had to pay for it. I got three hundred dollars from him and used it to buy a waterbed. I knew I wasn't pregnant. I know I can't keep livin' like this sober, or I won't be sober long. And if I'm not sober—I'm dead. I'm thirty-three years old and there's no more chances for me out there." Leslie sat quietly, rubbing her piece of satin.

Leslie was expressing the dilemma of people who are ambivalent. Her trust level was so low that she was unable to attach even to a sick man, so she used her ability to charm to con a variety of men into 'taking care of her,' as she put it. With Leslie, maintaining her addiction was not a primary issue. She did not have a particularly expensive habit. It was probably more important for her to play out her rage and distrust in a way that she could win the 'battles,' though assuredly, she was losing the 'war' she was waging. I wondered how her feelings affected her during her marriage as compared to the past three years.

"You never talked about your marriage," I said.

"Well," she answered, "it wasn't the happiest time in my life."

"Why did you get married?" I asked.

"That's another long story. Lemme go back to the beginning, okay? I guess I better go all the way back to when I was in my teens. I told you I learned to manipulate men. Well, I guess the truth is that I had to pay a high price for what I got. I would go out with five or ten guys during the same time and play with all of them. But I guess a lot of them played with me, too. I wanted to be popular and I reached a point where I would just make it with a guy to prove I could take him from his girlfriend. I was doin' a lot of dope—pot, ludes, downs mostly—and everybody was into it. But inside, even back then, it was tearin' me up.

"I'd have this awful dream where I would be attacked by a million guys. All I would see is their goddamn dicks wavin' in my face. One night, it got even worse. I was tryin' to slow down on the dope. I was gettin' pretty messed up and I had this dream that I was lyin' in a field, and dicks were growin' out of the ground like mushrooms. I couldn't get away. They were watchin' me and tellin' me, 'You're just a little whore, Leslie.' I started swingin' at them and chopping them off but they just grew faster and faster. I woke up shakin' and screamin'. My mom wanted to take me to the hospital, but I talked her out of it. I knew if I went to the hospital I would've told them everything and they would've told my mom. I don't even wanna think about what she'd've done to me if she knew what I was into. I had to be Snow White to her. And, anyway, I knew all I had to do was drop a couple of Quaaludes and I'd feel better——or at least I'd feel nothing for a while.

"It's funny. Back then, I really didn't like sex at all. It wasn't pleasant and it never helped me feel close to any of those guys. I really just wanted them to be my friends, but I thought that was what I had to do to make them like me.

"I guess you could call what happened to me a nervous breakdown, huh?"

"Or, maybe you were just giving yourself a message about how you felt about your life."

"I hope that's not what I meant when I said that life sucks," Leslie laughed.

I chose to deal with the pain Leslie felt throughout her life rather than the joke she was attempting to make of it. "Often dreams are symbols that are connected to your life, and that dream certainly portrayed an exaggeration of reality and a situation which brought you no good feelings, no matter how many men you slept with."

"At the time, I didn't know what to make of it, but for a while, it changed my life. It was about that time I went away to college. It's funny, all the drugs I took and I was still a top student. When I got to college, I had a room-mate and she and I had an affair. It was the most romantic relationship in my life. We were together for two years and it was the sanest time in my life. I got away from men and she made me feel really good—in every way—including sexually. I never experienced such tenderness from a human being. I almost got rid of the pain I had all my life. But, after two years, my mom found out and she sent me off to another school across the country. I was devastated. Not only did I lose the one person I ever really loved, but I lost my family, too. My mom told me that she didn't want to see me or hear from me again until I was married and had as she said, 'removed the stain' from her life. I didn't see my family for almost four years. I finally gave in to the pressure and started going out with men. I picked one who looked like he could make a good living and I married him." Leslie began to cry.

"Tell me about your marriage," I said.

"There isn't much to tell. My husband tried to control my life. I had all the children one after another, figurin' it would help me to make my life right, but all it did was make it more impossible. I did a lot of pills and drank some, but I kept it under control because of the kids. My husband had a real drinking problem and when he would drink, he got very nasty. He hit me, I think, four times. The last time was it for me. I was beaten enough as a kid. I wasn't going to take it as an adult.

"Three years ago, I packed up the kids and we moved back home. I figured I would go to my mom's house until I could get a job and figure out what to do with my life. When I got there, she told me I couldn't stay with her. She said, 'You made your bed, you can sleep in it.' I was left with five kids and no place to go. I found a place, got my husband to send some support—he never was a problem with that—he still loves me and thinks someday we will get back together. It wasn't enough, but I knew how to get men to take care of me. That's something you don't forget just 'cause you're married for six years! And my mom

Leslie

33

fixed it so I could never look at another woman. I don't care how much she rejects me—I can't reject her. She's all I have. Crazy as it sounds, I love her."

"That's a lot of pain you're holding on to, lady," I said. "Did you ever feel like ending it all?"

"Just every minute of every day—but I wouldn't. There's the kids, and sometimes—not very often—I think, 'Maybe God has some purpose for me here.' He sure has a funny way of showin' me what it is, though, don't He?"

"Leslie, perhaps, if you have faith, you will allow yourself to grow so that you can discover your purpose. Maybe you have to be more open to 'hear' that voice which tells you what you are destined to accomplish. But, you can't hear it or accomplish anything if you commit symbolic suicide every morning."

"What's that supposed to mean?"

"Simply that when you set out to live at your own expense or other peoples' rather than in harmony with your real needs, you lose that day—and you can never get it back.

"Life is choices. If you choose to put a band-aid on your hurt instead of fixing it—tomorrow it will still be there."

"You mean running to men, don't you?"

"Yes, as opposed to developing healthy relationships. A healthy relationship doesn't produce pain and insecurity the morning after. Nor, do you wonder if you will see that person the next weekend. Or, have to wonder if he loves you. Two healthy people won't settle for less than a commitment, nor do they need to.

"Leslie, the way you feel about yourself today, you aren't ready or able to form a healthy relationship. That is the only reason that so many people suggested to you that you should stay out of sexual relationships and give yourself some space and time to work on developing a positive sense of yourself. And, with your vulnerability, the only way to stay out of sexual relationships is to stay out of all relationships with men."

"You can't know how much pain I feel. I need something just to keep me going. I don't wanna keep livin' this way, but I can't help it. Well," she said, changing the subject, "now you know my whole story. Some wonderful life, huh?"

"Yes, I know your story and I shared some of your pain, and you're right—I can't know your pain just as you can't know mine. But I accept that yours came from the many terrible things that happened to you, and then a number of things that you caused yourself while you were trying to feel good.

"So, now what?" I asked. "Okay, you've had a difficult life, but there are no rewards or breaks for what you went through. Leslie, you're thirty-three years old, you have five kids, you have a college degree which prepared you to teach school, and you have social skills, as well as musical and writing talents which you mentioned one time in group. I didn't bring them up again because I got the sense that you weren't ready to do anything about it. But, perhaps it's time to think about what you want to do with your life. So, as I said, now what?"

"Now what," she repeated, almost in a stupor. "Now what? I'm supposed to just forget everything I went through and live happily ever after? Well I can't."

"What do you see as your future?"

"Takin' care of the kids for another fifteen years. Livin' from hand to mouth. Bein' dependent on my ex-husband and my mother."

"What can you do to make that picture a lot brighter?"

"I guess I could get a job. The kids are all in school and the older ones can take care of the younger ones until I get home from work."

Leslie

35

"There's a problem, though," I said. "Until you stop feeling sorry for yourself, there's no way you're going to do anything except make sure you have lots of reasons to feel sorry for yourself."

Sometimes, when a person has experienced only pain and failure, it becomes so ingrained that the person believes that there is no hope and that any attempts to make the situation better will only make it worse. Every move Leslie had made in her life brought further unhappiness to her. The one relationship which brought her pleasure was detroyed by her mother and her need to please her mother. In order to break a negative pattern, a large element of risk is involved. You need to risk a new failure, and place a great deal of trust in others.

"I never had any proof that anything can ever be different," Leslie said, "so how can I feel that life will change just because you say so?"

"If you don't take a chance, nothing is going to change. It's time to stop living in the past. Sure, you had terrible things happen to you, but in the past fifteen years, most of what happened to you was caused by you. It's almost as if you really want to continue living in the past. You lost your childhood, so now you are going to do your best to destroy the rest of your life as well. That's about par for the course when you are on drugs and drinking heavily, but when you stop, either you develop a new pattern of living, and get away from the chaos, or the pain just gets worse."

"I want to change, but I'm afraid."

"I know, Leslie. Nobody said it was easy. It's the fish hooks. You just can't leave them in much longer and survive."

Leslie continued fighting change. She remained in the relationship which brought her instant gratification, but at the same time, let her know that she was not really loved.

Stop the Merry-Go-Round

She was able to stop using men to survive financially, so her life was becoming somewhat more acceptable to her. She worked part-time and continued to live hand-to-mouth. It was as if she needed this negative pattern to justify her negative self-image. The emotional poverty of her existence was being replayed in the way she handled her finances.

"How do you feel about yourself now?" I asked her a couple of months later.

"I still don't like myself and I hate my life."

"What can you do to improve it?" I asked this for probably the thousandth time.

"I know, I know. Get rid of my boyfriend and look for a full-time job."

"You make it sound as though I asked you to cut off your hands." I watched her reaction. I expected anger which she had always used to fend off change.

"Robert, I can't take it any more. No matter what I do, I can't get rid of the damn pain. I hate my life. I hate being a mother to five kids. I just want to have fun. And I can't. Nothing is fun any more."

Leslie's attitude was typical of addictive thinking. 'Fun' is synonymous with absence of feeling, not enjoyment. The trio of 'sex, drugs and rock-and-roll' are all quick fixes. They alleviate pain for a few moments, but leave a void. That void can be filled only by qualities such as caring, involvement, commitment, direction, and identity. Leslie had yet to identify these elements in her life. She had played several roles which allowed her to survive a dysfunctional home and an equally dysfuntional adulthood.

"Who are you, Leslie?" I asked.

"I'm just a little wimp who can't make it in this world."

"Who said you're a wimp? That had to come from somewhere."

Leslie

37

"Nobody—I can't remember." Leslie looked away. She reached into her bag and removed the satin strip and began frantically rubbing it.

"Why don't you want to remember, Leslie? You know what's strange? That's one label I never thought anybody could apply to you. There are several which I would employ." She looked frightened, as though I were about to attack her.

"First of all, I'd call you a survivor. I mean that in the most positive sense. Regardless of all else, you took a brood of kids and with minimal help, you are raising them. Despite your anger and resentment, and considering the way you brag about their accomplishments, they seem to be doing pretty well. Then, I'd call you a good mother. Being a good mother isn't having good feelings—it's taking care of business. And, you've done that. Your kids are clothed and fed and given attention. So you live with negative feelings. You do sometimes take out your anger on them, but you are aware of it and you are working on minimizing it. No parent is perfect, and you judge yourself against real standards, not against perfection. I'm a parent, too, and I'm far from perfect—and that's reality.

"You have intelligence and I think you would make a wonderful teacher because you really do have a command presence as well as the ability to charm people. You are animated, and despite your pain, you can be sensitive to the needs of others."

Tears poured down her face. "I can't stand to hear those things. I don't deserve them."

"Yes you do. You always did. And the time has come to open yourself to your own specialness—don't wince. We all have special qualities and it is time for you to get in touch with yours."

"After all I did to mess up my life, how can you say I'm special? Robert, you're just handin' me a crock of shit, and I can't take any more."

"Would you rather listen to whoever it is who calls you a wimp?"

"Yeah! At least he knows what he's talking about." Leslie stared at me angrily.

"Who says you're a wimp?"

"My brother. But he only says it so I'll listen to him. He is recovering from an addiction, too, and he's helped me a whole lot."

"Did your mother used to talk to him that way when you were kids?"

"She talked to all of us like that when she was angry. So, now he talks to me that way? Maybe it makes sense."

"But it doesn't make it true. Maybe that's how he deals with his pain, but you don't need to be put down by anybody. Remember, it was the people who were closest to you that always did the most to hurt you."

Leslie was nodding her head in agreement. "I love him. He's the only one who stuck by me when my mom kicked me out. He stayed in touch. The rest of them just left me out there by myself."

"Maybe it's time to place limits on everybody who loves you. Do you have to take abuse in order to be loved?" I paused to let Leslie absorb this. "Your mother loved you, but she abused you—sometimes. You had to accept the abuse to keep the love. You don't have to do that to keep your brother's love. Maybe that's why you select men who don't love you. If they hurt you, you can get rid of them. The nice ones are harder to get rid of. You have to hurt them because you believe they are going to hurt you. If they really love you, you have to be rotten because you believe that eventually they will hurt you because nobody can be trusted. Leslie, you are in a terrible predicament because you always end up with nothing worth having."

"How do I change it?"

"You have to let go. You have to take a chance and give up your beliefs about the world. You have to begin accepting that not everybody is untrustworthy. You need to get out of old relationships and spend some time just learning who you are and working on building your life. If you aren't getting your good feelings from a man, maybe you'll push a little harder to make your life whole—like getting a job, dealing with the reality of being the mother of five children, and being responsible for everything that happens now. If you don't have casual sex to give you a quick fix, maybe you'll work on your feelings and try to come to some resolution that will allow you to live at peace with yourself.

"If you get your sense of worth from yourself rather than from others, it will be real and permanent. If you get it from a man at this point, you will pick a man who is worth what you feel you are worth—and today, that isn't very much. And, if he isn't worth much, he'll have to keep you feeling 'down' to keep himself feeling 'up.'"

"Yeah," said Leslie. "I've had a lot of men in my life who were like that. My ex, he was always putting me down and making me feel very small and worthless. But, when I finally grew a set of balls and left him, he was begging me to come back. All of a sudden, I was the most special woman in the whole world and he couldn't live without me."

"Leslie, we've been working on these concepts for quite some time in therapy, but until you let go of your old way of managing your life and take a chance that something different might work, you'll never be able to experience full growth. You've come a long way in many respects. But you need to take that one more giant step."

Stop the Merry-Go-Round

"I think I'm ready to listen to a lot of what you're saying," Leslie began. "I can't take the pain anymore, and I know I bring it on myself and I don't have to. It's like that terrible dream about the mushroom garden. After that experience, I did get away from the problems, but I just walked into new problems to replace them. I just didn't know it at the time. It isn't going to be easy. I'm gonna need a lot of help.

"Robert, I'm going to try what you're suggesting. I'm not gonna promise I can do it perfect, but everything I tried left me feeling like hell. Maybe if I had friends it would be easier."

"Maybe if you change the way you relate to men, you will be able to develop some friendships with women."

Shortly therafter, Leslie left therapy. I lost touch with her, but heard that she continued to attend NA and AA meetings regularly. I got a call from an employer several months later. She had used me as a reference. It told me that she was trying to build a career for herself. Perhaps Leslie had to move on to work on herself by herself. She and I had engaged in a painful process and maybe she had to put the pain behind her to continue healing. Even though therapy is defined as a helping relationship, it is also by virtue of what we do here, a painful process. Leslie had her fill of painful relationships. As I have often said, therapy isn't the answer to everything. I learned that there is a simple way to know when it is time to leave therapy, and that is when you realize that it could go on forever!

Leslie

CAITLIN

*I have learned that there are two words
I have to accept to be honest about my life
and to grow as a person.
They are: incest and victim*

The Empty Chair

As we have seen in Leslie's story, much of what people do, think and feel as adults relates, both directly and indirectly, to events which occurred earlier in life, during the developmental childhood and teenage years. It isn't necessarily a single, traumatic incident which alters a person's life-course. Sometimes, it is the overall effects of the conditions under which he or she lived. Our upbringing, with its positives and negatives, shapes the way we feel about ourselves, about those who will become close to us as adults, and about the world around us.

Often, the terrible and traumatic events which shape parts of some individuals' lives are buried because the pain of the incident or life-period was so great that the individual chose to escape from that pain by denying that it happened or, more directly, alleviating it with drugs and alcohol. But, whatever means the person chose, the pain did not disappear. It affected behavior, attitudes, values and feelings. The person became less able to feel whole and to live effectively in the adult world where we are expected to make competent judgments and live in harmony with others.

Discovering the hidden sources of a person's anguish is sometimes difficult. No one wishes to suffer through another exposure to his or her worst nightmares. When the anguish is caused by childhood sexual abuse, it often remains hidden because of shame or the immense pain and rage which it triggers. It is a fact, though, that by revealing the distressing incidents and allowing the pain to be shared with another person who knows how to deal with it, the pain is relieved and allows the individual to begin growing.

Pain and the fear of pain are like solid blockades to change and growth. If your experiences with parents and other significant people in your life were negative, rejecting or brutal, you will enter adult life believing that all of the world is negative, rejecting or brutal. This pessimistic view of the world becomes a self-fulfilling prophesy which will cause you to pick negative, rejecting or brutal people with whom to interact. Sometimes the beginning of self-help is simply the admission that you need another human being to help you find your own solutions to life's problems. Therapy doesn't provide better answers—simply better questions. When the trauma includes sexual abuse and incest, the taboo against discussing it with anyone is much stronger than it is when the issue is physical and verbal abuse.

Sometimes, the more extensive the problem, the more likely it is that the individual will choose not to deal with it. In the narrative to follow, the young woman, Caitlin, was confronted with life situations which so overwhelmed her, that she dealt with her problems by denying that they bothered her. She needed to build her life upon lies which allowed her to survive until she was ready to face the life-shattering pain she had been carrying.

Denying the existence of pain can impede your emotional growth. In the case of a recovering addicted person, the consequences can, and often do, include relapse because he or she has learned that drugs and alcohol can serve to alleviate the pain of the moment.

Some of the details Caitlin revealed about her past seem almost too bizarre to be true. Whether they happened is not the issue. The important thing is that this is how Caitlin portrayed her reality and she lived her adult life based upon that portrayal. I must add that in twenty-five years as a practicing therapist, I have heard other stories which demonstrated that Caitlin's story was, in all likelihood, accurately portrayed. Before I describe Caitlin's therapy, consider her own brief account of her problem and what happened.

"My adult life was made up mostly of lies and deceits—and constant pain. I spent most of my adult life in therapy, but it was only recently—very recently—that I began telling the whole truth. I guess when you've been the victim of incest, it can mess up your head so badly that you don't know how to deal with life.

"I always wondered how I would be able to like myself after what happened to me. Maybe if I talk about what really happened, I will feel better someday. Don't get me wrong, there are times now when I feel okay, but I never know when it is going to hit me—that screaming pain inside me that tells me it was my fault, or I am dirty when I know—at least part of me knows—that's not true.

"I have learned that there are two words I have to accept if I am to be both honest about my life and be able to grow as a person. They are: incest and victim. I have to accept that they are connected. I was a victim of incest. To accept that, I have to accept that I was not responsible. Maybe I'll have to tell myself I was not responsible a million times before I really believe it, but I'm going to keep on doing it until it works.

"This is the hardest thing I ever did. I'm sitting here telling you about my life and I don't know if I can get through any of it without crying or screaming or wanting to kill somebody. For ten years I took drugs to stop the pain inside me, but drugs only led to more problems than I already had. By the time I was twenty years old, I was in a year-long residential program for drug addicts. Not long after I graduated, I went back to drugs.

"I'm not telling you my story to try to justify what I did. I'm only sharing my life and my feelings so that maybe you—or somebody you know—might not have to go

Caitlin

47

through what I went through and what I'm still going through.

"I still haven't learned to trust people. Maybe that's why I even lied to my therapist. Here I was—trying to get my life together—and I was telling my therapist I was sober three years when I had been taking drugs almost half of that time—the most recent half. Maybe inside, it allowed me to blame myself for having sex with my father when I was twenty-two years years old and it was supposed to be all over. I'm still learning that once you are a victim, things continue to happen against your will until something stops it. Part of the reason you can continue to be a victim is that you begin to believe that it's your fault, not the fault of the person doing the things to you.

"One thing I learned to do a long time ago was to hide from my feelings. I don't know what will happen if I try to face them all at once. Sometimes I think I am crazy even though most of the time I know that isn't true. Maybe I've been hiding from my feelings, but they sure haven't hidden from me. They come out and make me do things that still make my life uncomfortable. They make me depressed. Sometimes I pick fights with my boyfriend because I am so angry at men. He doesn't do anything to deserve the pain I give him. But I think, I didn't do anything to deserve the pain my father gave me all my life.

"All my life . . .

"It was never easy. I don't remember much about my early years. I know I was a very outgoing kid. I guess you could call me a pretty girl. I was athletic and I had lots of friends. Things were tough at home—my dad left the family and my mom sometimes didn't have the time she needed for raising children. She was too busy just trying to get a little fun out of life. Sometimes, I feel I've been the same way with my son, but lately, I'm developing much more responsibility with him——even though it isn't always easy.

"When I came into therapy a year ago, I just wanted to feel better. My life was chaos. I went to AA regularly but I was taking drugs whenever I needed to feel better. Everybody thought I was stand-offish. Maybe part of it was my distrust, but part of it was that I wasn't really straight, and inside, I was ashamed——of that fact and of everything else about me. Thinking back, maybe it was easier to be ashamed of not being straight than being ashamed to admit that my father was having sex with me from when I was fourteen to when I was twenty-two.

"I played a role even in therapy. Now, what you see is what I am, but in therapy, I played a foul-mouthed, tough, closed, cynic who probably did to my therapist what I did to every other man in my life——try to set him up to prove that he was no good either. It almost worked, but he and I went through too much together to allow me to walk away in the end without dealing with who I really am."

For most of the time I knew Caitlin, she and I were engaged in a struggle in which she made some remarkable strides toward wholeness. It wasn't until just recently that I learned that she had held back some important details which may have affected the way in which her therapy evolved.

What people reveal in therapy is often less important in the short run than what they learn over the course of a program. Don't get me wrong, I'm not recommending coming into therapy and painting a false picture, but when you really look at life as a whole, much of what we do is to paint pictures. We play roles. If we are healthy, our roles are consistent with the things we do in those roles. For instance, when we play parent, we speak with a different voice than when we play lover, or employee, or student, or friend. Caitlin played the role she was capable of playing. She was as honest as her pain and her fear allowed her to be. In the end, she grew toward her full measure of humanity because she no longer needed to lie. She knew she had to face the hurt inside her or continue to live—not a lie—but a chaotic existence.

She sounded so different in therapy than she does now, but that hour a week was just one small piece of Caitlin's reality and she shouldn't be judged by it. I remember that first time we met . . .

Three Years to Get Ready

Caitlin came into therapy when, after what she claimed at the time was three years of abstinence from drugs and alcohol, she relapsed and began using prescription drugs. When she called to make her first appointment, she was casual and non-committal. She said that she had been recommended by a friend and that she had a few problems she had to work out. She emphasized that she was sober for three years.

Caitlin presented a picture of perfection, externally. She wore elegant clothes, had a stunning hairdo, and used considerable make up. She possessed a classic beauty which needed far less help than she gave it. Her face demonstrated no emotion, not even the nervousness which most people show when they enter therapy.

"Tell me what brings you here," I said, noncommittally. I wanted to give Caitlin the opportunity to develop her own agenda.

"I don't know where to begin," said Caitlin. She squirmed uncomfortably in the chair and picked at her fingers, and looked down at her lap. "I guess I better tell you the truth. I picked up drugs the other night since I called you to make this appointment." She couldn't look at me as she spoke. "You know, I could've lied to you. You would've never known. But then, I would only've been lyin' to myself, wouldn't I?

"It wasn't just that one night you picked up, was it?" Her appearance said that she was at that moment under the influence of drugs.

"How . . .," she stuttered, looking totally mortified. "You're not the first to ask that. No . . ." She looked up for the first time. "I used tranquilizers for about a week. I was usin' when I called you last week. I have to stop. It doesn't work anymore. All it gets me is sick, depressed and ashamed. I was sober for three years, and now I've lost my three years," she added, almost in tears. "Who'm I kiddin'? I can't lie any more. I'm gonna be straight or I'm gonna be dead. I can't play with drugs—not for one more minute. I came here because I want to be sober."

"How do you mean, lost your three years?"

"Well, you know. I'm going to have to go to the AA meeting and tell everybody I'm one day sober—again! I have to face that, and it's not easy, let me tell you." As she spoke, Caitlin became more animated, but it was as if she were playing a role. She was not coming through as real. I knew that in three years she had learned all of the correct responses. I barely had to question her. She had all of the questions and answers pre-prepared.

I thought to myself that perhaps it was the effect of the tranquilizers or perhaps this was the way she related to people all of the time. After a moment, I answered her. "It beats telling them you're still getting high, doesn't it? And, you can't lose what you learned. Maybe you just missed something along the way that you need to add to what you already know. Yes, in terms of consecutive time, you are one day sober, but the knowledge you learned about

Caitlin

51

recovery in the last three years will all come back to you once the drugs are out of your system. You're alive, you're back on a healthy track and you're trying to find out why you got a danger signal. Sometimes a slip can be positive because it tells you that you need to deal with something else."

"When you put it that way, it beats bein' high by a mile!" I sensed that she was beginning to relax just a little. "One of the women in AA told me to come to you. I thought I had enough therapy in the rehab three years ago when I was first getting sober, but maybe I'm one of those who is sicker than others and needs more help."

"What was happening that got you to pick up drugs after three years without them?" It was time to help her focus upon why she was here.

"Well, about a week ago, I just felt so bad that I went out and got high."

"You mean you had no warning?" I used the question to help her order the time prior to her brief relapse.

"Well, yeah, I wanted to get high, but I didn't know it until I was out of the house and headed for one of my old places. It's funny. I had the choice. If I walked up the street, it would've taken me to an AA meeting. I went the other way and it took me to the bar where I used to hang out. One of my old crowd was only too happy to get me some pot. And then, I went home and took some of my mother's tranquilizers. I told myself I was only gonna take them for one day—until I was feelin' calmer, you know?

"Hey, wait a minute! Are you sayin' I planned it?" Caitlin began to get angry and defensive. "I mean, after three years, I should know what I'm doing!" She stared at me angrily. I noticed that although her voice expressed anger, her body language gave another message. She sat half-turned away from me with her arms folded across her upper body. "Shit! Who'm I kiddin'? I knew what I was doin' all right. If there's one thing I learned in three years, it's that there's no such thing as a slip."

"Did anyone ever tell you what S.L.I.P. stands for?" I asked, keeping the conversation at a comfortable level until I could figure out what was really bothering Caitlin.

"There are some who think that it stands for 'Something Lousy I Planned.' There is nothing that you do that you can't understand if you know what to look for." I looked to her for a reaction, but there was none. "Okay," I continued, "it really isn't that important because we're not here to blame you, but to help you figure out what you need to do to remain sober. Let me ask the question a different way," I said, realizing that there was much more going on than I could see or hear at the moment. "Maybe that was an unfair way of putting it. No, I do not believe that you intentionally did anything to jeopardize your sobriety. Thinking back over the past few months, was there anything different in your life?"

"Well," she became very flustered, "uh, . . . there was this guy. I met him in AA and afterwards I found out that he was drinking and doing drugs. But he wasn't doin' them around me. I thought—I think I'm in love with him. Maybe I am. I'm not sure. Hell, I'm not sure of anything right now."

"How were you feeling about yourself around the time you met him?" I hoped for some clue from her as to the reason she needed to resort to drugs after such a long period of abstinence.

"Lousy—like I always feel." Caitlin began playing nervously with her fingers again. "Are you sayin' that it's connected? I knew I was . . . You know, you're not the only one who told me that. Everybody was sayin' that I was headin' for a fall. I guess I had to learn the hard way, didn't I?"

Caitlin

It was as if we were playing some kind of game. I felt that I didn't know all of the rules. She was giving so many different messages. I was more interested in what she wasn't saying. That seemed to be dictating what was happening. "Lousy, like I always feel?" I thought to myself. I wonder how long 'always' has been for Caitlin. I wasn't quite ready to ask her straight out about what made her feel so lousy, but I knew. It was in her body language. It was in her mannerisms. I wondered if she had ever told anyone what was torturing her.

"Caitlin, tell me what you learned the hard way."

"I . . . I'm not sure," Caitlin answered, with uncertainty. "Maybe to listen to other people. I don't let anyone get close to me."

This was yet another statement which begged me to ask the question about who did the terrible things to her.

She sat silently, pondering. "Right now," I interjected, "you're not letting me get close either, so I guess I can't give you advice or opinions either, but I rarely do that, anyway. I figure my life isn't so perfect that I can tell other people how to run theirs." Our eyes met briefly and both of us smiled. Caitlin looked at me intently for a moment as if to learn something which she could not see earlier. I allowed her to take all the time she needed to begin to feel comfortable. Sometimes the most important moments in therapy are when nothing is said.

"It's like I'm not learning anything from experience. That's it, isn't it? You mean, everything I do connects up? That's what you're saying?" Caitlin leaned forward in her chair, though remaining in a defensive position.

I felt as if we were going in circles. Caitlin kept looking at the principles behind what we were saying, but she was not providing any new information about herself. Perhaps she was afraid that she would not be able to keep control if she opened up. Control appeared to be a real issue for her.

"Caitlin, tell me. Does the guy . . . ? What's his name, by the way?"

"Joe."

"Joe have anything to do with your picking up drugs?"

"Yeah. Sort of . . . You know, another sick man in my life. I had a life full of sick men." She spoke in a detached manner without feeling, as if she were talking about another person's life, and at that, one who didn't matter. Her face and eyes were blank, but her body was twisted almost into a pretzel as she continued: "There was my father, and my girlfriend's father. Both of them had sex with me. I never told anyone about my girlfriend's father. I was only nine and I didn't think it was important. My baby's father, my ex-husband, he beat me and cheated on me. I'd come home and find him in bed with girls who were supposed to be my friends! After I got divorced, other guys, they shit all over my life.

Until I met Joe, I'd stayed out of relationships for a long time after I got straight. For almost a year, I didn't have sex with anybody. Then this . . . He's just like all the others. He tells me how much he loves me, but we fight all the time and he's been gettin' real rough with me. You know, when I came in here today, I pretty much decided I had to blow him off, but I didn't know why." A bit of anger came into her voice. "He's just like all the other sick motherfuckers I've known. He lied to me. Hey, I know what I have to do. It won't be easy because I have feelings for him, but I can't go on beating myself up.

"Well, now you know my whole story. But, I talked about most of these things three years ago in rehab and they don't bother me any more."

"Caitlin," I said softly, "if those things don't bother you any more, how come you picked up drugs last week? And how come you are still going out with 'sick mother-fuckers?'" I looked at her and she became even more uncomfortable. "Maybe you talked about some of the things which hurt you, but maybe you really didn't deal with some of them. There's a difference, you know. Sometimes, what you do in rehab is only to lay the groundwork for what you have to do later. Some things take years before you are ready to *really* deal with them— and the more painful they are, the more you have to do to prepare yourself to really deal with them."

"You think because my father was a scumbag, I'd intentionally pick somebody else who was going to hurt me? Come on!" Caitlin stared at me, challenging me to contradict her.

There are all kinds of denial. Sometimes the most difficult kind of denial is when the person admits to the facts, but denies the emotional impact which was involved, or the after effects which do not stop just because you tell someone. The emotions need to be released, and Caitlin covered hers so well that if it were not for the disaster in her present life, it would be impossible to tell that she had experienced trauma in her earlier life. What Caitlin was doing was admitting that terrible things happened to her, but her behavior implied that she was not bothered by any feelings from those events and that she had not let it have an impact upon her life. Saying that black is white doesn't make it so. It is not possible to wish away the pain and rage of assaults upon our beings. If something hurts, we have a right—no, an obligation—to appropriately scream bloody murder!

We sat quietly for a few moments. I felt that there was no answer to her question that would help Caitlin at this moment. Of course, she didn't intentionally repeat her past. It is simply that we will pick what is familiar over what is healthy until we are able to understand what we are doing. Sometimes, the fear of facing overwhelming pain, rage and shame is enough to keep a person from dealing with them. I waited.

Enormous tears began streaming down Caitlin's face. Her eye liner ran down her cheeks in huge black rivulets. "Why do I act like I do?" she said, between sobs. "I want to like myself. Why can't I?" She paused, and her face froze back into a mask; a rather dirty one. "I never cry!" she exclaimed. "It makes me ugly." She was not aware her makeup had run, and for the moment, I decided not to tell her about it. I didn't want to distract her from feeling her frustration. It wasn't the feeling which she ultimately needed to get to, but at least she wasn't being defensive. "I'm sorry," she continued, "I don't allow myself to get upset like that. It's not good for me."

"Maybe you came into therapy partly because you need to learn to like yourself. To really like yourself, you have to be honest with yourself. And, to like yourself, you have to first get past all of the old feelings you've been stuffing. You can't hide from your feelings. Keeping it all in doesn't allow you to experience your present feelings, and they could become a lot more pleasant than the old ones. Perhaps you can't hold back the tears all the time anymore. It uses so much energy that you might not have enough left to stay straight. Caitlin, now that you are feeling a bit more under control, I just wanted to tell you that you have a wee bit of eye makeup on your cheeks."

"Oh my God!" she exclaimed. "I must look a mess. I look bad enough when I am fixed up! Lemme go straighten myself out. That's a funny one! Straighten myself out? Well, at least I can fix my makeup. I can't stand it for you to see me like this."

"No matter what your makeup is doing, you are a very beautiful person, and a very attractive woman too. Maybe

Caitlin

when you learn to like yourself, you will see yourself the way others see you."

"Oh, I know that," she said in an almost offhand manner. Sometimes I feel good lookin' an all, but I feel really ugly on the inside, and that's what's really important. I mean, I ain't no Miss America, but I know guys'll look at me. But that's 'cause they don't really know me. And they all only want one thing from me!"

The hour was nearly over, but Caitlin had opened the doors to describe, though not deal with, some of her real feelings. "Our time is almost up. Should we talk about what you need to do to stay straight?"

She answered without hesitation. "No, I'm gonna be okay. I'm gonna go to a meeting tonight and keep goin' every day until I'm back in control. Mentally, I'm already straight. Drugs won't solve anything. And I'm ready to start dealin' with all the things I gotta deal with. I needed three years to get ready, but I know I can't sit on all this shit no more—any more. Can I come in again tomorrow?"

"If you're ready to handle it, sure," I answered. We selected a time and I felt that she was in for a long and painful journey, but one she had to endure—if she was going to live an effective life or maybe simply live.

Righteous Anger

Caitlin looked a bit more animated than she had the previous day. She still looked as though she had spent four hours getting herself ready. Her hair, face, nails and clothing showed great care—more than the situation called for. This, I thought, was perhaps a way of controlling some measure of her life. She painted her exterior to hide the interior. She had already said that she didn't like herself. And her entire life was spent denying her negative feelings—and perhaps her positive ones as well.

"How was your night?"

"Lousy. I went to a meeting, like I said I was gonna, but Joe was there, and we ended up gettin' into a big fight. I blamed him for my gettin' high—I guess that was wrong of me. I got high. Then he started cursin' and threatenin' to hit me, and a whole bunch of other people came over. I was so embarrassed. Here I just got done tellin' them I'm one day sober, and then, I'm outside actin' like I'm in a bar! But, I didn't let it get to me."

"You seem to say that about a lot of things, Caitlin—you didn't let it get to you. Yet, you say you were acting like you were in a bar. Maybe things get to you more than you are able to see. It's like you allow your anger to come out but you can't accept that you have it." She sat quietly thinking about what I had said.

"Yeah . . . I never looked at it that way. When I was married, I'd beat up on any girl who looked at my husband. And I beat him up a few times, too. I don't take anything from anybody, but I never thought I was an angry person. Everybody in AA is always tellin' me I'm angry, but I can't see it."

"Do you feel anything when you are acting angry?"

"No, I just react. A lot of the time, I can't even remember it afterwards. I don't want to be out of control." There was fear in her voice. " Maybe I'm crazy. When I was in my addiction, I had the excuse that it was the drugs, but it's still happening."

"Where did violence start in your life?"

"It was when I was little—maybe seven or eight. My mom would leave me and my sister with my brother. He was older—like maybe fourteen. He would beat on us every day. I tried to get between him and my sister—she's a year younger than me. After, it was funny—not funny but strange—she would have to hold me and rock me to sleep. We were so close then. Sometimes, I was afraid he would try to have sex with one of us. Maybe, I'm just feeling that way now because of what did happen to me later. But, who knows? Maybe I should consider myself lucky! At least that never happened."

"What was your mother doing all that time?"

"She was out having a fuckin' good time with her boyfriend of the week! Then, when I was eleven, she got married again and I didn't get along with her new husband. He thought he was my father and tried to boss me around. I never had a real father until I met him again when I was fourteen. He left when I was two, so I was used to just mom. I really rebelled and he told her she had to choose —him or me. Well, guess what? She sent me to live with my grandparents."

"Was that any better for you?"

"Better?" Caitlin stared at me and for the first time, there was real anger in her eyes. "I had to take care of my grandmother, who just had her leg amputated, and my grandfather was mean and treated me like a servant. I had to clean a three story house all by myself. I begged my mother to take me back, but she told me she couldn't take care of me. She kept my fuckin' brother and my sister but I was too much for her! Up until then, I was a good kid. At least I thought so.

"Y'know? I just thought of this . . . Besides being mean to me, my mom's husband always wanted to hug me and I wouldn't let him touch me. After what happened with my girlfriend's father, I wasn't about to let any man put his hands on me!"

"Did you think he was going to try something with you?"

"I never really thought about it, but you know, maybe he was and I'd just gone through so much I didn't even take notice." Caitlin looked at her hands. Her expression was blank.

"What are you feeling now?"

"Uh, angry, I guess."

"You guess?"

"I don't like to deal with feelings. I . . ." Caitlin stopped. "Damn," she exploded, "this is what the people at AA were talking about when they said I am the angriest person in the room. Everything in my life would make anybody angry and I didn't understand it when they asked me why I couldn't feel it. What good would it have done to feel it when I was a kid? Nothing could help me. I figured if I was invisible, I could keep the situation under control. Like when my brother would come in the house, I would hide in the closet. Sometimes I would stay in there all day and night. I couldn't even go to the bathroom. I had to just keep it in 'til I almost exploded.

"Even now, I sometimes just disappear. If I feel like just being in my own head, I just walk away and nobody better try to stop me!"

"Caitlin, that was then and now is now. The old rules don't apply any more. It's like you are still living in your childhood world. There aren't as many enemies out there. Before, it was everybody. Now, you just need to select the healthy people and reject the unhealthy ones."

"But how do I learn to tell the difference?" Caitlin looked confused.

Caitlin had lived twenty-three years and had yet to see her first, truly healthy day. She was presently living with the same mother who had rejected her as a child. At best, she had to have ambivalent feelings with which she never dealt openly. The mother who had rejected her was now supporting her in her recovery. And, at the same time, her

Caitlin

61

mother was taking care of her as if she were a child. Caitlin had a seven year old child of her own, yet it was her mother who gave the child most of the parenting he received.

"Before you can pick new friends and lovers, you need to begin to deal with your feelings about yourself and your feelings about the people who helped you feel that way." Caitlin looked at me and appeared uncomfortable. "What are you thinking?"

"I worked so hard to forget everything that happened to me and now you're sitting there telling me I have to remember it all over again. I don't know if I want to go through that." Caitlin looked as if she might leave, and frankly, I wouldn't have blamed her. She leaned forward in her chair and suddenly sat back. "Yeah, you're right. If I had been able to live with it, I wouldn't be here after three years so-called sober, would I?"

Another session was ending and Caitlin had already made several important discoveries. She accepted that she possessed righteous anger. She knew that her chaotic life was connected to her dysfunctional past. She accepted that she would have to deal with her feelings if she wanted to change those things about her life which prevented her from living in a healthy manner. Today, her life was in neutral. However, that certainly was an improvement over two days earlier when she was in free-fall!

Old Anger

"Hi!," said Caitlin as she breezed in the door a week later. "I don't know why or how, but after our session last week, I started to feel better than I ever did. But I started thinkin' and dreamin' about all the things from my past. I don't know whether that's good or bad."

"Maybe it isn't good or bad—maybe it just is. Your past is a part of you and either you deal with it or it will deal with you. Oh, and you look beautiful when you smile!"

"Thanks!" she said, "an' you don't have to tell me—I should smile more often. Everybody tells me that."

"When you have less to feel bad about, you will have more to feel good about. That's how it works—at least it always worked that way for me."

"What should we talk about today?" She tried to keep the focus away from herself.

"How about telling me something that might help me understand who you are and why you are the way you are."

Caitlin sat pondering for a few moments. She got up from the chair and began pacing the room in an agitated manner. She stood behind her chair and began squeezing the back of the chair so hard her knuckles turned stark white.

"I never told anybody what I'm gonna tell you now. I don't even like to think about it. You know how I told you that my girlfriend's father molested me? I never told anybody what happened and I still have nightmares about it. It was like the end of my childhood." She paced about the room and finally sat down. I sat silently and waited for her to continue.

"Like I was sayin'. I went swimmin' with my best friend. I was about nine. You know, even though things were tough at home with my brother beatin' me and all, I still had a lot of fun. I had lots of friends and we did all kinds of fun things together. Anyway, we went back to her house and I had permission to spend the night. We played in her room—her dad was in the kitchen drinkin.' I was scared of him, but Debbie—that's my friend—said as long as we stayed out of his way, it'd be okay. When we went down to get some milk and cookies, he looked at me in the strangest way, y' know? I wasn't dumb. I seen that look before. My brother's friends were always teasin' an tryin' to get me alone in the bedroom. But that was different——they were kids and this was a grown man.

"Anyway, I was scared, but we went to bed. He was still downstairs drinkin.'"

"Where was your friend's mother?"

"She left when my friend was about seven and it was just her and her father. So, we went to bed and she took the inside of the bed next to the wall. I didn't think anything of it then. Well, in the middle of the night, something woke me up an it was him, holdin' me down an doin' oral sex on me. I still get sick just thinking about it. I was so scared, but I still tried to kick him off of me. He just laughed. He told me how much I was going to like it! After, he just got up and left like it never happened. I just lay there shakin.' I felt so . . . dirty, and like my childhood just ended.

"My friend just lay there with her face to the wall the whole time. I knew she was awake. Later, when I was older, I figured that I saved her for that night. But he was doin' it to her——and probably more. And the next morning, he jokes with me about how much he liked his snack last night! I hated myself after that. I always felt dirty and spoiled. And I always hated sex. It was just somethin' I used but I never liked it. It's a way to hold a man and that's all. I never feel anything——you know what I mean." Caitlin was shaking, and rocking back and forth, hitting her head against the chair with each rock.

"What are you feeling?"

"Nothin'. What good does it do?"

"Caitlin, what are you doing?"

"Oh, you mean the rockin'. I been doing that since I was a little kid whenever I get upset." She continued rocking violently.

"If you are upset, what is it you are feeling?" I probed.

"What the fuck is it any of your fuckin' business anyway? All these goddamn questions. What do you get out of it? You like hearin' sex stories?"

"Who are you angry at, Caitlin? Did I cause your pain, or force you to tell me about the hurt?"

Caitlin paused to think about that. She stopped rocking. "You mean, I'm really angry at that bastard and I'm takin' it out on you? Yeah. I do that all the time. I get mad at my mother and rag all over my sister—or the other way round. Or I snarl at every man I meet at AA because I let one guy hurt me."

"How do you feel about your girlfriend's father?"

"I hate him," Caitlin said without expression.

"So, what you're saying, is that you do get your anger out, but never at the person who caused you to be angry."

"Yeah, I guess that's so. Damn! You know I never really looked at it that way. I thought that I just never let the past bother me." Caitlin seemed genuinely excited by her discovery. "How do I learn to get my anger out?"

"I can show you a technique that might help you do that when you're ready. I use a method called 'the empty chair' which sometimes can help people practice dealing with their anger safely. It can be very painful, but it works for many of the people who try it."

Caitlin began nervously picking at her fingers. "I guess I'm willing to try anything. My way sure didn't work, did it? And the way I felt this past week tells me that somethin' that's happening in here is workin' for me, that's for sure!"

"It's too late to begin today, but next week, if you want to, we'll have you try to talk to someone who hurt your life. It's one way to get out old anger or to practice dealing with a situation that you are really going to face. I'll explain more about it next time, okay?" She looked both disappointed and relieved that we were not going to work on her anger any more that day.

Caitlin was beginning to believe that she needed to deal with her old rage so that she could have a chance to grow. However, after twenty-three years of holding it in, she was not able to make an instantaneous change. At least she was beginning to have hope, and sometimes that is enough to hold off the pain temporarily.

"Real" Problems

Caitlin appeared to be very depressed.

"Is everything okay?"

"I don't know what it is," she began. "I've been havin' these dreams—about my father and all. I don't like it."

"Your therapy is stirring up old memories you've been trying to keep buried. But the price you've paid to silence your memories is a dysfunctional life and a relapse into drugs. It comes down to which pain you choose to have, Caitlin."

"I don't think I'm ready for that empty chair thing today. I got some real problems I have to talk to you about." I sat silently, and she continued. "I think I'm a little pregnant."

Sometimes reality rears its ugly head and yesterday needs to be put aside. Many of the vulnerable women who enter sick relationships are the ones least likely to take precautions against pregnancy. Perhaps it is a fatalistic view of the world or, equally likely, it is a fantasy about creating a perfect family and living happily ever after. At the moment of impact, there is not the luxury of sufficient time to explore the reasons. There is only time to decide how to handle a reality from which there is no escape through denial. Caitlin's words appeared to be attempting to minimize reality. ' . . . a little pregnant?'"

Caitlin continued: "I gotta talk to Joe. I can't handle another kid. No way. Unless he's ready to help all the way."

"You mean marry you?"

"Well, or something," she answered, with uncertainty. "I can hardly take care of the one I have. I mean, I was a mother when I was sixteen and I need some time for me. Do you know what a baby would do to my life? I'd be a prisoner."

Caitlin's predicament was not uncommon. She had been a victim in every sense of the word since early childhood. When a person, after sufficient negative experiences, believes that her fate is sealed and that she will always be a victim, she no longer needs a perpetrator in order to be victimized. She becomes adept at setting up the circumstances of her own victimization. Caitlin was pregnant by a man who was an active addict and alcoholic and who also abused her. Regardless of which alternative she chose, she would emerge a victim. In such a case, the best she could accomplish would be to cut her losses. This was a no-win situation. As a therapist, I could not offer her advice about the person with whom she chose to spend her life, and whether or not to terminate a pregnancy, because these issues are so personal. Her own beliefs needed to be sorted out, but it was her beliefs that had to be used to make the decision.

"How late is your period?" I asked, trying to bring the discussion down to practical reality. There was no use dealing with the emotional issues of pregnancy if Caitlin was not pregnant.

"I'm about two weeks late now," she answered, once again showing no emotion.

"Well, before you do anything else, why don't you get a pregnancy test so you can be sure one way or the other."

"I'm afraid. I really don't want to know." She stared, stony faced.

"Caitlin, this is one of those issues that will exist whether you want it to or not. If you are pregnant, you can't wish it away and you have a lot of important decisions to make that don't allow you a lot of time."

"I just don't have the strength to face any more problems right now," she said, with resignation.

"I know you don't, Caitlin, but there are some things which can't be put off no matter how you feel. This is one of them." I paused and saw that she was trying to close out the whole conversation. "Caitlin . . ."

"What?" she answered with annoyance. "Okay," she said, after a moment, "I know I can't run away. Why do I always do these things to myself? I could've stayed on the pill. I could've, I should've, I would've. Yeah, I know all the right answers, but I still do everything to fuck myself up. This one is really somethin'! You'd think I'd learn something from experience, wouldn't you? I mean, I sometimes resent havin' one kid—how'm I supposed to deal with another? I sometimes don't even give enough attention to the one I've got, for God's sake!

"I gotta get a pregnancy test, and if it's positive, then I gotta decide what my next step is. Sounds easy, don't it?"

"Caitlin," I answered gently, "I hear you saying you are emotionally tired, but besides finding ways to deal with your feelings, part of your recovery is to create a more effective life for yourself by making healthy decisions— even if the circumstances are difficult ones."

"There's no sense puttin' it off another day, is there? I'm gonna stop off after I leave here and pick up one of those pregnancy tests. Here's one time in my life where I hope I really flunk a test!"

"When you find out, give me a call, okay?" She nodded her assent. "Whatever the results are, you can find a way to deal with it. Sometimes you have to start recovery by accepting that there are some things left over from your sickness that have to be dealt with. Part of getting well is—no more running away from yourself. Remember, if you could handle everything you had to deal with in your life, you can handle this."

"I guess so," she answered, morosely.

"Hey!" I said loudly, getting her attention for the moment. "Do you think you are going to use pregnancy to get away from dealing with yourself and gaining a sense of your specialness in this world? No way!"

"You're right. My mother used her kids as an excuse to fuck up her life, and not do anything for herself. I'll be damned if I'm gonna do that to myself. I didn't get this far to throw it all away.

Caitlin left the room feeling better about herself than she had an hour earlier—in spite of the fact that she had a real problem with which she had to deal.

Caitlin called me the following morning to let me know that she was pregnant. She decided to inform Joe and to discuss what they were going to do because it was his child also. She called me the next day to schedule an emergency appointment.

"That bastard!" she began. "How the hell could I have been pulled in by his bullshit? You know what he did? I asked him to come over to my house. First thing he does is start apologizin' for the fight, so I think, now everything's gonna be okay, right? He starts pawin' at me and wants to get me into bed. That's when I backed him off and told him I was pregnant, and you know what he does? He asks me, 'How do I know the baby is mine?' He knew I wasn't with anybody else for a year! I freaked out and started screamin' at him and tryin' to tear his face off. He keeps sayin' that I'm tryin' to get over on him so he'll have to pay for my kid, and I picked him because he had a good job!

"Before this, even though we had plenty of fights, he was always tellin' me he really cared, but now I see it was just bullshit."

I asked her what she was feeling.

"Now, I'm really angry. I wanna kill the motherfucker. I wanna rip his face off." Caitlin paused, and her expression changed from anger to pain. "I also wanna beat myself for lettin' it happen. I should've known better."

"Who said you should have known better? Where did you learn anything different from what you were able to do? Did your parents teach you how to develop healthy relationships? Or for that matter, anybody else in your life?"

"Well, when you put it that way, no." Caitlin was now more under control. "But to survive, you have to know those things, don't you?"

"Yes, Caitlin, you do. But you never even saw a healthy man, so how could you be expected to know the difference. Joe was like all the men in your life. He even used the same words, didn't he?"

"You bet your ass he did—oops! Excuse me!" Caitlin looked embarrassed.

In the same breath Caitlin used street language to refer to herself and her life, but when it was directed at me, she got embarrassed. Shouldda, wouldda, couldda—that's what it's all about, isn't it?

"That's okay, Caitlin. There's nothing I haven't heard—or said. One thing about this place is that you don't have to censor words, ideas or feelings. This is a place where you can tell it like it is. Nobody can get hurt—they aren't here to hear it. And just as important, they can't use it against you for the same reason."

"Yeah, I know, but it's so damn hard. I been feelin' these things all my life, and now I can't live with it anymore. Maybe it's too late for me, sometimes I don't know."

Don't give up no matter how scary it is. You have enough pain in you for ten lifetimes and just the thought of having to bring it out has to be . . . you know, I can't even put a label on it. I can't even say I know what you must be feeling, because as bad as anything has been in my life, I have nothing to compare it to. All I can say is I will be here for you and with you when you go through it. You won't be alone. That is one thing I can identify with."

"I'm not goin' to give up. It's just that sometimes I get so tired of all the pain. And I know that I bring a lot of it on myself."

"Maybe one of the things we can work on is to help you to make healthier choices in the future." Caitlin stared at me. At the moment, we were speaking different languages. So, I got back to the practical issue with which she soon must deal.

What do you plan to do about your pregnancy?" I asked.

"I hate this," she said. She shook her head back and forth as if to deny the existence of the situation. "I could have had an abortion when I was fifteen. I decided I wanted to keep my baby, and now I'm twenty-three years old and have a seven-year-old son I don't want some of the time—I shouldn't say that, but it's true. I never had a chance to be a kid—well I never would've anyway with what was going on in my life.

Caitlin
_____

"Anyway, what am I going to do? I guess I have to have an abortion. It makes me sick thinkin' about it, but I can't be bringin' another kid into the world now."

Caitlin made the decision to have an abortion. She believed that her life was too chaotic to attempt to bring another child into it. She was barely able to attend to the one she had. She worked through the feelings rather quickly because she handled this issue with the same denial which helped her survive all of the previous trauma in her life. Her philosophy had been, "If I don't allow it to hurt, maybe I can survive another day." Her method obviously was flawed. The fact that she turned to drugs clearly established that.

I Can't Handle This!

"I want to forget about the abortion," began Caitlin. "Maybe some other time, we can talk about it, but for now, I'm okay and I want to just move on and start dealin' with what makes me the way I am."

"Okay, if you're certain you don't need to let out some of your feelings about Joe or the abortion." I looked at Caitlin and saw no reaction. "Maybe we can talk about something that really ties it all together—men."

Caitlin almost jumped out of her chair. "Yeah, men. I guess there's no way to avoid that subject, is there? Yeah, I guess I have to go through it. Where do you want me to start?"

"Tell me about the men in your life."

She pulled back into the chair and folded herself up behind her arms. Her eyes were the only indication of the depth of pain she was facing. Caitlin's face was a blank.

"Well, you know that sex is the biggest problem in my whole life. I never really liked sex—I still don't. But I have trouble saying no to men I date. I guess after your own father has sex with you, not much matters, does it? When you feel that dirty, sometimes it's not easy to really care what happens to you today."

"Caitlin," I stated firmly, "I want you to know before we go another step forward, that the one thing in this room that matters is you. From now on, you can choose to be in control of your life. You had no choice with your father. You need to learn that. That means you dump the pain of the past and no longer use it to beat yourself or cheat yourself. Every time you use the past as an excuse to put yourself down, you are depriving yourself of a chance to be whatever special self you were meant to be—and when you are ready to let yourself be special—you will be. I have this theory about people. I believe that everybody is born perfect and if experience didn't get in the way, we would all live contented lives. Well, maybe there are a few exceptions, but for the most part, I believe that people want to trust, love, care, share—at least most of the time. But when you grow up in a family which teaches you that you can't trust and that you aren't worthy of love; which shows that they don't really care; which shares only their own pain; you come to believe that what you learned from your family is the truth for the whole world. If you want to make a fresh start, you have to believe in trust and love, in caring and sharing."

"I want to believe. I *have* to believe if I want to live. I can't go on fucking up my life anymore."

"You were starting to talk about the men in your life."

"This is difficult." Caitlin squirmed in the chair, unable to get comfortable.

"Why don't you sit back and physically relax. Sometimes, when you stop feeling today's feelings, it is easier to

Caitlin

talk about the past." Caitlin leaned back in the chair and draped her arms over the armrests. She tried closing her eyes, but found that too uncomfortable. For a woman who has been sexually violated by the man who is supposed to be closest to her—her father—it would take an immense amount of trust for her to sit in a room with a man with her eyes closed.

"This is better," she said, sounding just a bit more at ease. "Anyway, like I was sayin'. I'm all mixed up about men. I'm all mixed up about everything. But men . . ."

"What's the first thing you remember about men?"

"I guess that would have to be my brother and his friends and how they treated my sister and me." Caitlin paused for a few moments to gather her strength and continued: "I told you how he was always beatin' on us. I couldn't even protect my own sister. I was about eight years old, so I guess I really couldn't have done much. And when that thing happened to me with my girlfriend's father it was almost like I was being told, 'See. If you had helped your sister, this wouldn't've happened to you.' I know that's silly, but back then, I really believed it."

"So what you're saying is that you blamed yourself partly for what your girlfriend's sick father did to you?"

"That's silly, isn't it?"

"No, not if you are nine years old it isn't. Children believe in magic and it is easy to convince them they are responsible for everything that happens. For instance, did you ever hear of a child who was certain that she'd caused her parents' divorce?"

"Okay, maybe I wasn't responsible for what he did, but I just feel like I could have done something to help my sister." Caitlin began nervously twisting a tissue and tearing off pieces which she meticulously placed in the ashtray.

"Let me ask you something. If your seven year old son was in the room and someone was robbing you or threatening you, what would you expect him to do?"

Without hesitation she replied, "Get the hell out of there and protect himself!"

"Were you so much different at eight than he is at seven?"

"When you put it that way, not really." She looked somewhat relieved.

"I gotta talk about my father now," she blurted. "You're gonna hate me when I tell you the whole story. Nobody knows. I told them one time in rehab that he had sex with me, but it's a lot worse than that."

"No matter what happened, I care about you. Sometimes, when you've been carrying something around with you for a long time, you feel you can't tell. It is far worse hiding it than sharing it with someone you trust. Let's deal with that first. Do you trust me enough to share a deep and painful secret?"

"I put my life in your hands just by coming here. I was ready to go out and kill myself with drugs when I came here, so I had to trust somebody. You've helped me a lot and you never judged me, or tried to tell me what to do like a lot of people in my life. I needed that because I sure judged myself. You couldn't know how much."

Caitlin was sitting all the way forward in her chair as if she was preparing to run, but that was simply fear of the unknown. She had never placed trust in anyone as an adult, and this was probably as important a challenge as she would ever face in her recovery. At a point similar to Caitlin's many people choose to run away rather than risk giving trust to another person because every time they chose to trust in the past, that trust was violated. In Caitlin's life, every significant adult violated her trust. As an adult, she learned to pick only those people who most

Caitlin

75

resembled her dysfunctional family, so she was always let down. The most recent example was her boyfriend who all too willingly impregnated her and then denied responsibility when the inevitable occurred.

"God, this is so hard!" she exclaimed.

"Caitlin," I said, so softly that she had to lean forward to hear me, "tell me what you cannot tell me."

"I . . . my father had sex with me for almost eight years. I was still doing it when I was two years sober. It didn't stop until he had a stroke and was completely paralyzed. Two years sober, that's really funny! How could I call myself sober when I was . . . Oh, shit, I can't handle this. I gotta get out of here!" Caitlin stood up but did not move toward the door. "I finally told somebody, didn't I?" She sat down and leaned back in the chair, breathing raggedly.

I again asked for her feelings.

"Mostly relief. Like okay, I did it, so what? I can't change it. I never thought I would tell anybody. I go to AA meetings every day and what am I supposed to do, get up and share with the group that my father was fuckin' me since I was a little kid and it would still probably be goin' on if God hadn't given him a stroke to stop him? Oh, Jesus Christ, I been livin' with this since I was fourteen. How can you say a twenty-two year old is being forced to do somethin'? This is one you can't blame on anybody but me!"

"Before you blame yourself, what were the circumstances?"

"He threatened to kill me if I didn't do what he said. Once, he put a gun to my head and another time he strangled me and tried to drown me in the bathtub. And worse than that, he threatened to kill my son if I didn't cooperate with him. He was really sick. He would sometimes say that we were meant to be together——like boyfriend and girlfriend. He even had a girlfriend who was only a couple of years older than me."

"It doesn't sound like you had any choices. Caitlin, why were you living with him at that time?"

"He had all of my furniture at his place and I had no place to go when I got out of rehab."

"Aren't you the slightest bit angry at your father for what he did to you?" Anger rose in my own voice.

"What good would it do to be angry with him now?" Tears were streaming down Caitlin's face, but she was so upset that she didn't realize she was crying.

"Caitlin, just stop for a few minutes and let it go."

"I . . . don't . . . want . . . to . . . cry," she said in ragged bursts.

"It's too late to hold it back now. You need to let it all out. It isn't just for what your father did. Let it go."

She did. She cried silently. She was not yet willing to accept that she was entitled to express her pain fully and openly.

"It feels so strange," she said, after her crying subsided. "I never let myself show any feeling—except anger—and even that's never when it should be.

"I just decided something. I don't ever want to let anybody control my life again. This time, I'm going to stay out of relationships until I learn to like myself and learn that I'm important. I really needed to trust somebody, and I'm glad it was you because now that it's out, I know I have a lot of work I have to do to make myself well. It's funny, I was thinking of dropping out of therapy because I was doing okay again and was telling myself I didn't need to talk about the past. Robert—thank you. That's so hard to say when it is real. I told Joe 'thank you' when he brought me flowers, but he only did it because of the night before. He had been drunk and didn't show up for a date.

Caitlin

77

Boy am I rambling on! It's like somebody pulled out a cork and everything wants to come out at once. Wow!"

"It's okay, Caitlin." I looked at her carefully. She seemed to have an inner glow. "Just don't try to do everything on your first day out of prison—yes, prison—a prison you constructed to keep yourself in and everybody else out.

"And, I just noticed something that I want to share with you. It's a small thing but maybe it has some meaning. I noticed when you were talking during the past few minutes that your speech was different. You usually talk tougher—you drop the last letter of words—like gettin' instead of getting. You stopped doing it. Also, your tone is different—softer, more feminine. Maybe even the way you speak is tied to trust and comfort about yourself."

"I can talk very nicely when I think about it. It's just that it was always so much easier to talk street talk, y'know?" She smiled, indicating that the last words were said intentionally.

"There is no end to the wonderful things that are there to be discovered within you, is there?"

She looked at me to see if I was serious, and looked pleased to discover that I was.

Caitlin had trusted one person with her deepest secret. This particular secret is one which haunts untold numbers of women—and men. Incest is devastating enough in the life of a child. It is often made far more traumatic because there is no one to protect the interests of the child. Whom can she tell? The perpetrator often threatens her with violence, or worse yet, blame. Often, the mother doesn't want to hear terrible things about her mate—he is her source of support and comfort. So, the child is sacrificed. In Caitlin's case, her mother sacrificed her long before sex was involved. She was placed in jeopardy so that the mother could have a peaceful relationship with her new husband. Caitlin was already a 'trained victim' long before her father touched her. She needed to fully understand this so that she could begin the process of relieving herself of guilt for what was, from its inception, a terrible injustice perpetrated upon her very being.

Euphoria

"I feel great today!" Caitlin began. "The nightmares stopped and it's like I had something ugly and rotten cut out of me. Everybody who's seen me in the last week has been doing a double take. They can't believe it's me. I've kept a stone face for so long, maybe they thought I was born with it. I have a smile for everybody and they really think something is wrong now! Even my mom thinks something must be wrong.

"You know, I even feel attractive. I want to tell the whole world—'Hey, I'm Caitlin and I'm okay! You hear?' I never experienced anything like this. It's like a constant high."

"That's just what it is Caitlin, a genuine high. You've been in pain for so long, that just simply relieving some of it makes you feel better—maybe better than you ever believed you could feel."

"I would never let myself feel this good before because I always believed that if you let yourself feel too good, someone or something would come along and take it away. I can't stop smiling."

Caitlin and I spent the rest of that day talking about good feelings. She deserved to ride the crest of her relief for a little while. There was plenty of time to get back to dealing with the roots of her bad feelings. I didn't choose to tell her that the euphoria she was experiencing would pass as soon as reality presented her with a new problem. She had relieved some of her guilt by sharing a terrible secret, but she hadn't begun to change her old attitudes and values, so it was inevitable that she would repeat the past—until she developed new ways of dealing with reality.

Too Good to Last

"You look really down today," I said when Caitlin had seated herself.

"Yeah, I am. I knew it was too good to last."

"More important, did you enjoy it while you had it, and do you want more of it?"

"Sure I do, but I already told you the worst thing that I ever did. What do I have to do to get it to come back —kill somebody and then come in here and confess it to you?"

I couldn't help but laugh, and that got Caitlin laughing, too.

"I know I'm just sittin' in my own shit today, but I'm so used to feelin' bad that I guess I just wanted to feel good for a little while longer. I guess I gotta work some more to get it back. Nothin' ever comes easy for me.

"Talk about your anger today, Caitlin."

"What makes you think I'm angry?"

"Because you're depressed," I said.

"What's that got to do with it? Maybe I should talk about my depression instead." Caitlin was beginning to become impatient.

"Okay, so talk about your depression."

"What's there to talk about? I feel lousy."

"You know, it's funny. Last week, when you were happy, you couldn't stop talking. Now . . ."

"Yeah, like when I feel down, I haven't anything to say."

I stopped for a moment and looked at her. Caitlin was looking off into space. It was as if she knew what she had to say, but was still resisting the need to say it. "We seem to be going around in circles today. What's wrong?"

"I don't know. It's not like I'm doin' it on purpose or anything. I want to let it out. It's like I . . . never mind."

"Say it Cait. 'It's like I' what?

"It's like I'm not allowed to talk about my feelings," she blurted.

"Who said so?"

"My father—my father. My brother. My father, when he was—you know—he threatened to kill my son if I ever told! My brother, if I told my mother, he would've beat me even worse! I learned to keep it to myself."

"No, Caitlin, you learned how to hide from yourself. What do you think the drugs were all about? And the kind of men you chose to go out with? And stuffing your feelings all the time? But it was there the whole time, and a couple of weeks ago when you let some of it out, you felt really good for the first time in years."

"I can't talk about feelings. I just can't." She sat shaking her head violently back and forth.

"What would happen if you allowed your feelings to come out? Caitlin, what are you most afraid of?"

"I'm afraid that if I ever took the lid off, I would get a gun and kill every one of those motherfuckin' sons of bitches today! I hate them all." She grimaced and sat clenching and unclenching her fists.

"Caitlin, I would like you to do an exercise with me. It's called 'the empty chair.' Remember, we talked about it before. In this exercise, you talk to some of the people

Caitlin

81

who hurt you. It lets you get to some of your deepest anger without hurting anybody, because the person really isn't here. Are you willing to try it?"

"Right now, I would try anything. I can't live with this inside me anymore. Let's do it."

I set up the room with two chairs facing each other and asked Caitlin to sit in one of them. "First, get yourself relaxed and comfortable," I began. Caitlin nervously adjusted herself in the chair. "You comfortable?"

"I'm okay, I guess."

"Now, I would like you to close your eyes, relax and breathe deeply. This is just to get yourself more comfortable and get your mind off everything else, okay?" Caitlin followed the simple instructions and began to feel more at ease physically.

"Okay. Now that you are more relaxed I want you to picture your father sitting in the chair opposite you. You can open your eyes now. Picture what he looks like. Remember, he cannot speak or move. He can only sit there and listen to you. This is your turn to tell him what you need to tell him so that you can feel better. This cannot hurt him because he is not really here, but his image is here for you to use to get out your feelings.

"When you talk to him, address him directly, don't simply talk about him. Picture him in the chair. He is waiting for you to begin. Remember, you can stop any time you want. You are in complete control."

Caitlin stared at the chair opposite her. There was pain, rage and terror in her face. "I don't know how to start."

"What did you call him?"

"Dad," she answered softly, as though the word might explode.

"Then, begin with the word, dad. If you're ready . . ."

Caitlin began crying. "I can't."

Stop the Merry-Go-Round

82

I sat silently. I knew at the moment, there was nothing I could do to relieve the pain she was feeling.

"Dad," she began hesitantly, "why? Why did you do it? I'm your daughter, not some fuckin' whore you picked up on the street. I was fuckin' fourteen years old and I never knew you. For fourteen years, I wasn't good enough to be part of your life. I was on the streets and I couldn't go back to mom and I wouldn't go back to grans'——no way. You said I could come live with you and we could get to know each other. Yeah, get to know each other!

"Sure, I was already into drugs, and that was okay with you. You were the only one who didn't condemn me and call me all kinds of bad names like mom and grampop, and mom's fuckin' husband. You were my hero and my last chance. I needed you, goddamn you. I didn't have nobody. You even got me drugs and said we would have a good time together. You took me to a motel like some tramp and you told me it was alright to sleep with you because you loved me and we were finally together. I was so damn confused and I was wasted. I didn't know. I should . . . I was just a kid, damn you.

"Afterwards, I even tried to justify it to myself. I tried to believe all the bullshit you told me about how it was alright. I figured maybe it was a way I could have somebody for myself. Sure as hell nobody else wanted me and if this was the price I had to pay—well I paid plenty of other prices, didn't I now? But I was never sick enough to really buy that. I lived in hell because of you.

"An'. . . an'. . . then, I wanted to get away. I knew it had to stop and you said, if I ever tried to leave you that you'd kill me and you put a gun to my head and I thought you were really gonna do it. But where could I run? I had nobody and no place.

"Once it started, it just went on and on, like some nightmare. I got a boyfriend,and that didn't stop you. I got

Caitlin

83

pregnant and had a baby and that didn't stop you. I justified the lousy way he treated me just so I could get away from you. I got married, and that didn't . . . I got sober, an' . . . I can't go on with this. I wanna kill him. I hate him so much, I just wanna kill him!" Caitlin cried in deep, body-racking sobs.

"Let it all out, Cait. Don't hold back now. It's okay. This is your time. He had his." My own voice was shaking with rage, but as I had said, this was her time. "Tell him how you feel about him."

Caitlin paused, building her courage and emotional reserve, and began, "I hate you. You are slime. You don't deserve to be on this earth with human beings. I'm glad you got your fuckin' stroke. I couldn't stop you so God did it for me! I hope you rot in hell! I wish you would drop dead!

"I just wanted somebody to love me, and somebody to love, and look what you did to me. I needed a real father. I had nobody in the whole world who cared about me and you were my last chance and look what you did to me. You made me worthless. How am I supposed to go on livin'? You destroyed me. I always feel dirty. How can I face people? No, how can you face people? How the fuck can you look at yourself in the mirror and not wanna kill yourself? I mean, you threatened to kill your own grandchild just so you could keep on fuckin' your own daughter. How sick can a person get?"

Caitlin simply stopped. She slumped in the chair, drained, physically and emotionally. "I think I'm gonna be sick," she said.

"Just relax. It's going to be okay now. That was a lot of rage that had to come out. It's like having an operation. You need some time to recover. Want a glass of water or something?"

Stop the Merry-Go-Round

84

"I'll be okay. Was that me? I guess it was. I never expected anything like that to come out. You mean that was inside me all the time? I feel . . . lighter. Boy, I wouldn't want to go through that every week!"

"That gets rid of some of the feelings you needed to deal with. It really does help to get them out. Maybe the rest will come easier. No matter what you still need to accomplish in therapy, it will never be that painful."

Caitlin had confronted a large part of her rage and could now accept that her anger wouldn't lead her to homicidal behavior. She had feelings that were strong enough to wish someone dead, but her feelings were normal for her circumstances. She spent a lifetime having no outlet for her feelings. The same people who were destroying her life were the ones who provided the basic necessities of life. There was no escape—until she took control of the direction of her own life—and that process was just now occurring.

Accepting Her Own Worth

"Talking to my father last week really helped," Caitlin began. "It's like I don't feel as bad about it any more. You know, I don't care who knows now. There's really nothing I can do about any of it and I just have to get on with my life. Don't get me wrong, I'm not about ready to forgive and forget, but I can't spend the rest of my life letting it eat me up inside. I still don't want to see him or talk to him, but I don't have to do that to get better, do I?"

"No, you don't have to see him. Recovery may require that you forgive the people who hurt you, but forgiveness simply means that you don't carry grudges any longer. It doesn't mean that you are supposed to go back and let them hurt you again. You simply need to let go of the feelings that are eating at you and keeping you from having a healthy life today. You were so hurt by what your father did to you—both the rage at him and the guilt you developed by blaming yourself—that you couldn't develop healthy relationships. After all, if all men are rotten and you are worthless, as you came to believe, then how can you even think about finding a man who has decent values? Because you are normal and healthy, you did seek relationships, but you only looked for a man who fit the image of what you believed all men to be—rotten—and he would be low enough to accept you for what you thought yourself to be worth—nothing! It was a terrible, vicious circle."

"Caitlin, how do you feel about yourself today?"

"Today, I feel pretty good about myself. Yeah, I know what you mean about letting go of the hate. It's something that really doesn't do me any good at all. When I feel angry, I just want to hurt somebody."

"Let's get back to your feelings about you, okay? What kinds of things about yourself make you feel good?"

"You won't let me out of this one, will you?" she said, smiling, but defensive.

"Nope," I answered, in my best stone-faced imitation.

"Okay, what do I like about me? I don't know. That's a tough question." Caitlin squirmed nervously in the chair.

"Let me ask it differently. What are your good qualities?"

"Well, I'm not stupid and I'm not ugly. I try to be a good person. This is difficult!"

"What nice things have other people said about you?"

"The only nice things I can think of are what guys say when they want to get into my pants. Then, it's 'Baby, you're the most beautiful girl in the world!' Or, 'I ain't never met nobody like you.' But the rest of the time, I guess not too much. Everybody always tells me I should smile more, or I should get a job, or they tell me how to raise my son." Caitlin was speaking matter-of-factly, and didn't seem bothered by what she had been saying.

"Do you expect to get compliments?"

"No! Why should anyone want to compliment me?"

"Caitlin, why shouldn't they want to, and more importantly, why shouldn't you expect some compliments?"

"Cause I never got any," she said, wistfully.

"Do you ever give people compliments?"

"Sure. Today, I told my mom her hair looked nice and she looked real young."

"Does she tell you those kind of things, too?"

"Yeah, I guess so. Sometimes."

"Do you hear it when she tells you nice things?"

"What do you mean?" Caitlin was confused.

"Well, you said before you never got compliments. Maybe you just are unable to accept compliments. And, maybe she also criticizes often, too."

"Oh yeah, she's great at that. 'Don't yell at Bobby! Why didn't you straighten the house?' For god's sake— straighten the house—I'm here takin' care of two kids all day—mine and my sister's. What does she expect—I'm gonna keep them chained to a wall? Kids play."

"Do you do a good job with kids?"

"Yeah, as good as anybody could. I don't neglect them. I do plenty."

"Then that is something else you can say you are proud of about yourself, right?"

"Yeah, right—right." Caitlin was not used to receiving compliments or giving herself credit for doing anything right. "I guess if I really thought about it, I could find a lot of things I do pretty good, couldn't I?"

Caitlin

Caitlin needed to begin accepting that she had worth. She had been a victim for a long time, and part of the nature of victimization is that good feelings are withheld and doled out very stingily by the person who is making you a victim so that you will always feel indebted to him or her!

Caitlin was now learning that there is only one person who had the right to judge her and that was herself. She could consider the opinions of others, but her self-worth had to be determined by her alone. Placing a value upon yourself requires that you accept your right to feel good about yourself, that you can forgive yourself for mistakes, and that you are willing to take responsibility for changing those changeable things about yourself which you do not like. As Caitlin grew, she learned of the existence of many assets within her. She came to see her softness and nurturing ability. She began to learn that she was intelligent, although she had not tested that intelligence in a formal way—such as school—since she was a teen.

Why Can't I Say No?

"I'm really starting to see some differences in me," said Caitlin. She often began a therapy session with a report on her progress. Caitlin was anxious to gain confirmation that what she was seeing was real. "For instance, I'm not so angry all the time. I don't run away and hide so much. Everybody is starting to notice the change. Don't get me wrong, if somebody rubs me the wrong way, I can still be pretty nasty, but I don't distrust everybody. I'm talking to people now, and I like it.

Stop the Merry-Go-Round

"There is one thing, though, I gotta talk about. I met a guy. He was pretty nice and all, so I went out with him, and we ended up in bed that night. I really didn't want to but I couldn't say no. Why did I do that? I mean, that's not the way I want to be. Don't get me wrong, I've been with a few guys—not really that many—considering I've been in an addiction since I was twelve."

"Why did you go to bed with him?"

"Because I wanted to—I thought. The more I think about it, the more I think it was because he was so persistent. I was weak. He just broke down my will. But afterwards, I felt so lousy about it. I don't know. I'm really confused. Then he wanted to see me the next night and I freaked out and told him to get lost. He must think I'm nuts!"

"Why did you go to bed with him?"

"Because I didn't want to lose him."

"But, the very same night, you really lost him—you told him to get lost!"

"That's why I stay away from men most of the time. I'm totally confused and I don't need this. I have enough to deal with." Caitlin picked at her fingers nervously.

"Caitlin, what do you want from a relationship?"

"Love, respect, somebody who cares about me. Is that wrong?"

"No, its perfect. What went wrong?"

Caitlin thought for a moment. "I guess I didn't show those things for myself. If I respected myself, I wouldn't have jumped into bed with him."

"Then, why did you?"

"I was afraid. Afraid I'd lose him, I guess." Caitlin began biting her lower lip.

"Caitlin, what are you worth?"

"Yeah. It keeps comining back to that, don't it? What am I worth? I've been thinking about that a lot this week.

Caitlin

89

I'm worth a lot. I'm a good person. I can be fun. I'm a giving person. I'm pretty nice looking. I'm pretty intelligent. I'm not bad, am I? Then why can't I say no to somebody I think I like?"

"Who says you can't?"

"Nobody. I just have to learn how. I mean, who is he? I can get a guy without jumping into bed. Anybody who doesn't like me for me isn't worth having anyway, isn't that so?"

"Maybe the only problem you still have in that area is you believe it, but your belief is still not absolute. You still have to ask permission to like yourself, isn't that so?" I asked, parodying her question.

"I'm going to keep working on it. I don't want to spend the rest of my life jumping in and out of beds to find the right guy. I want to be able to go out and say no—to everybody. I want to get married again someday. I like the idea of sharing my life, and it won't happen until I get control of myself. And, it's not like I'm promiscuous or anything like that. I don't go out much at all, but if I think I like a guy, I'm afraid to say no."

Caitlin was beginning to develop a much needed tool in her recovery—the ability to critique her own thoughts, feelings and actions. She had an analytical mind which was finally being given a chance to work in her own interests. Earlier in life, she used her intellect simply to survive in a capricious and dangerous world. Now, she was able to look at her own actions and test them against her developing knowledge about the world outside her earlier purview. Once this factor was in place, Caitlin needed to find a direction in which to take her life.

Caitlin was beginning to take control of parts of her life. Her social life was an important factor she needed to consider.

"I went out on three dates with the same guy and didn't let him touch me. You know what? He still calls me back!"

"You sound surprised by that."

"I never tried it before. The way I stayed out of bed was to stay out of relationships." Caitlin looked very pleased with herself.

"How does it feel to say no?' I asked.

"Great! I can say no and somebody will still like me. And, even if he doesn't, I still like myself!

"There's something else I have to deal with. I don't know what to do with my life. I could get a job, but I don't want that. I really would rather do nothing but I know that I can't. If I don't learn to take care of myself, there'll always be somebody able to control me—my mother, some man—and I don't want that any more. I would rather just stay home and take care of a house and my son, but I have to be able to take care of myself, even if I marry some rich guy.

"I always got in trouble when I let somebody take care of me. When I was little, I didn't have much choice, but if I could've gotten out, I would've saved a lot of pain. I started running away when I was twelve, and look where that got me. Eventually, that put me with my father, and that was one hell of a person to have to depend on, wasn't it?" Caitlin paused to allow her anger to course through her.

"So, I've got to do something so I can have enough money so I'll always be independent. That way, I can choose. Now, I can't."

Caitlin

"What do you think you would like to do?"

"I've been giving it some thought. Eventually—this is gonna sound crazy—I'd like to go to college, but for now, I want something I can do quickly—like in six months or a year."

"That makes sense in your circumstances," I said, "and, by-the-way, it is not crazy to want to go to college. If you have a goal, the only obligation you have is not to blow yourself out of the water getting to it. You need to be able to take care of yourself financially so you don't have to live with your mother anymore or depend on some man to take care of you, but you need to look at two kinds of goals—short-term and long-term. If your long-term goal is to get a college education, it can be something you begin part-time after you get a good job and feel independent. There isn't any rule about how you get an education. You simply have to set your priorities and start going for it."

"I've been thinking about what I want to do now, and I thought about something like medical technology. It makes sense. I think I could do real well and the course is only about nine months. The pay is enough to get my own place, and then, later, I could worry about doing something else."

"Caitlin, it sounds as if you have been doing a lot of thinking about the future. It says a lot about how you are beginning to feel about yourself."

"I never looked at it that way," she said, "but it does, doesn't it? Oops! I forgot. I'm not going to ask when I should know the answer myself. Yeah, it does say a lot about how I think of myself!"

Caitlin's life was coming into order. She had begun to learn how to function in a healthy relationship, but she had overcome all of the other obstacles and this last important goal was one for which she was ready.

Stop the Merry-Go-Round

At this late juncture in her therapy, Caitlin admitted she had not been sober after she left the rehabilitation center. She had been forced by circumstances to go to her father to have a roof over her head and there was no way she could handle being near him without drugs. Even though she knew what it meant to go back to him, what choice did she really have?

Caitlin left therapy shortly after she reached this point in her development, but she kept in touch. She did meet a man with whom she is attempting to make a healthy life. He is the same one with whom she was able to develop a relationship before sex became a component. He knows about her past and perhaps he is even more able to forgive and forget it than Caitlin herself is. Both she and her young man come from dysfunctional families and are recovering from addictions, so there are times when their relationship is stormy. Both accept that learning how to relate appropriately is a serious after effect of their upbringing. Neither saw a healthy relationship in his or her early life. They came to therapy for a brief time to work on developing methods that would improve their ability to relate without arguing and fighting.

The purpose of therapy in Caitlin's life was not to give her a crutch upon which she could eternally lean. Rather, therapy was a relationship in which she could develop a set of values that would allow her to see herself as a positive human being, able to make healthy choices. She now had the tools through which she could lead an effective life. She had made the attitude and value changes which allowed her to live with her traumatic past without finding it necessary to repeat it.

The year that Caitlin spent in therapy was fraught with pain, but it was a new kind of pain which proved more tolerable than the pain of the previous twenty-three years of her life. She learned that it was not necessary to forget

Caitlin

the past, but rather she learned that she simply had to relieve the pain it continued to cause her.

During her last session, I asked Caitlin to review some of the things she learned about herself.

"You began therapy just one short year ago, Caitlin," I said. Is there anything you feel stands out particularly?"

"Just that I never pictured myself as being as hard as I sometimes was. Did I really use all of that foul language? That isn't me—at least not the way I like to think of myself. You know, I wasn't aware of the way people saw me. I always thought they didn't like me anyway, so what was the difference how I acted. I learned that the only one who really didn't like me—was me.

"I never realized how my anger made me sound like a truck driver. I never talk like that anyplace else." Caitlin smiled with embarrassment.

"Anger has to come out some way, Caitlin. Sometimes, you can't recognize it yourself as anger, but a lot of times, how you talk can tell other people what you are really feeling."

"Sometimes, I don't believe that I let so many negative things happen to me as an adult. Maybe it's like you said—part of me was trying to self-destruct because I didn't feel much worth."

"Or. maybe it was simply that no matter what you planned in the past, it never turned out to be worth anything because somebody was always coming along to mess it up for you."

"It's still so difficult to talk about," said Caitlin. "I still have the pain and the rage, but it isn't every minute any longer. I can have days when I really feel okay now."

"The pain never completely goes away, but the more you deal with your feelings, the easier it becomes to live with yourself, Caitlin."

Stop the Merry-Go-Round

"I don't think I'll ever be able to think about—see, I can't even use the word without getting sick inside—incest. I was a prisoner and a victim. Thinking of myself as a victim is difficult, too. There is that little part of me that keeps trying to blame myself for some of what happened. I really am learning that now. It keeps haunting me and a sick part of me keeps telling me it had to be my fault. Most of the time, I know that nothing I could have done would have made anything different.

"Sometimes, I still have trouble feeling I'm worth something, but I keep working on it every day."

"The change in you is apparent to everyone else, but it takes the most time to see it for yourself. Caitlin, we all have self-doubts—even therapists sometimes don't like themselves as much as they—I was going to say should, but the better word is need to."

"Yes, need to, I believe that."

"That sure changed, didn't it, Caitlin?"

"Once I met the guy that was right for me, we didn't touch each other for over a month and we were together every day. That felt so good to know he wasn't there for sex. He wanted me and he was willing to wait until I was ready. That helped me feel better about myself."

"Sometimes, what you thought were the most difficult things to do, turn out to be both simple and profound. A little two letter word, 'no' can entirely change your outlook on life. When you were a child, you didn't have the power to use it. It was forbidden to you. Now, Caitlin, you are empowered."

"Empowered," she said, as if she had discovered some inner magic. "Empowered," she repeated, and smiled—one of her now more frequent smiles.

Caitlin had endured unremitting anguish throughout her life. She was rejected, abandoned, and abused in every sense of the word. Yet, at age twenty-four, she had new

Caitlin

hope for a bright future because she was now more in control of her own life, and that control allowed her to deal with the day-to-day difficulties all of us must face. The difference was that she now could also face the day-to-day triumphs which are also available in the world. She was now allowed to succeed, and as she used to say, "That's something, isn't it?"

MARIANNE

It was all over. I was free
I don't know where life will lead,
but I will never again be anyone's victim.
Of that I can be certain.

To Dream The Dreams
You Dared Not Dream

The Home Years

I don't know quite how to begin my story. How do I tell people that I used to hate myself? How do I tell you that I allowed myself and my children to be abused by a sick husband for five years? Even now, over a year later, I still can't reconcile how I allowed it to happen. You know, I always thought I was a winner. I never drank, I never did drugs. I was a good student and a model teen. I don't want to blame mom and dad, or Dan——that's my ex-husband.

My therapist asked me to talk to you——to tell my story. He said that maybe it could help someone. I don't like talking about these things, but maybe, if going through the pain of talking about it one more time can help even one other person escape what I went through, it will be worth it.

You know, when I first went into therapy about two years ago, my therapist asked me to tell him about my childhood. Without thinking, I told him that I couldn't remember anything about it. I learned later that not remembering their childhood is very common among abused people. When you do begin to remember, the thing that stands out most is the pain.

I'm not good at telling my story. For so many years, I was better at hiding it. Everything I remember is like pieces of a puzzle. I painted pretty pictures of my 'perfect' family. To the world, I was Marianne Lovely, Marianne Bright, Marianne Mature. I guess I was all of those things, but inside, I felt like Marianne Worthless, Marianne Punching Bag.

I'm sorry, I don't mean to cry. Yeah, I was also **Marianne Waterworks!**

My childhood. I guess that's as good a place as any to begin . . .

I remember the street where I grew up. Talk about something right out of *The Brady Bunch*! The street was lined with beautiful trees—oak and maple—so even on the hottest day, there was shade and a sense of privacy and permanence. Maybe my street helped save my sanity when I was growing up. When I was outside of my house, I always felt more real, more protected. The houses had huge lawns with lots of shrubs.

Our house was the biggest on the block. It sat back on the property, and dad was always saying that it allowed us to have the privacy we needed. Dad added on an extra bedroom every time he and mom had another kid. There were six of us, and I was the oldest. I remember dad insisting that every kid have a room of his or her own. He said something about how when he was growing up there were six kids and his parents in a three bedroom house and he would be damned if his family was going to live like that.

I loved my mom and dad, I really did. Mom was so perfect—at least to the rest of the world. She was the president of more organizations than I could name. I was always polishing her collection of gavels and plaques which they'd give her after her term as president or chairperson. "To Mary, for dedication above and beyond," they would all say. "Above and beyond." Yeah. And dad, he was—and is—the Vice President of a big company and he did it all on his own. He never had the opportunity to get an education. He never missed a day of work, and when people from his office came over to the house for a party or something, they were always telling me how great a guy my dad was.

Maybe if I tell you some of the things I remember it will help you understand how my life worked out the way it did. Don't get me wrong, I'm not making any excuses for myself. I'm an adult, and I'm responsible for my own actions. But, I've learned through therapy that sometimes what you see and what you learn as a child is what you become as an adult—until you accept the responsibility to change it.

I don't remember much from before I was twelve or so. I can remember mom screaming at the kids, but there are so many blanks that I can't fill in. Anyway, I remember enough after that to give you a picture of what was happening in my life.

The first thing that really sticks out in my mind is one day when I was coming home from school. I was in about sixth grade. It was in the spring. I was feeling great because I just got a writing assignment back from my teacher. I'll never forget her—Mrs. Lindner. She said that it was the most beautiful thing she had ever read. I wasn't used to getting compliments—I still have a difficult time accepting them. It was the story of a young girl who had everything—a new bike, a stereo, her own TV, lived in a beautiful house—you know, all the material things that are supposed to make a kid happy. Anyway, the girl gave all of the beautiful things away to the poorest child in the neighborhood and moved into the doghouse in her back yard. I can't remember the details of the story—it was a long time ago but I remember that Mrs. Lindner cried when she handed the paper back to me. I remember that she wrote on the paper that I was the most sensitive and caring student she ever met.

I think I flew from the bus to my house. I don't think I ever felt so good in my life. As soon as I got in the door, I came back down to reality. I could hear my brothers and sisters screaming upstairs. Mom was in the living room, sprawled out on the sofa, her ever-present cocktail glass on the table next to her. The ashtray was overflowing and

Marianne

_____

101

there was a dish of leftover something which looked like it had been chewed and spit out. I shuddered in disgust and hoped mom hadn't noticed. I judged what condition she was in the same way a woodsman tells the age of a tree—by the number of rings. There were plenty of wet circles on the table that day. It meant she had had no meetings and probably started drinking by mid-morning.

"Whatcha got there?" Mom's speech was pretty slurred.

"It's just a story I wrote for an assignment for school. Mrs. . . ."

"Well, while you were out becoming a goddamned Ernest Hemingway, I've been here all alone, trying to take care of your five brothers and sisters. Can't you see I'm sick today and you were supposed to come right home after school?" When mom was that drunk it didn't pay to argue with her. "Lemme see the damn paper. I guess I worked hard enough for that privilege."

Mom read the paper in that funny way she had when her eyes wouldn't focus. Afterward, she looked up and said, "You are a damn ungrateful bitch. That's us you're talking about, isn't it? Don't we do enough for you around here? What did you tell that nosy teacher about our family?"

Any good feelings I had disappeared at that instant. All I felt was I had done something bad, and I didn't know what it was. What had I said that was wrong?

"But, momma, . . ."

"But, momma! Listen, you. Get upstairs and start taking care of your brothers and sisters. You don't care about me at all, do you? I have to take care of all of you and this damned palace. Do you think your father will listen to any excuses I have if the place isn't perfect when he gets home?" Mom struggled to get up off of the sofa, but she slipped back because she was—I have trouble saying it, even now—she was drunk.

Stop the Merry-Go-Round

I felt so guilty. "I'll try to get home earlier from now on, momma. I know you need my help. The kids are a real handful." I felt like about a hundred years old when I went up the stairs. All the kids ran up to me and hugged me. Sometimes I almost believed I was their mother. "C'mon, let's play in my room," I said. That was a real treat for them. Because I was the oldest, I had the right to keep my room private.

I loved my room. I got to pick out everything in it. For my twelfth birthday, mom took me shopping and told me that I was going to have a room any teenager could be proud of. She let me know that when she was a kid, she had to share a room with her sister and that all their furniture was hand-me-downs. We picked out a fairy tale bed with a huge white canopy. I always imagined that I was a princess when I was in my bed. All my furniture was white and we picked out soft colors for the curtains and carpet. And, I picked out the biggest bookcase I could find because I had more books than any ten kids.

Usually, I read stories to the other kids until mom had dinner ready. Sometimes, though, when mom was too "sick" to cook, I made dinner. I did it pretty good, too.

When mom was "sick," as she used to call it, I tried to be extra careful and extra quiet. The little ones seemed to learn how to become part of the scenery when mom was having one of her tantrums. I tried to protect them as best I could. Maybe that is why I have so much trouble remembering. I did get hit a lot.

That day, when I got upstairs, I remember feeling like I was going to throw up. I was too young then to realize that it was because another little piece of my dream had been stolen. I just thought then that I had a weak stomach. Mom's friends always said I was so delicate. I thought that was what they meant.

Marianne

103

"You keep those damned kids out of my hair, do you hear me Marianne?" I shuddered when mom screamed like that. Her voice would cut right through me. It wasn't until much later that I learned to turn it off. I remember how she talked to herself while she was making dinner. "Damn all of them. Always wanting, wanting, wanting. Who ever took care of me?" Sometimes, I could hear her crying.

At exactly ten to six, I would tell the kids to get washed for supper. Dad liked all of the kids clean, neat and at the dinner table when he came in the door at exactly six o'clock. Dinner had to be ready or there would be hell to pay.

Dinner wasn't exactly the most pleasant experience at my house. Dad would come in, inspect the living room to see that there was no mess, and without saying a word to anyone, go wash for dinner. When he came downstairs, it was like the general inspecting the troops. Everyone had to have clean hands and face, a clean shirt, and be sitting silently at the table with our hands folded in our laps. Mom would bring the food in from the kitchen just as he sat down, and serve dad first. If he didn't like what she served, she had to start cooking all over. Back then, I thought that everybody lived like that.

We ate in silence that night, like we always did. After dad would finish his dessert, he would ask mom if anything happened that day. That was the moment of truth for us kids. It meant that mom would report what we did wrong and dad would go for the strap.

"Anything happen today I should know about?" You could have heard a pin drop in a snowbank. I looked at mom pleadingly. Dad caught the glance and stared at me belligerently for a long moment. I felt like I was going to throw up my dinner.

"Well," mom said, dragging out the moment for what seemed forever, "Marianne was a little late getting home

from school, but I took care of it. It won't happen again."
Dad looked almost disappointed.

"You kids better listen to your mother, or you'll answer
to me, do you hear?" When dad raised his voice, you
couldn't help but hear. He gave me a look that said I was
off the hook for now, but that he was going to count this
one and add it on to the next time I did anything. A lot of
times, when one of the little ones would make a mess or
break something by accident, I would take the blame and
the whipping. I remember the first time—I was only about
four years old. Funny how bad memories can flash back
when you least expect them. Maybe that is why I have such
a hard time remembering anything from my childhood. I'm
sure there must have been some good things, too.

After supper, I walked as quietly as I could out of the
dining room, up the stairs, and into my room. I wanted to
be as invisible as possible in case dad was thinking about
changing his mind about punishing me. The last thing I
saw as I began softly climbing the stairs was dad making
his daily pilgrimage to the liquor cabinet to pour his first
drink of the night. I noticed that he used the tallest glass
on the bar. That usually meant a lot of drinking and
trouble later. Mom asked him to pour her one, too.

I made it as far as the bathroom at the top of the stairs
and threw up my dinner. I had to be careful to be very
quiet. Afterwards, I felt very sick and went to lie down on
my bed for a few minutes. My composition was lying on
the bed. I picked it up carefully, like it might explode. I
read Mrs. Lindner's comments maybe five times. Then, I
began tearing the paper into the smallest pieces I could.
I remember feeling very cold inside. I stuffed the pieces
into my pants pocket.

For a little while, I just lay there staring at the canopy
over my bed. It was so white, like a cloud, I remember
thinking. I picked up the book I had been reading—I

Marianne

105

remember—it was *Alice in Wonderland*. I reread the part about the Mad Hatter's tea party and began crying. I thought about our dinner table and for a moment, pictured my dad with a funny stovepipe hat on. I was sitting there with mouse ears and whiskers.

"Marianne, did you give the kids their bath?" Mom's voice exploded into my consciousness and I jolted out of bed, startled and frightened. "MARIANNE, DAMN YOU! ANSWER ME WHEN I'M TALKING TO YOU!"

"I'm getting them ready right now, momma," I answered, my voice shaking.

The two next oldest to me had just finished their baths, so I felt a little better. I could use that as an excuse for why I hadn't started with the three little ones.

"Why do you always make me scream like a maniac to get anything done around here?" Mom always had to get her last digs in. "If someone doesn't keep an eye on you kids every minute, there's no telling what you'll get into. And I better not find any mess in that bathroom when I get upstairs, do you hear me?"

"When you get up here, you'll be too drunk to see what the bathroom looks like," I thought, and then felt immensely guilty. "Mom really has it tough," I added, more to make myself feel better than because I believed it.

You know, maybe it's good for me to talk about myself like this. It helps me remember a lot of things I'd forgotten—or needed to forget.

I had one friend back then. It was an old teddy bear with one eye and the stuffing coming out in two or three places where the stitches were coming apart. Teddy was the only one I could tell my secrets to. That night, after I got the kids in bed and told the little ones a story, I just sat in bed rocking my teddy. Oh, yes. Before I went to bed, I pulled all of the scraps of my paper out of my pocket and one at a time, threw them in the trash. I didn't fall asleep for a long time that night.

You know that old saying, "When it rains, it pours?" I guess it's so old because it's so true. I don't know what time it was—maybe two in the morning. Anyway, I guess I finally had fallen asleep. I had the bedroom next to mom and dad's. I called their bedroom the battlefield because there were so many fights there. Maybe that's one of the reasons I stayed out of bed with guys for as long as I did.

That night was one of their really bad ones. I was awakened by dad's shouting, and like I said, when he raised his voice, the whole house shook. It felt as if their voices were attacking me. I could hear by their tone that they were both pretty drunk.

"I wish somebody would give a damn about me around here once in a while." When dad started on that one, it usually meant that he was getting ready for a real fight. You know, that was the way he could justify whatever came next. I just sat up in bed holding teddy real tight. Then it came. I almost had it memorized by the time I was twelve. "All you do is watch your damned TV all day and you don't do a damned thing around here. The place is a mess; the kids are all over the place; dinner's not ready on time. I work hard all day and I deserve a break when I get home. And you, lying around the house like an old whore. That's what the hell you are—an old whore. I don't know why I put up with you. Well, don't just stand there. What do you have to say for yourself? Well?"

I just sat there in bed, hugging my teddy. I rocked, trying to make myself feel better. Mom came right back at him. "What do you want me to say. I work plenty hard. I really try for you, you know that. I made your favorite dinner tonight and you just sat there looking at it."

"You were lucky I could even look at it. What did you do, use a blowtorch on the meat—or were you just so

Marianne

107

drunk that you forgot it was cooking? If you have to drink all damned day, at least get that lazy daughter of yours to do the damn cooking. She has to be good for something."

They always had to get me into it somehow. They were both drunk and screaming, and I guess I was happy they didn't come into my room and beat me unconscious. Sometimes, I really believed that if I hadn't been born, they might have been happier. I knew what was going to happen next. Mom couldn't leave well enough alone. It was almost as if they wanted to keep escalating things until it became a fight.

"Drink all day?" she screamed. "Look who's talking about drinking all day. You come home with half a load on and don't stop until you pass out. It's no wonder I need a few drinks to get me through the day."

"Why don't you just shut your mouth?" By that time, dad was really sounding dangerous. "I'm sick of listening to you and sicker of looking at you. I just want to get some sleep, so shut up." I rocked harder and I felt sick to my stomach. The usual routine at this point was for mom to tell dad to shut up and that would be his excuse to hit her. Then she would threaten to leave, he would apologize and they would go to bed and—I almost said, they would make love. If that's love . . .

I can still hear their words. It happened so many times. I sometimes have a difficult time knowing what is real. How can people do that to each other? Now, when I hear the word "love," I cringe.

Life went on like that. I stopped writing about anything real and I grew into my teens—somehow. The beatings increased as I got older. It seemed that any excuse was enough. I got home five minutes late, dinner wasn't ready. By the time I was thirteen, mom turned over the responsibility for all the cooking to me, except when they had company. Then, she was the perfect hostess.

Stop the Merry-Go-Round

As soon as I started developing, they started accusing me of sleeping with every boy in town. What's funny, I was so scared of boys, I wouldn't let them touch me. I didn't really know what sex was all about, but I tried to act like all the other girls and I pretended to be sophisticated. You know, mom and dad were so repressed when it came to teaching about sex that I'm still uncomfortable naming body parts that have to do with sex.

By the time I was fifteen, I had a best friend. Her name was Bridget. We really got along even though we were different. She was always egging me on with the boys and maybe I needed that because I was so shy. She was always talking about sex and we spent hours on the phone just dreaming about going out with the best looking boys in school.

I remember one day we were talking about Eddie Hughes—only the best looking jock on the football team. He asked me to the soph hop and my heart just stopped! Bridget was giving me the lowdown on how to seduce and trap him into going steady. I felt very daring even having a conversation like this. If mom had ever caught me, she would have skinned me and dad would have finished the job later.

"Brige," I remember telling her, "I'm so excited."

"That's great," she answered. "That'll make it better for both of you!"

"I don't mean it *that* way," I answered, indignantly.

"Hey, you gotta start sometime. D'you want to be the last virgin in Eastland High?"

I remember I thought to myself that if sex and love was what my mom and dad had, I wanted to be the last virgin on the planet Earth.

"Brige," I asked, "Did you ever—you know?"

Marianne

109

"More than you want to know," she answered, in a voice that really scared me. I didn't find out until much later what she meant.

"Marianne, MARIANNE, WHERE THE HELL ARE YOU?" Mom's screaming brought me quickly back to my real problems. Finding out how to handle Eddie Hughes would have to wait.

"Gotta go, Brige. My mom's throwin' a fit and I better see what she wants. I'll talk to you tomorrow after my date with destiny!"

Just as I hung up the phone, mom came charging into my room. She never knocked—she just came in any time. Dad did it too. I felt that I had no privacy at all. I took to changing in the bathroom because a couple of times dad barged in when I was undressed and it made me really uncomfortable. Maybe it was something about the way he looked at me just a little too long. He never did anything, but when he would come in like that, it was when he was drunk. He'd just stand in the door and not say anything. It was spooky.

"Marianne, are you gonna lie around in bed the whole damned day? I'm going to a meeting and somebody has to take care of the kids. Dammit, I expect some co-operation out of you. Your room's a mess. Straighten it up." Mom looked her ever loving best that day. There were no signs that she had been drinking half the night before. She was really beautiful when she fixed herself up. She bragged about being the best looking of the O'Ryan girls. Everybody said that I looked just like her. At that moment, that made me feel really proud.

"I just made one phone call to Bridget. I've been with the kids all morning while you were getting ready," I said, maybe a little too sarcastically, because what she was doing most of the morning was trying to get ready to get out of bed.

"Don't you talk back to me, you arrogant little bitch. I'll show you who runs the show around here." I remember her coming toward me with her hand raised. I heard more than felt her hand hit my face. It's funny, all I could think about was whether I would have a bruise when Eddie Hughes saw me that night. Otherwise, it was just business as usual at the O'Ryan house. I didn't cry. I had learned to keep my tears to myself. I later learned how to stop them altogether.

My date with Eddie Hughes confirmed my opinion about men. Things went great at the dance and we were chosen the most popular couple and got to dance a solo in front of everybody. I felt like a princess for one brief moment. After the dance, all the kids went out for sodas, and I was in dreamland.

"Eddie, I've got to be home by eleven," I said. "It's already ten of."

"Just finish your soda first, an' then we'll go. A few minutes won't kill you."

"You don't know my parents."

"Okay, but you'll miss all the fun. The gang is gonna go down by the river an' have some fun—you know. An' you just happen to be with the most fun guy of all, babe!"

"Maybe some other time, Eddie. I really did have fun with you tonight, but I have to get home." I began to feel a little scared. Eddie was two years older than me and a lot more experienced—or so I'd been told. I put the lid on my soda and asked him again to take me home.

He didn't say much during the drive home. When we were about five blocks from my house, he pulled into a side street and turned off the motor.

"How's about a kiss goodnight before I take you home?" he asked.

I was getting more and more scared, but I figured that if a kiss would get me home, it couldn't be that bad. I had never been kissed by a boy and he was cute . . .

In a matter of seconds, Eddie's hands were all over me and he was trying to get the zipper of my dress open. I tried to tell him to stop, but he wouldn't listen so I poured my soda right in his lap. After, he had the funniest look I have ever seen. I didn't wait to find out what he was going to do next. I jumped out of the car and ran home.

Mom and dad were waiting up. Actually, they were just in the middle of Saturday night drinking. It was way after eleven and I was pretty shaken up by what had just happened.

"Well, look who it is!" mom slurred. "What were you doing, making it with half the sophomore class? The dance ended at ten-thirty. Where the hell were you? You had us worried out of our minds."

"Eddie took me out for a soda. Everybody went. I was the first to leave. I told him I had to be home." I wanted the floor to open up and swallow me because I just knew that this was building up to a real beating. No matter what I said or did, they were going to justify it. Dad just sat there, boiling and saying nothing. I prepared myself for the worst. I remember I used to turn cold inside and pretend I wasn't really there.

Mom was just warming up. By then, I could almost write the script for her. "Sure, and I'll bet he took you straight home, didn't he? What's that all over your dress? You took it off, didn't you? Tell me, damn you. You're turning into a real slut aren't you?"

"Answer your mother, damn you. Or you'll answer to me, you hear me. YOU HEAR ME?" When dad chimed in, it was over.

I thought to myself, "What the hell, as long as I'm going to get beaten, I might as well just tell them what I think."

Stop the Merry-Go-Round

"I didn't . . . He . . . he . . . Oh, what's the use. You'd never believe me anyway. The hell with you. The hell with both of you. You can beat me, but goddamn you, you can't break me! Come on. Kill me. I don't care. That's what you really want anyway, isn't it? Maybe I should go out and have sex with the whole school. Maybe that would satisfy you. You'd have something to tell your clubwomen then, wouldn't you? Why? Why do you hate me so much? What did I ever do to you? Oh, what's the use."

I was so frustrated that I wasn't afraid anymore. I ran up to my room. For a moment, I thought about running away, but where could I go? I was fifteen years old and had a 'great' job bussing tables in a neighborhood restaurant one day a week.

I heard my mother still screaming from downstairs; "You don't run out when I'm talking to you. Do you hear me? Get back here, NOW! John, you handle this. She can't do this. I won't take it. She just won't listen any more. Teach that little bitch a lesson she won't forget."

My dad came through my door like he was really going to enjoy this. I just looked at him and said; "Hit me all you want, I won't cry." I don't remember anything after that, except that I couldn't get out of bed the next day. I still have a couple of souvenirs from that night that won't ever let me forget it. I have a scar on my forehead above my right eye, and a permanent lump on my lip that makes me look like I'm always pouting. So much for my pretty face!

I made up my mind that I would not stay in that house one day longer than I had to. I figured I would have to last until I graduated from high school so I could get a job and support myself, but after that, I would never look back. So much for my great plans to go to college and become a successful business executive—just like my—God forbid—just like my father!

Marianne

113

The only two really good things I remember in all the years I lived at home happened at school. I guess I had some fun times, but inside, I was always hurt, depressed or angry, so I really never let the good times feel good. My therapist told me that this is very typical of abused people. Anyway, the first time I felt really good was the time I told you about in sixth grade when my teacher complimented my writing. The second time was when my English teacher in twelfth grade told me that I should give serious consideration to becoming an author. Serious consideration, me, Marianne!

His name was Mr. Laffer. I'll never forget him. I never heard a more appropriate name for a person. He always seemed to pay special attention to me, and once when he called me into his room after school, I almost blew the whistle on my family. When I got the note to report to his room after school, I was scared out of my mind. The first thing I thought was; "What did I do wrong?" I was so used to the way things were at home, that I automatically assumed that I was going to be blamed for something.

I stood in the doorway shaking. "Come on in and sit down, Marianne," Mr. Laffer said in that soft, smiley voice. "Do you know why I called you in?

"I must have done something wrong, but I can't think what it might be," I blurted, "I try so hard, so hard . . ." Tears began pouring down my face and I couldn't stop crying. Mr. Laffer reached over to me with a tissue and I automatically jolted backward. After so many years of ducking slaps and punches, it was a reflex.

I'll never forget the look of horror on his face, followed by a look of recognition.

"What is it, Marianne? Is anything the matter?" Mr. Laffer looked at me with a concern I hadn't ever seen in my life. I didn't know how to handle this. So, like the good and loyal O'Ryan that I was, I covered up.

Stop the Merry-Go-Round

"No, I'm fine, Mr. Laffer, really. I was just thinking of something. I just cry over nothing. I'm okay. Don't mind me. I'm always crying. If there is ever a drought, just call on good old Marianne and she will cure it in a minute."

He must have known that I wasn't about to tell the family secrets. It was then that he told me how talented a writer he thought I was. Then he added, "I just want to let you know that if you ever need an adult to talk to about anything—anything at all, I'm here for you, okay?"

I almost told him everything, but I was too well-trained. I just put on my best smile mask and told him that everything was really fine.

When I got out to the hallway, though, I really lost it. It was what he said. "Me, a writer," I thought. "If I live that long."

It's funny. The next really good thing I remember in my life was when I went into therapy when I was twenty-four. Maybe something good is supposed to happen to me once every six years. I really shouldn't talk like that, but sometimes, it is difficult to really see the good in life, even though, for the most part, my life is now in order.

The night of my high school graduation was independence day for me. I had planned all year that I would get my own place and move in the day I got out of school. It meant giving up the scholarship I had won. I figured that I could go to school part-time but I had to work full-time to make it. I have a lot of regrets, but at the time, I didn't believe I could last another day in my parents' house.

I was counting the minutes until I got home after the ceremony. I skipped the graduation parties. I was so full of rage that I didn't feel I had anything to celebrate. I didn't know how I was going to tell my parents I was leaving. I had hoped to avoid one last scene. I was too worn out to face it.

Marianne

115

When I got home, they were in the living room, drunk as usual. I'll never forget that scene. It was the last time I really spoke to my parents. I see them at the obligatory family gatherings, but generally it's just hello and goodbye. Even when I had one foot out the door, I was wishing that there was some way I could get them to talk to me—to see me. Even at seventeen, I had pretty much given up that dream.

"Look babe, I'm sorry I couldn't make it to your graduation today. You know how hectic it can get at work. Meetings all day. Here, have a little drink to celebrate the occasion and give dad a hug." He reached out for me and I could smell the liquor on his breath.

"You know I don't drink, dad," I said, sarcastically. "Anyway, I made it through another occasion without you." It was almost as if I had to pick a fight with them. Maybe I felt that I owed myself one. They couldn't throw me out and I could run faster than they could swing. I knew it wouldn't do any good to tell them off—well, it wouldn't do them any good. I needed to do it for myself.

"What's that supposed to mean?" Good old mom. I could always count on her to make a bad situation worse. "Doesn't your father do enough for you, you ingrate? Who put the clothes on your back and the food on the table?"

Seventeen years of pain exploded out of me in a single burst. Needless to say, I felt guilty about it afterwards, but not until I was out of there and safely in my own place. "Mom, dad, That's it. I've had it. Dad you put the clothes on my back and then both of you ripped them apart seeing who can beat me the hardest. As for the food on the table, as long as I can remember, *I'm* the one who cooked most of it. I already decided. I'm leaving this house today and I won't be back. I got my own apartment. I've been working part-time for five years and I saved every cent. I can take care of myself until I get a job.

Stop the Merry-Go-Round

"Mom, dad, I love both of you very much. I wish . . ."

Mom never could let anything go. She had to keep the pot boiling. "You can't leave here without our permission and I for one won't give it. Your place is here with your family. You kids, all you ever want is freedom, freedom, freedom. At your age, I was already preg— . . . married." Mom looked like she had just been caught naked in church. I've never seen her look so scared, and vulnerable. For an instant, I wanted to hug her and reassure her that everything would be alright. But, too much pain had accumulated for me to let it go that easily. I wasn't interested in her excuses—at least not then.

"Mom, I've known since I was ten that I was an 'early baby.' I saw your marriage license. It doesn't matter. What were you trying to hide? You called me a bitch and a worthless bastard enough times so I almost believed it anyway.

"That's all you think about isn't it? Your reputation. Well, if they only knew . . . Oh, don't worry, I won't tell all your little secrets. That's one thing I learned in this family—how to keep little secrets.

"Dad, you don't even care if I leave, do you? One less mouth to feed. You never did care, did you?"

I've never seen dad look so lost and defensive. It was as if the cruel warden was being held captive by the prisoners and was begging for his life. "That's not true! I always loved you. You're my favorite."

"Well you sure had a funny way of showing it." I stood over them like a raging tyrant. For a moment, I thought that I was their parent and was disciplining them. "I still have scars on my face, back and legs from some of the little 'lessons' you were always teaching me."

"Well, somebody had to teach you," dad retorted. What do you think my parents did to me? If I had mouthed off

Marianne

117

the way you did, I would have been picking up my teeth—
if I was conscious. And I turned out okay."

"And if *I* had done some of the things you've done, I would have been tanned and then thrown out," mom added.

I was shaking inside. "You'll never understand. If *I* had done . . . Mamma, I've never even been with a boy—never! I never drank. I never took drugs. What do you two want from me? *What the hell do you want from me?*"

We all stood there like a frozen montage. I read that in a book somewhere. It was too late to change anything. Mom and dad began making apologies. I didn't want to hear that they didn't know, or that they loved me.

"It's too late for words and it's too late for tears. I can't even cry any more. I can't feel anything. I'm leaving tonight. I *have* to." I couldn't trust them. I'd heard apologies before. Mom had spent the whole weekend nursing me after the soph hop. And dad, of course he took me to the best plastic surgeon to try to fix up my face after that same weekend! In my bitterness I believed that if only they hadn't beaten me up, there wouldn't have been a need to nurse me.

They didn't try to stop me. Maybe a little part of me wanted them to. At least it would have shown they cared.

On My Own

The first night in my own apartment was scary, but at the same time, I felt a sense of relief to be away from the beatings, the drunkenness, and the constant put-downs. I didn't have any furniture yet, and all of my belongings were in bags and cartons, which I had moved into the apartment during the previous week, but it was my place. You can't know what that meant to me. Even though I had plenty of doubts about making it on my own, I had a feeling of safety for the first time ever.

It was nearly dark when I got to the apartment. I was shaking so hard that I had trouble getting the key in the lock. I discovered my first mistake when I tried to turn on the lights. I had forgotten to buy light bulbs. There I was, in the dark, no furniture, no food, no light except for the bulb in the bathroom. I opened my sleeping bag, got undressed, and tried to go to sleep. Pictures of my beautiful canopy bed and down comforter kept flashing through my mind. Frantically, I searched for my teddy—I still couldn't sleep without him. I recalled seeing him on my dresser, standing his lonely vigil. "Well, one of us got out, anyway. I hope mom and dad observe the Geneva Convention rules and don't hurt him." I began crying, first for teddy, then because of feeling lonely and scared, and finally, because I just needed to let it out.

Early the next morning, I awoke to find everything looking so much brighter with the sun streaming through the uncurtained window. The apartment was small, and far from fancy; but it was clean and had 'potential,' as I liked to call anything that really wasn't that nice but could be fixed with a lot of effort. I remember saying the same thing about Dan, my ex, after I first met him. I had a lot to learn.

I discovered quickly that I had forgotten a few other necessities like soap and towels, but I managed to get myself fairly presentable and went out to look for a full-time job. By afternoon, I found a job as a secretary in an insurance company. The salary was nothing to write home about—if I had had a home to write to—but it was a start. It would pay the rent, and more important, it left my

Marianne

evenings free so I could begin taking courses at the local community college.

The next two years passed quickly and my life was better than it had ever been. I worked, I went to school and I studied. My apartment began to look more like my room at home. Marianne never stops reading—that's me! I didn't visit my parents' home until two months after I moved out, and when I did, the tension was terrible. None of us knew what to say. Mom looked a lot older—maybe it was just my imagination. At least, I did liberate teddy and was so happy to have him back. When I got him home, we had a little party for the two of us. It felt a little silly, but there was no one there to see us, so it was okay.

Occasionally, I dated, but for some reason, every guy I met was boring. Some were educated and were doing well. One really developed a thing for me, but I didn't have any interest in any of them. I rarely dated the same one a second time. My girl friend, Bridget, teased me about being the last virgin in the country, but it wasn't a big deal. I continued getting flashbacks of mom's and dad's relationship, and the last thing I wanted was to repeat their life. Anyway, I was beginning to make a dent in college and at work. I was promoted to group supervisor and the company was now paying for my college courses so I transferred to the best school in the city. I continued getting A's in almost every course and was now majoring in business administration.

I was beginning to really feel good about myself. Sometimes, I had nightmares about being beaten or hearing dad beat mom, and once I had an awful one in which I went berserk and killed my whole family. However, most of the time, I felt at ease with myself and the pain of my childhood became more remote. I made new friends in school and at work, although I spent little time with them. My goal was to build a career for myself so I would never have to depend on a man, the way mom depended on dad to take care of her.

It's funny how life revolves around a few critical moments. I learned that in therapy—but only after it was too late to put it to use when it was needed. Life was going well, and the spring semester had just ended, so my evenings were free until September. I decided not to go to summer school that year because I wanted some time to travel and the strain of work and school was getting to me. Bridget talked me into going out with a guy I had known casually in high school. Back then, I never looked at him twice. His name was Dan. He was very popular, but he was on the wild side and was always trying to impress the girls with how macho he was.

Dan called on Friday to ask me out for Saturday. He was very polite on the phone and sounded surprised that I accepted a date with him. That impressed me. I had dated one of his friends—Eddie Hughes when I was 15. That was a really unfortunate experience and left me with bad feelings and scars all over my face from what dad did to me because he thought I 'did it' with Eddie. And, of course, didn't Eddie brag all over school that he got in my pants! So, to say the least, Dan wasn't beginning with an advantage in my life.

Sometimes the most important events in life begin insignificantly. I don't know why I was so concerned over a date with someone I had known and ignored for five years. Although Dan never did say where we were going, I dressed for a dinner date. I looked nervously at the clock and noted that he was already a half hour late.

I was ready to give up waiting for him when the doorbell rang. I opened the door and gave my best woman of the world imitation and . . . There he was, in dirty work clothes and work boots. He had a scraggly mustache, chin fuzz, long hair, none too neatly combed looking very

Marianne

121

distracted. We stood staring at each other and I felt totally out of place in my dinner dress.

"Uh, come on in," I began, really not knowing what to do or say. I don't know why, but I felt like I was the one who was out of place all dressed up.

"Yeah, well, I'm uh, sorry I'm, uh, late," said Dan, "but I was workin' on my pickup an' I didn't realize what time it was. I guess I'm makin' a real lousy impression, huh?" Dan smiled an awkward, sheepish smile, and for the first time, looked attractive in a little-boy way.

"Maybe he has 'potential,'" I thought to myself. I shuddered as he walked across my clean carpets in his dirty work boots, and prepared to sit on my sofa in clothes which had obviously been worn to fix his pick-up truck. "Pick-up truck?" I added, putting another point in his negative column.

I had already given up on going out, so I asked him if he would like something to drink.

"Yeah, that would be fine. You got any beer?" Dan looked at me with his head tilted to one side and a half-smile on his face. I began liking him at that moment.

"No, I'm sorry, I don't. How about a soda or some coffee?"

"That's okay," he answered, looking somewhat disappointed. "Hey! What d'ya wanna do tonight?"

I looked at him and at me and was too embarrassed to tell him I would have to change if we were going out. "How about if we just stay here and talk so we can get to know each other?" I hoped he didn't get the wrong impression, but for some reason, I felt that he wasn't about to try anything. I didn't know then why I was getting strange feelings. Therapy later taught me that I was seeing something familiar in Dan and already knew that he could fill a level of need which I didn't even understand.

Stop the Merry-Go-Round

We sat and talked until four in the morning. I didn't even notice whether his dirty clothes were leaving marks on my furniture. I opened up and told Dan about my family and he told me about his. He was abused, too, by his dad. His dad was a mean drunk and had no redeeming features that I could see. Dan's mother put up with him and made excuses for him which really angered Dan. His dad and mom brawled right in front of the kids. It's funny, when I say that, it's almost like I'm excusing my parents because they did their thing in the bedroom where it was private. Maybe that's something I have to look at. I noticed that Dan was shaking all over when he talked about his family. But, at the same time, he talked like it was somebody else it happened to. I thought, "I'll bet I was doing the same thing!"

Five years later, in a therapy group for abused women, I talked about that first year Dan and I were together. I was just beginning to figure out how our relationship had deteriorated from a loving one into an abusive one. I've really come to love the people in the group. For the first time in my life, I can talk about what happened to me and not feel like I am talking about somebody else. When I heard the others talk with such honesty about the same kinds of situations I was in, it helped me to begin to do the same thing. I was raised to keep the family secrets, but maybe that is what helped me to accept so much pain in my adult life. Maybe I'm getting ahead of myself but everything from then on in my life is so tangled up that it's difficult to separate past from present. I loved Dan—I still do love him—and that made it more difficult to separate my feelings from his actions. I always made excuses for him—just like my mother and father did for themselves and each other. And, just like Dan's mother did for Dan's father—and later, for Dan.

Marianne

It was just a few weeks after I went into therapy. I had told Dan he had to leave because he had really beaten me up—worse than ever before. I was talking to the group and had so many mixed feelings that I wasn't certain what I wanted to do. The group asked me to tell them about my relationship with Dan. I didn't want them thinking that he was a bad person:

"When I met Dan," I told the group, "I really didn't like him." I got very defensive when I talked about Dan. I really tried not to. I was learning in the group that it is so common for an abused woman to make excuses for the person who is abusing her. "I, no, I guess I really can't say that. There was something about him, but he really wasn't the type of man I thought I wanted. He had no education and no real goals, but I could talk to him. He was so nice to me. It was—how can I say this—I think it was that I could trust him. I thought I knew him.

"That first year—before I got pregnant—was so great. I totally fell in love with him. He would listen to me and he was so understanding and gentle. He would sometimes just hold me for hours and not—you know—try anything. He really respected me. That was very important to me. After we had been going together for almost eleven months, we decided that we would live together. I was a little frightened, but we both felt that it was right for us.

"He was so helpless sometimes, like a great big baby. He had to be reminded to take off his work boots and he couldn't remember anything. I guess I really liked taking care of him. Maybe that was one of the things that made him so attractive to me."

Robert, my therapist, said that it sounded like there were some really good things for me in the relationship.

"Yes, there were. You know, I really resent it when the group puts him down. I know I have to deal with what he did to me, but you have to understand——Dan isn't a bad person."

It was at this point that Ellen, another member of my group, who always told it like it was, chimed in, "Mare, that isn't the issue here. The son of a bitch almost killed you, and you sit here defending him. Where is your anger? Goddamn it, until I felt more for me than I did for my fuckin' boyfriend, I stayed a victim. I mean, if that's what you want . . ."

I wasn't used to the way Ellen expressed herself. Sometimes, I resented someone who was only nineteen being so wise, so I would dismiss what she said because she used street language or because she was so young. Maybe I needed it put to me that way and to hear the truth from someone that young to get me to see past my own denial. To listen to me most of the time, you would think I lived the life of a princess. Maybe that was because in my head, I always did. It kept me from going crazy or killing myself. I pictured myself as a teenager lying in my beautiful canopy bed, but I left out the bruises, cuts, and the need to remove the bloody sheets the next morning. And, later, I was Marianne——perfect mother and house-wife——taking care of the little ones and making gourmet dinners for my loving spouse. I left out living in fear of the next beating and trying to believe I had any worth after some of the things Dan said to me when he was angry. "But I love him," I would say. "I know he'll change because he loves me, too."

Ellen always had an answer that forced me to look at reality. "Yeah, sure, he'll change. From beating you to killing you, maybe. I've been out of my sick home for over a year now and I still can't get rid of the anger, dammit. I wake up in the middle of the night shaking and some-times I want to take a gun or something and . . . Oh, Christ!" Ellen began crying, and although I was having a

Marianne

125

difficult time feeling my own pain, at that moment, I still felt her shame, rage and frustration. "I still hate to cry." Ellen was obviously upset with herself for losing control. "Haven't I cried enough?"

Robert's statement to Ellen helped me to see what I was going through, and what Ellen had already been through. "It's okay. It's really okay. Sometimes, it's only after the pain is over in reality that you can even begin to deal with it inside yourself."

One of the other women in the group, Robin, went to Ellen with a tissue and comforted her while she wiped her eyes and blew her nose. I was still unable to show any feeling for anyone in the group even though I wanted to go over to Ellen. I seemed to be able to show all kinds of feelings toward someone who was threatening my life, but I couldn't reach out to someone who was trying to help me save it.

"See," Robert continued, "most of you in this group were never allowed to cry, or even complain. You got so used to being a victim that you almost believed that it was right."

"Sometimes, I am so confused," I told him. "You know, I'm supposed to be so independent. I did ask Dan to leave like the . . ." I almost said, like the group told me to, but I realized that I was making the decisions in my life, not the group. "No, I did it, not the group. You know, it's funny. I've been so independent in the rest of my life. I moved into my own place when I was seventeen. I have a good job. I take care of two children—not counting Dan— and I still get good marks in college. Why can't I deal with this thing the same way? I know that he could talk his way right back into the house if I don't keep him really distant. It's like I know I can't live with him, but I keep hoping he'll change."

Everyone sat quietly looking at me. I sat quietly, not really feeling anything. Maybe, as Robert said, it was too early for feelings, but as Ellen said, it was time for action. "I guess it doesn't happen overnight," I began, with increasing certainty. "You know I was thinking about what I said before about being so confused. You know Dan could be the greatest guy in the world. Everybody likes him and you know, nobody could understand why I wanted to leave him. I mean he was every girl's dream—quarterback on the high school football team, good looking, built like a—you know, but . . ." I paused to gather my thoughts. "Maybe what we think is important when we are nineteen isn't what really is important in a relationship when you grow up, but how do you know what anyone is really like? How do you know . . . ?"

Ellen always seemed to be able to say the right thing at the right time for me. This time was no exception. "The trouble is, that what you don't know can kill you!" She had a way of getting right to the heart of things. I both envied and admired her strength. I hoped that someday I could develop some of that forcefulness.

"I love you, Ellen." I said it so softly that I thought no one heard me.

"I love you, too, Marianne." Ellen mumbled just like I had and stared at the floor.

"She's just like me," I thought, and although I couldn't understand why just then, I began to feel less confused.

How did things change for the worse in my relationship with Dan? I used to ask why, but I learned that at best, I could only guess why anything happened. But I can look back and see when the changes began and what was going on during that time. Maybe why isn't really that important. Why is sometimes just an excuse to allow problems to continue. Why only helps when you already are working on changing something and you want to understand it better.

Marianne

127

But, when the something is abuse, there isn't any time to deal with why he does it and why you accept it. I learned that you have to get to safety first, and then worry about why it happened. Sometimes, when I talk about this, I can almost hear Robert or Ellen talking to me——or maybe it is through me. That makes me feel very . . . valuable.

During the year we dated, Dan was my best friend as well as the man I was falling in love with. He was always there for me and I could tell him anything. He respected the fact that I wanted to wait before we got involved sexually. He respected the limits I set. When we decided to live together, I started seeing signs that there might be problems, but, hey, I was in love, and love could conquer all! The first sign that something was wrong was that Dan would go out a couple of nights every week and come home late and ripped. I later figured out that he had been getting ripped a couple of nights a week long before I knew him, but when we were dating, he did it on the nights I was in school and we didn't see each other.

The next thing that went wrong was that when we tried to have sex the first few times, he——this is embarrassing for me to say——I don't like to put him down, but he couldn't perform. I was the one who suggested that maybe if we had a couple of drinks, it would help him relax. I know I was scared out of my wits. I didn't know what I was supposed to do. Because I was totally inexperienced, I really didn't think anything of it. From then on, the only time that Dan could have sex with me was when he was drinking or high on pot. When he was lit, he was Mr. Passion, but he acted as if he were the only person in the room. I didn't complain for a long time, because I didn't know the difference. And, when I learned a little about what goes on in the world, and suggested that he try something different, he got all bent out of shape and slapped me. He had never raised a hand to me in the year

Stop the Merry-Go-Round

or more we were going together. He convinced me that it was my fault for questioning his manhood. That time, I accepted his reasoning and let it go. I apologized to him for being so insensitive.

My life changed imperceptibly after we moved in together. At first, it was just that the apartment looked a little dirtier. I was so in love and so wrapped up in being the perfect mate that I really didn't see or care. I dropped out of school because Dan complained that I didn't pay attention to him. I rationalized that it was okay—I would go back the next semester when I got more used to my new responsibilities.

The time we had spent together talking and being close began diminishing, but there was still enough that I figured that was the way it was when you lived together. I rationalized that we were both busy, and that Dan had a lot on his mind.

Now that we lived together, one thing I found occupying Dan's mind was that he couldn't hold a job. This wasn't apparent when he was dating me. He never talked about it, and I assumed he was working during the day—maybe because I was. He always seemed to have enough money, but that was because he had lived with his parents and had no expenses.

I remember the night that life went from having problems to being a problem. I came home from work and, as usual, Dan was stretched out on the couch. I didn't ask him if he had worked that day—I knew he hadn't. But, under normal circumstances, that would have been okay. I was earning enough to take care of all of our expenses, and Dan did work a couple of days a week in construction jobs, so he was contributing something. I didn't even resent that he wouldn't even fix supper when he had been sitting at home all day. I rationalized that he was such a poor

---

Marianne

cook that it wasn't worth the effort. I made a lot of excuses for him back then.

"Dan, we have to talk." I was trying not to look as anxious as I felt. I busied myself by taking off my jacket and making a display of kicking off my high heels.

Dan didn't move, but looked up and said pleasantly, "I'm all ears, babe!" I was happy to see that he was in such a good mood until I noticed how red his eyes were and knew that he had been smoking pot.

"Dan, we've always been able to talk to each other, and you're my best friend in the world, but I want you to know that I'm not going to try to push you into anything." I was trying not to be angry, but I knew that when Dan was high, he really was not going to be able to deal with anything.

"You gonna talk about marriage again?" Dan said, beginning to become defensive. "I told you I love you and I want to marry you, but we have to wait till I get a better job. I mean, you think I like it—you having to work? Just be patient with me, something will break for me soon. Mare, I love you more than life. I couldn't live without you."

"I know Danny. I love you, too. Nobody else ever really understood me or accepted me." I sat down next to him on the sofa and held his hand. "I don't want you to feel any pressure and you know I believe in you. But . . . I, uh we, I'm pregnant, Dan."

"What do you mean . . . ? Oh!" I looked at Dan in disbelief. I couldn't forget that look, like I was trapping him into something. It passed quickly, and I rationalized that away, too, but it was there. "Well, we have to get married right away. Nobody is ever going to say I didn't do the right thing."

I got really angry and almost decided to end it right then, but I was pregnant and frightened. "Well, you don't have to do me any favors. I've been taking care of myself for three years and I can keep on doing it. If this isn't what you want, you can just leave." For a moment, I was afraid that he would do just that.

But, Dan did love me, only at that time, I didn't realize what his love meant. He needed me, but on his terms. He wasn't able to deal with a real relationship—especially one where he would become responsible for a child.

For a while after we got married, things did get a little better. I worked through my ninth month and that kept our finances in balance. My parents gave us a generous wedding gift—I guess guilt is good for something—so we were doing okay. But when the baby came, I had to quit work and I wanted to stay home with the baby for at least a year or so.

Dan began drinking more often, and complained that I paid more attention to the baby than to him, so, of course, he went out for a little fun with the guys! I spent a lot of time on the phone with my friend Bridget who was in the same situation as I was, except she had two kids and a husband who ran around with other women. We each lied to the other about how great our lives were. We were both taught to keep family secrets. I think each of us knew that the other was lying, but we were afraid that if we confronted each other, we might lose the only real friend we had. In one of our conversations, Bridget did admit that Bob had hit her after an argument, but she felt that she had pushed him into doing it. Where did I hear that line before?

Dan and I began to have more frequent arguments and he would often threaten to hit me, but other than grabbing me by the arms, there hadn't been any more violence. I'll have to learn to stop saying 'other than,' I do know now that violence is violence, and abuse doesn't begin physically—it simply ends there. I suppose when

Marianne

131

you grow up ducking hands, fists, straps and occasional hair brushes, being grabbed seems almost like fun. Let me tell you, however, I had to wear long sleeves in the summer because of the bruises from those grabs.

Our arguments took on a pattern. I called it fighting to make up. I guess it appeared that I started most of the arguments, and maybe I did. Usually, it was because of Dan's drinking or irresponsibility. When I couldn't take it anymore, I would confront him. I remember one argument in particular which lets me understand just how much I depended on what I learned later was a sick life style.

I had spent the day chasing my son Jeffy around the apartment. He was a 'terrible two' and could exhaust an army. I had also done the laundry, picked up after Dan who was always leaving his dirty clothes and towels all over the place, vacuumed, shopped for groceries, and had a special dinner ready for Dan when he came home from work. As usual, he was late and smelled of beer when he finally got in the door. I still was planning to restrain myself, because I felt that an argument was not what I needed that day.

"Hi, babe! Loafin' round—as usual?" The fact of the matter was that I had just sat down for the first time in twelve hours. It was as if he wanted to push my buttons, and boy, did he know which ones to push!

I could feel it coming before we even started. I had that same hollow feeling in my stomach I used to get when I knew my dad was winding up for a battle. My anger began building rapidly, and I thought, "Oh, well, as long as it has to be, I might as well give as good as I get!"

I became belligerent, and oblivious to what might happen to me. "Where were you?" I said, indignantly. "Supper was ready two hours ago. If you're not coming home, you could give me a call. Would that be too much to expect of you?" I should have known that was all it would take to really set him off.

"Hey!" Dan's voice rose to match and surpass mine. "Who do you think I am—your kid? You don't tell me what to do—you hear! If I want to spend a little time with my friends after a hard day's work—I damn well will. I mean, who the hell do you think you are. I work my ass off for you and your kid . . ."

"Oh, so it's my kid, now? I suppose you were out watering the lawn when he was conceived?"

"Hey! I can't even be sure he's mine," Dan used his best snarl, and arrogantly stood with his face right in mine. "How do I know what you were doing when I was out?"

I reacted as though he had just punched me in the stomach. For a moment, I was unable to reply. "Just like dad and mom," passed through my mind. Nothing mattered at that moment. He wasn't going to get away with that! "Boy, let me tell you—you are some prize. First of all, when the baby was conceived, you were never out. I was working two jobs while you were lying around the house. You *know* there was *never* another man in my life. I don't know what's wrong with you lately."

"What do you mean, wrong. Are you sayin' there's something wrong with me? I'll show you wrong!" Dan raised his arm and looked like he was going to take a swing at me, but he stopped himself. I felt relieved. I know now that was part of my problem. When I think about that kind of behavior now, I feel incensed!

"See how angry you get me?" Dan calmed down as quickly as he had become angered. It was so hard to figure how to react to him. "I know Jeffy's my baby. How else could he be so smart and good lookin', huh? C'mere babe. I'll make it okay. Come on. Come sit with me." Everything in me told me to stand my ground, but I seemed drawn to his side. He gestured for me to sit on his lap and I did. He

Marianne

133

began biting my neck and fondling my breasts roughly. I allowed him to continue, and I suppose, appeared to be cooperating. I felt empty and detached. He ran his hand up my leg and under my panties and said; "Hey, how about makin' a little sister for Jeffy tonight. What about it babe?"

It was as though I was reading from a script. It wasn't really me. "Well, we can try. But, no more fights, okay? I hate it when we fight. Mom and dad were always fighting. I couldn't stand it. I don't want us to be like that."

"Yeah, mine always were, too. I promise. I'll be good from now on. I love you Mare—you'll never know how much."

I wanted to believe him. Maybe this time, he finally learned how good I am for him. "I love you, too, Dan. I always will," I said to him and really meant it. I thought, "Maybe another baby will settle him down." I was still looking for a magic answer.

The Merry-Go-Round

I felt completely trapped and totally defeated, yet, I did nothing to change the situation. I was not yet twenty-five years old and all I could think about most of the time was the peace that death would bring to me. Dan became more abusive as the years passed and pressure on him to perform and conform increased. I managed to minimize the amount of time we spent together by taking a series of meaningless jobs at night when he could watch the children. It's funny, he was always home when I needed to go to work. I guess the money meant more to him than I did. I felt that it was outrageous that I had to work as a cocktail waitress when alcohol had played such a large part in destroying my life. But, the pay was good and Dan couldn't be depended upon to bring home enough money to take care of his responsibilities. I rationalized that at least it kept a roof over our heads.

Sometimes, when Dan and I were fighting, I became completely detached and could actually see my mother and father doing and saying the same things. Dan could always be depended upon to criticize my cooking. That was always a good fight starter. If that didn't work, he would call me fat, stupid or ugly. I can see how women can become anorexic, or give up working on their own goals. Even though I never weighed more than a hundred and ten pounds, I began to see myself as fat and ugly. I never did go back to college after I dropped out—until after I separated from Dan.

The worse things got, the more I fought back—just like mom. The fights usually ended with Dan storming out, and begging for forgiveness the next morning. I always forgave him that one more time, and for a few days or weeks, things would actually seem to improve. Then, some little thing would set him off, and another round of fighting would start. At least I did learn one thing—having another baby wouldn't help anything.

I had this dream all the time. I would replay the night I left my parents' home. I was carrying a suitcase that was bigger than I was, and as I ran, it would pop open and I would have to stop every few steps to put everything back in. And, the faster I would run, the closer I would be to the house. I kept running past the same places, and I would always end up back in my room. When I got there, I was a prisoner. I was locked in the room with a menacing stranger. Sometimes the dream became violent and sometimes sexually violent, but I was consistently the victim. To the rest of the world, I was still Marianne Perfect.

Marianne

135

About a year earlier, Bridget had left Bob. I was really surprised. She didn't talk about it but I assumed that she must have had her reasons.

I knew things weren't right when I began losing my temper with my children. They have always been good kids and I knew I was taking my pain out on them. After what happened to me as a child, I had sworn I would never do that. So much for best intentions.

I remember one particular incident. It was just before things came to a head with Dan. We had been sniping at each other for a few days, and I knew that there was a blow-up coming. Dan, as usual, was over two hours late for supper and the chicken I had made rivaled one of those rubber ones you get in the prank stores.

Jeffy was whiny because he hadn't eaten. "Mommy, is dinner ready yet?"

"I'm waiting for daddy, Jeff. You know he likes to eat with the family." The truth was that I used the children as a buffer when I knew he was about to start up with me. He did try to keep somewhat better control in their presence.

"But mommy, I'm hungry." I couldn't stand his whining.

"Didn't he know that if I fed him now, I could be facing a beating later?" flashed through my mind.

"But mommy, but mommy!" I screamed at him, and drew my arm back as if I was going to hit him. Didn't he know? Couldn't he understand? How could he know? He was five years old! He flinched and ran out of the kitchen, crying. I stood there, staring at my hand and my mother's screams and slaps filled my mind. Tears began streaming down my face. "I have to do something. I'll cut my hand off before I'd ever hit one of my children!" I didn't know yet what I was going to do, but when I became a threat to my own children, I knew that it was time to make some kind of change.

Stop the Merry-Go-Round

Perhaps it was fate that the phone rang at just that moment. It was Bridget. It was time to tell somebody. I couldn't keep it to myself any longer. I swallowed the false pride which was the legacy of a lifetime of keeping family secrets, and said, "Brige, I need to talk to somebody—right now. I think I'm cracking up. I really am. Can you come over?" I almost started telling her everything over the phone, but I really needed her to be there with me, or I wouldn't have had the courage to talk.

I felt a sense of relief, like a child who has lied to her parents and finally confessed. I had been carrying my truths which were everybody else's lies for a lifetime. I thought, "Maybe telling somebody I can trust will help." I busied myself straightening up the living room to fill the time until Bridget got there.

Dan came storming into the house and I could tell just looking at him that he was getting ready for a fight. I forgot about Bridget for the moment, because I knew that this one was going to be violent. He was drunk or high. I could tell by his clothes that he hadn't worked that day. The smell of beer and stale cigarettes on him told me he had spent the day in a bar. His eyes looked like tunnels. He probably had been doing speed, too. When he did speed and drank, he was really radical.

That whole night stands out in my mind. I replay it like my nightmares, which still won't go away.

Dan stomped into the living room and stood in the middle of the room with his fists clenched and a wild look in his eyes. I stood quietly, trying hard to be invisible. I guess I must have been staring at him, because that was his opening line. He always needed something to start with.

"Well, what are you staring at, stupid?" Dan didn't need to build up to his rage this time. It was there as soon as he came in the door. "I swear, sometimes I think you

Marianne

137

get dumber, fatter and uglier every time I see you. I'll bet you didn't even make me anything for dinner, did you? I don't know why I bother with you at all!"

I don't know why I fought back. Call it a reflex reaction. "Dinner's been on the table for three hours. Look, if I don't know when you are going to get home, how do you expect me to make your dinner?" I really believed that no matter what I did or said, Dan was going to find some way to twist it into whatever justified what he was going to do.

"Well, maybe if I had something worthwhile to come home to, I would come home. All you seem to do is bitch——maybe 'cause you *are* a bitch." Dan knew that one word, 'bitch' pushed all of my buttons. I heard it so much from my mother that once he did that, I didn't care what happened.

I felt the same as I did that last night in my parents' house. "That's it! I can't take this anymore. Maybe if you got a job like a normal person and didn't sit around in a bar all day, you wouldn't be so nasty all the time." Well, now, I just pushed all of his buttons, too! If there was one thing that got to him, it was being confronted with his irresponsibility. Maybe that is why he used violence. Nobody could confront him——especially the one person who knew how weak he really was!

"And whose fault is it I don't have a job? Maybe if I had something worth working for, I would have an easier time finding something. You sit there like a freakin' judge and tell me how to live my life. And I don't sit around in a bar all day. I'm tryin' to make deals for work . . ." The veins were standing out on Dan's neck, and his hands were balled into fists as he was screaming at me, but I couldn't stop fighting.

". . . and spend what little you make on beer and crank." I just had to have the last word. It seemed as if I really believed I could win this kind of argument. Dan

Stop the Merry-Go-Round

came after me, but the doorbell rang at that moment. I remembered that I had asked Bridget to come over.

I stood frozen and Dan said, "We'll finish this later, bitch. Well, answer the damn door, or are you too stupid even for that?"

I was completely numb. Bridget had never seen me looking like that and asked, "Hey, Mare, are you okay?" She saw Dan standing sullenly in the corner and looked back at me with the same knowing look that Mr. Laffer, my English teacher, had given me.

Dan was not great at playing the innocent, and in an angry and resentful voice said, "We'll finish our little conversation later. I'm goin' out." He couldn't hide the anger that was written all over his face, either.

"Wow! What was that all about? You two love birds have a little spat?" I couldn't tell if Bridget was serious, or being sarcastic.

I didn't know how to begin. My first impulse was to cover up like I always did. "Oh, Brige. I—I . . ." I paused and then chose my words as if they might explode. "Things are not going so great. Dan is under a lot of pressure because he is having trouble finding work and it seems that everything I do upsets him."

Part of me just wanted to blurt out the truth, but all the years of keeping secrets stopped me. Tears began pouring down my face and Bridget came over to give me a hug. She couldn't miss my look of pain. She was holding me tightly right on the spot where Dan had punched me a couple of days earlier. "What is it?" she asked me.

I continued to try to minimize the problem. "Oh, it's nothing. I hurt my back trying to lift Krissie. It'll heal. I'm tough." I smiled through the pain. Bridget gave me that look which said, "Sure, that's what happened!"

Marianne

139

"What? You act like you don't believe me." I became totally defensive and I was shaking inside. Inside, I was crying out to her, but I couldn't drop the act.

"C'mon Mare. You need to talk. What are friends for? We could always count on each other. Tell." When she said that, it was like a dam burst inside of me.

I stalled for one last moment while I poured us a cup of coffee and put a plate of cookies on the table. I remembered when we were kids we always did our most important talking at the kitchen table—except then, it was milk and cookies. Not much has really changed. "Oh, Bridget, I don't know where to begin. What am I doing wrong? I love Dan, but everything I say or do just seems to get him angry."

"Did you ever stop to think that maybe it isn't you? Maybe it's him?" Bridget paused and really looked at me. I felt as if she could see right through me and it made me very uncomfortable, almost like when my dad would walk into my room when I was undressed. "Mare, maybe it's none of my business, but I'm your friend and . . . we've been through a lot together. So, I'll just come right out and say it. That bastard beats you, doesn't he?"

There was no place to run and no place to hide. I panicked. This was what I had hoped for, but now that my opportunity was right in front of me, I still wanted to run away. "Well, it only happened a couple of times when I really got him angry." I did my best to minimize the situation. "Dan loves me. It's just that he's under so much pressure . . ."

"Hey! This is me you're talking to, kid. I had one beat on me for five years until I finally got up the nerve to walk the hell out. The nerve and almost two years of therapy. When I got together with him, I was almost grateful that he would even look at me after . . ." She stopped and looked like she had opened something she hadn't planned to open.

I just sat and waited for Bridget to continue. "What the hell, I may as well tell you everything. I know you won't broadcast it to the world." She took a deep breath and continued. "When I was a kid, my father . . ." Tears began pouring down her face. "My father had sex with me from when I was ten years old until I got the hell out of the house with Bob when I was seventeen. He threatened to kill me if I told, and when that stopped working because I didn't care anymore, he said I had my choice—it was either me or my little sister Kathy. Remember, Kathy ran away when she was fourteen? He must have done it to her anyway. Marriage to Bob seemed like heaven after that! So everything I did was . . . Oh, Mare, I'm sorry. You need me right now, and I am really okay with all of this. Therapy really helped me to accept myself and know I don't have to hide other people's dirty secrets any more. Sometimes, I feel like all men can rot in hell, but that passes. Maybe someday, I might even want a healthy relationship—whatever that is."

Now, all the missing pieces fit. I should have . . . No, there is no way I could have known, just like no one ever could have known what I was going through. "I didn't know, Bridget. You never said . . ."

"Neither did you, kid. Neither did you." We sat and held each other and Bridget was careful not to touch my bruises. "Wanna talk about it now? Punch, kick or throw?" She had a way of cutting right to the bone!

"You don't understand. Yes, he beats me. Yes, punch, kick and throw, okay? But I love him. I can't just walk out. Dad used to be that way, but it stopped and he and mom have a decent marriage now. Is there any chance Dan might change?" I was still looking for a magic answer.

Marianne

Bridget reached over and held my hand and I felt like a small child whose mother was trying to teach her how to tie her shoes. "Sure, but he has to want to. Mare? Why don't you go for help? That's one sure way of changing things. Change yourself."

I reacted as if she had just spit in the kitchen sink! "Help? You mean like to a shrink? I couldn't. Tell everything to a stranger? God, never! I'd die first!"

Bridget looked at me with the hardest and coldest look I'd ever seen from her. "It *could* come to that, you know."

After what I'd been through in twenty-five years of living, I wasn't convinced. I felt better now that it was out in the open, but I felt that Dan and I could still reason with each other. "I have to try on my own. I'll talk to Dan. I know he loves me and we can work it out."

"I love you too, Mare. You're the best friend I ever had. I don't think I would have made it this far without you. You sure you don't want me to stay? Dan had that look when he left. I've seen it plenty of times before. First my dad and then Bob. I learned to spot Bob's signal. He always got this cold look in his eyes before he started with the physical stuff. It was like he was just looking for an excuse." No matter what she might have said, I wasn't ready to take any real action.

"I'm not ready to give up. Dan just has problems, and I have to try to help him. When we got married, it was supposed to be for better or for worse." Old beliefs die hard, even when all the evidence contradicts them.

Bridget knew that I wasn't ready to pack a bag and move out, but she did what she had to do. She gave me the whole picture as only she could. "Yeah, but when the priest said, 'till death do you part,' he didn't mean that the guy was allowed to kill you!"

"Oh, Brige, don't exaggerate. He loses his temper sometimes, but he still wouldn't really hurt me." It was like an automatic reaction. I couldn't stop making excuses for Dan.

Bridget came right back at me. "No? You wouldn't want to show me your back right now, would you?" Maybe I needed to hear this. It made more sense than what I was saying!

"Look, this is something I have to work out my own way. Really, thanks for letting me talk and thanks for all the help . . ."

She knew that this was my way of closing the issue. She finally let me off the hook. "But you're not ready to do anything about it. Okay. I was the same way. But if you need me . . ." At that moment, that was enough. I had someone who knew—and cared. After what she had been through, maybe my situation wasn't that bad.

Bridget let me know before she left that I should call anytime if I needed her. She gave me her therapist's business card and told me to call him when I was ready. I told her that I would, and put the card in the cookie jar with about a thousand other names and numbers which I never intended to call.

I washed and dried the dishes and put them away. Even now, I was doing all the little things to keep Dan from getting upset with me. It was a relief to be alone for a while. I thought about Bridget and what she must have gone through as a kid—hiding—I couldn't even think it, let alone say it. I didn't think things like that happened to nice people like—us! It struck me that my father sometimes was close to crossing that same line. Those nights in my bedroom. I shuddered involuntarily just thinking about it.

A thousand thoughts tumbled through my mind. Every word that Bridget said was burned into my brain. I heard all of the voices. Dan, Mom, Dad. The blame, the put-downs, the anger, the pain. "Why me?" "Maybe because

Marianne

143

you're the strongest and the healthiest," my own voice answered. What a strange idea. Everybody picks on me because I am the strongest and the healthiest. At that moment, I didn't feel much of either.

It was almost midnight. I decided to go to bed. Dan would be ready for a real brawl when he came in. I knew he was at the bar with his no good friends—all of them were single or divorced. He was probably telling them all what a no good, fat, ugly, stupid bitch I was. And, for good measure, he probably was telling them that I screwed around with every worthless bum in town. That was a good one. Right now, he was with every worthless bum in town! I thought, "Maybe if I'm asleep, I can get through the night without trouble and talk to him tomorrow morning when he sobers up."

I went upstairs. I began undressing and was having trouble getting my sweater over my head. My back still hurt from where Dan had punched me 'playfully' the other night. I looked at my back in the mirror and saw the ugly bruise turning from purple to a gruesome yellow. "It's starting to heal," was all I could think. I climbed carefully into bed and curled up on my side which was the least painful position for me.

The door slammed and I snapped fully awake. I lay still, hoping that if Dan thought I was asleep, he would just bitch for a while and then go to sleep. That was often the way he was when he was drunk.

"Where the fuck are you? We have some unfinished business and you're not gonna get off that easy! Where are you, you stupid bitch?" His voice was more mean than drunk. I lay still and tried not to breathe. He pushed the door open so hard it bounced off the wall and closed again. He rammed it open again, cursing, and came storming into the room.

"You think I'm stupid? I know you're awake!" I lay there frozen. I was not going to respond to him. It's strange what can happen to a person when she is in a situation which she can't get out of. My recurring nightmare passed through my mind, except it began where it usually left off. I was trapped in my bedroom with a menacing stranger. It was like I was outside of myself watching it all happen.

He just stood in the doorway for what seemed like forever. It was like he was a cat playing a game with a trapped mouse. He knew that he could do whatever he wanted. I was sitting on the dresser watching, like teddy used to. I saw the form move slowly across the room. I was under the covers and hadn't moved. How could I? I was sitting on the dresser, invisible.

"Get the fuck out of that bed, you stupid cunt or I'm going to pull you out by whatever I get a hold of!" I shuddered involuntarily when he used that word. He must have seen me move because he pulled the covers off the bed and reached over to pull me out of the bed, but I rolled out the other side onto the floor. I watched with total detachment as Dan climbed over the bed and grabbed for me again. I tried to crawl away, but Dan grabbed me and turned me over on my back, then, he sat on top of me. I covered my face with my arms, and I still refused to look at him or react.

Dan's knees were pressing into my shoulders and I felt pain coursing through my arms and back. He smiled and said, "Hey! I'm not going to mess up your pretty face. See?" He punched me in the ribs and breasts. I involuntarily lowered my arms and Dan pinned my arms to my sides with his knees. He began slapping my face, first almost playfully, and then harder. I refused to make any sound, or give any indication that he was even there, which made him even angrier.

Marianne

145

"You won't learn, will you. What did you tell that stupid cow, Frigid Bridget?" I continued to stare blankly, with no sign that I even heard him. "Goddamn you! I'll show you!" Dan pulled me up by the neck and choked me while at the same time, he pushed me again and again into the wall. I just hung limply like a rag doll and Dan got angrier. He finally let me go and I dropped to the floor like a bundle of discarded rags. I lay still. I wondered if I was alive.

Dan stepped back, gave me a hard kick and left the room. A few moments later, I heard the front door slam. I lay still, in an almost fetal position, trying to breathe. I began to feel the pain. My body felt like it was on fire. I was choking on something and realized that my nose was bleeding into my mouth. I turned my head to the side and wiped my nose with the sleeve of my nightgown.

I rolled over and tried to get up, but I was too weak and fell back. I looked around the room and it looked like a bomb had dropped. The bedclothes were scattered all over, all of my makeup was on the floor, including overturned boxes of powder. My rocking chair was on its side, and finally, I noticed teddy, keeping his solitary vigil on the shelf, undisturbed by all of the chaos.

With immense effort, I turned on my back, and lay staring at the ceiling, too hurt to get up. My nose was still bleeding, my lip was swollen and there was blood all over the front of my nightgown which had a torn sleeve and was torn at the bottom where Dan had grabbed it, trying to get hold of me. I began breathing in deep, ragged bursts. I still didn't feel anything emotionally.

Painfully, I dragged myself into the bathroom. I somehow got out of the bloody nightgown and got into the shower. I kept feeling like I was going to pass out.

I must have blanked out, because the next thing I knew, I was standing in the kitchen, naked and dripping all over

Dan's perfect floor. I took a sharp knife out of the rack and stood in the middle of the room, staring at it. I held it over my wrist, but made no move to cut myself. I don't know how long I stood there like that.

"Mommy, you're all naked and dripping!" Jeffy stood in the doorway, his eyes open wide in shock, or surprise. I was usually very modest around Jeffy, especially now that he was five, but I was oblivious to myself.

"Naked and dripping?" I slowly came to him. "Jeffy, what are you doing up at this hour?"

"I heard you and daddy fighting and I got scared. I thought he was trying to kill you, it was so loud. Mommy, are you going to take that knife and kill him back?" Jeffy was rocking uncomfortably from foot to foot, not knowing what to make of the situation.

I stared at the knife, aware of it for the first time, and dropped it to the floor with revulsion. "No, Jeffy, mommy wouldn't hurt daddy. The fight is over. Everything is going to be okay now."

"Mommy, I was so scared."

"Come here, baby. Come to mommy." For a moment, he just stood there, and I realized that he was confused by my nakedness. "It's okay, baby." He ran to me and hugged me, and I felt a wave of love pass through me for my child. For the moment, I didn't feel the pain from the beating. I didn't feel the pain from a lifetime of abuse. I was holding my baby in my arms and everything was going to be all right.

"Now I'm all wet, too!" Jeffy started laughing, and I began laughing hysterically with him. Out of the corner of my eye, I saw the knife on the floor. It had no meaning anymore.

"C'mon, baby. Let's go to bed. We've had a long night." I thought to myself, "I've had a long life!"

Marianne

147

The next morning when I woke I felt every muscle in my body aching. I dragged myself out of bed with a grunt. I looked at myself in the bathroom mirror and almost threw up. I didn't recognize the bloated, battered, distorted face that stared blankly back at me. I took my robe off so I could inspect all of the damage. There were large bruises on my arms, chest, and breasts, and distinct fingerprints around my neck. I could see and feel a lifetime of bruises and cuts, one layer on top of another. "I can't take it any more." I was startled, because I had said it out loud.

I limped slowly downstairs, and began preparing breakfast for the children. The cookie jar caught my eye. I reached in and pulled out the card on top of everything else in there. I read it, cautiously. It said, "Robert Sand, Psychotherapist, specializing in women's issues." It was after eight-thirty, and I took a chance and called.

Imagine, me, Marianne, calling a shrink?

The secretary put me through to Dr. Sand. "Hi! Robert Sand speaking. Can I help you?" I wasn't able to say a word. "I have trouble with opening lines, too. Here, let me give you one of mine," he said.

I began smiling despite everything I was feeling, and asked him if he worked with marriage problems. I was very noncommittal, but I did tell him that my husband and I had been having difficulties in our relationship and we were considering seeking outside help. I told him that I needed to talk it over with my husband before I made a decision. He was very nice and didn't try to talk me into anything, or offer any advice. He ended the conversation by telling me that I could call anytime, with or without my husband being involved. After I hung up the phone, I thought of Mr. Laffer for the first time in a long time.

"Any time you need an adult to talk to . . ." I never took him up on his offer.

I gave the children breakfast, and had a cup of coffee. I was tempted to call Bridget, but I wasn't ready to tell her that she was right. I still wanted to try to talk to Dan and get him to see that he and I both needed help.

Dan came home about ten in the morning, happy and looking like he had just been sleeping for ten hours. "Hey, babe, what's for breakfast?" After he said that, he looked at my face and then looked sheepishly at the floor. He came toward me with his arms out to hold me. "Oh, God, I must have been drunk. I . . . I'm sorry, babe. How could I do that to you? I . . . it won't happen again, I really promise. I'll cut back on my drinking. I was just under a lot of pressure. Did I really do that to you?"

"Dan, don't. We have to talk. I called a therapist this morning and asked about our getting some help." I held my arms out in front of me so he couldn't get close.

"Help? You mean see a headshrinker? No way. Are you saying there's something wrong with me? I told you, I'm just under a lot of pressure. When I get my business straightened out, I'll be fine. I didn't mean what happened last night. I was drunk and you got me angry. Look, I'm sorry, I'll make it up to you. What do you want me to do? It won't happen again, I promise." The words were the same ones he always used to get me to go along with him one more time. They were the same ones dad used to get mom to go along with him one more time.

I just sat, shaking my head. "I'm sorry Dan, It won't work this time. I already decided. I heard that promise too many times. Whether you go or not, I'm going. And, I've decided that you have to leave. Until we get things worked out, I can't have the kids exposed to your violence."

"Marianne, please, I love you. I can't live without you." I could see huge tears forming in his eyes.

Marianne

———————————

149

In his own way, I knew that Dan was telling the truth. He did love me, and he probably thought he couldn't live without me. For a moment, I almost said that I would give him one more chance, but I kept my resolve. "No, I'm sorry Dan. I'm really sorry, but we've been this route before and nothing changes."

It was like there were two people living inside one body. The tears and soft look were replaced by his snarl and swagger. "Don't think that I'm going to take this lying down. You think you can take my house and my kids? No way!" He stopped, and suddenly became the other Dan. "See, you have a way of getting me all worked up, but I can control myself if I try. Look we love each other. No one else could understand us like we understand each other. Hey, we grew up with families that fought, so we fight, but we do love each other. Doesn't that count for something?"

I just looked at him like I had never really seen him before. "Dan, if you won't get help . . . Look, I told you just how I feel. Don't you think I want to just wish the problem away? Dan, I have to think about Jeffy and Krissy. They don't need to see their mother beaten. I used to see it happen to my mother and now my kids are seeing it happen to me. Until you get your life straightened out, I can't live with you. You are going to have to leave—for now. I began to cry, but I had decided I was not going to change my mind.

"Please, Mare, just one more chance. I'll change, you'll see." In most of our fights in the past, this was where I would give in. I stood silently, shaking my head emphatically, no. "Okay, don't think I'm going to make this easy for you. You can't kick me out of my house. You won't get a cent! I'll see to it that . . ."

I cut him off without waiting to hear the rest. "See, you can't even keep a promise for two minutes. You don't get your way, and you are already threatening. It just won't work any more. I know I need help, and I was hoping that you'd see that you do too. But I guess you have to do what you need to do. I just hope . . ."

"Yeah, you just keep hopin'. But you better change your mind quick, or I'll be gone for good."

I promised myself I wouldn't get into a fight with him, but I was angry and my voice began rising. "You don't even know what you did to me, do you? You think you can just beat me and almost kill me and then either sweet-talk me or threaten me the next morning. I saw my mom go through that for a lot of years, and even she got wise in the end. No Dan. I'm not giving in." Dan stormed out the door. That was the last time we lived under the same roof. Later, when I thought about how we ended our marriage, I felt cheated. It wasn't the first time in my life I felt that way.

As soon as Dan was out the door, I called Dr. Sand and made an appointment for the following week. I was ashamed of all my bruises and wanted to give them some time to heal. "Still the proud one, aren't you?" It was ironic. The ship was sinking and I was worrying about my makeup!

After I hung up the phone, I called Bridget. I told her that I had called Dr. Sand. I wasn't worried how I looked any more with her. She knew. She said that she would be over in ten minutes. I didn't even have a chance to dress and she was there.

"Thanks for coming over again. I don't know——did I do the right thing? I love Dan. Maybe if I give him . . ."

"You were going to say, 'maybe if I give him another chance?' Mare, I went through the same thing, and I can't tell you what to do, but I learned in therapy that this is a natural step in your recovery. You were taught to be obligated to the person who hurt you. Hey, will you listen to me? I'm not the therapist here. Wait till you meet Robert—Dr. Sand. He's special. I don't know where I would be without his help—probably in the hospital—or the morgue, or at best in a nut house! Mare, if you can't talk to him, you can't talk to anybody. He'll wreck your stereotypes about men—and about therapists! Hey! Enough. You'll see for yourself." She reached over and held my hand. I squeezed hers to tell her all the things I couldn't put into words. We knew what real friendship was at that moment.

I still had doubts that I was doing the right thing, and Bridget listened patiently as I talked about it. "But, it's not like Danny is my enemy or something. He's my best friend, except for you—but you know what I mean. I married him in sickness or in health, and we're both pretty sick."

Bridget came right back at me. "Mare, I can't tell you what to do, but in sickness or health stops when he becomes violent—or maybe even before that. Hey, I was your best friend before Dan ever existed in your life. Did I ever beat you up?—not including that time in third grade." We both laughed at that! "You are giving him a chance to change himself, but in the meantime, you have to protect yourself—and the kids. Mare, I've been out of it over a year now and I still have parts of my body that won't heal and I have nightmares all the time. And, yeah, I *still* do love the son-of-a-bitch in my own crazy way, but I wouldn't let him within a mile of my house!"

"But, what am I supposed to tell Dr. Sand? I can't tell about . . ." Old habits die hard.

"Don't plan it in advance. When you get in there, you'll just know what to say. Hey, you won't be alone in the room. Robert will help you—if anybody can." We both laughed the way we did when we were young and . . . I guess we were never really innocent, were we?

That first night alone was like the first night in my own apartment. I was scared and relieved at the same time. The kids were very upset, and kept asking, "Where's daddy? Where's daddy?" I didn't know what to tell them, so I said that he was on a business trip. I had yet to learn how to deal with the truth with them.

The week until my appointment with Dr. Sand passed uneventfully. The bruises healed—especially when I covered them with a little makeup. It's funny, the only time I used makeup was when I was covering bruises—except for a little lip gloss and eye shadow.

Bridget was right. Robert broke all of my stereotypes when it came to therapists. I was expecting Sigmund Freud, Jr., and I got a man who looked like your next door neighbor—if you were lucky enough to have a good one. He smiled a lot, was very soft-spoken and didn't give much advice, but kept me talking even though I had sworn I would have nothing to say. You could tell he was really interested. He hung on every word, and when I talked about the abuse he was crying for me, even though I wasn't ready to cry for myself.

I was expecting the old psychiatric couch and instead, it looked like a comfortable den with a bunch of comfortable mismatched chairs.

"Come on in, Marianne. I've been looking forward to meeting you. Sit wherever you are comfortable."

"Which is your chair?" I was taking no chances on offending him.

"They all are, if you want to believe the loan company who is collecting for them, but if you'd like to make one your own, I'll get the contract rewritten." I couldn't help but laugh, although it was going to take a whole lot more to get me to tell my story to a stranger.

I picked a chair and sat sedately, with my knees together and my hands folded in my lap, just like my parents taught me. I was wearing a business suit. I hadn't dressed in a business suit since Jeffy was born. It's funny how old habits will pick a time like this to come out. I felt the same way I did on my first date with Dan. Robert was dressed casually, in jeans and a pullover. I thought to myself, "He doesn't look like he just crawled out from under a pickup, though. He's like all the good men in my life I ran away from." I began making a decision that this was one time I wasn't going to run—or hide. I just didn't know how to start.

I was sitting waiting for a cue and feeling very uncomfortable. Just when I was convinced that he was going to leave me sitting here until I said something, Robert began: "You know, the toughest thing to do is start a conversation with a stranger. I don't know about you, but for me, opening lines are awfully tough."

"God, thanks! If you had left that to me, we'd be sitting here until next week. I really don't know what to say. I've never been in therapy before. What am I supposed to do first?" I felt as though I had taken the first step in a long journey to an unknown destination.

"You've already done several things. You called, you came, you spoke. Now that the hard part's over, we can finish what we came here for. Which is?"

Dr. Sand rested his face in the vee between his thumb and index finger and waited patiently. "Like someone who knows what he is waiting for," crossed my mind. I was becoming more and more intrigued by this therapy thing. I figured that if I was going to do this thing, I better just jump in. "I'm not sure exactly where to begin. Well, I'm having some problems with my marriage and I want to try to get them resolved." I made the statement with all of the joy of a child taking medicine, but it was a start. My mind flashed back to a scene seven years earlier. Mr. Laffer was saying, "Anytime you need an adult . . ." "Dear God, I need one now!" came my answer. "What do you want to know, Dr. Sand?"

"First of all, please call me Robert, if you are comfortable with it. If you decide to stay in therapy, we are going to be taking what may be a long and very trying journey together and we need to feel comfortable with each other. Does that sound okay to you—Marianne?"

I liked the sound of my name coming from this man. I thought of other times in my life I heard my name, like my mother screaming it, Dan snarling it, Dad never using it at all (funny, I never really took notice of that before), and Mr. Laffer—saying it just the way Robert did. I thought, "I never called myself by my name. Maybe I ought to try. The way he says it makes it sound so nice." I didn't answer his question, but he knew that he would be Robert from then on.

Robert took my silence as my consent to continue. "Maybe instead of answering your question—you'll find I do this a lot—if it annoys you, yell or something—(We both laughed at that!)—let me tell you my definition of therapy. That might help you to focus on what you can use this time for, okay?" I simply nodded in agreement. "To me, . . ."

For the first time, he spoke more slowly, emphasizing each of his words. "Therapy is an opportunity to tell the things which you cannot tell so that you may yet dream the dreams you dared not dream."

I was caught off guard. It was like—I can't explain what came over me. "To tell . . . to dream . . ." My whole life flashed through my mind. The beatings, the drunkenness, the threats, the lies, the cover-ups. My eyes filled with tears which I tried to hold back.

"It's okay, Marianne. Sometimes, you have to start by letting out the pain—to make room for the dream." For the first time in my life, I had someone's permission to cry.

Marianne

155

I let go and must have just sobbed for maybe ten minutes. After I regained my composure, I knew I was ready to tell what I could not tell. It felt so right, when for twenty-five years it had felt so wrong.

"You know, when I first came in I was planning to do what I always did. I was going to give you a song and dance about how everything was just a little out of line and thank you for your help and leave. I can't do that anymore. Why am I here?

"All my life, I lived with fighting—and violence. My dad beat my mom. My mom—and dad beat me. I got married. We fought. My husband started getting violent. They all blamed me. If you would only this or if you would only that, you wouldn't make me hit you. It's all my fault? It's all MY FAULT? What did I ever do to any of you? WHAT THE HELL DID I EVER DO TO ANY OF YOU? WHAT THE HELL DID I EVER DO TO ANY OF YOU TO DESERVE THIS?" I sat trembling with rage, and as it passed, I felt totally embarrassed. "Oh, I'm . . ."

Robert cut me off. "Don't say it, Marianne. What? Sorry? Embarrassed? Say what you feel, not what you were taught to say. What are you feeling about your life?"

"I guess I feel angry." I was confused. I didn't know what he wanted. I've learned that I have to react to what I feel, not what other people expect me to feel, but I hadn't learned that yet.

"You guess?" Robert was being sarcastic with me for the first time and I began to understand that all he was doing was giving me the freedom to look at myself.

"No, I don't guess. I feel angry." I really didn't feel anything, but I knew I was supposed to feel angry from all of that abuse.

"I don't hear or feel anger in what you are saying, Marianne." I felt very defensive. It was as if Robert was trying to provoke me. "How angry?" He said it so gently that it made me feel almost able to let my anger show. "How angry are you Marianne? How much 'angry' are you *allowed* to show, to feel or to be?"

"It's hard to feel it after all these years. You're not supposed to air your dirty linen in public."

"Who said so?" Robert came out with it so suddenly that I was caught off guard—again.

"Who told you that you aren't allowed to share your problems and your feelings?"

"Why, mom and dad—and Dan . . . The people who . . ."

"The people who what, Marianne?"

"The people who had the most to lose if I told! Damn them! Damn them!" I was shaking, almost uncontrollably.

"What are you feeling at this very moment?" Robert sat back in his chair. He looked as though he had just finished doing something very important.

"Anger, I'm feeling *anger* . . . No I am feeling rage. How dare they? HOW DARE THEY!"

That was two years ago. I still had a long way to go in therapy. Just because I was encouraged to show my true feelings for the first time, didn't mean I was able to change the way I handled my life. All it did was give me a start toward being able to deal openly with my problems. I was still convinced that Dan could be changed into the husband I thought I needed.

As I grew in confidence, I began to make changes in my life. I went back to school at night, and took a full-time job. Jeffy started first grade and I found a good nursery school for Krissy. I was amazed at how much ability I had to take care of myself and the children. Dan was true to his word. He provided almost no financial help at all. At Robert's insistence, I joined his women's group. I wasn't much for talking in group, but I began finding that

Marianne

157

I really was able to develop relationships in which I could be honest. The group jokingly referred to me as 'The Sphinx' because I talked so rarely, but I didn't mind. I knew there was real caring in that room.

Robert worked with me in therapy to help me see myself as a whole woman who had choices. We dealt with my rage and frequent bouts of depression. I was beginning to feel better about myself and had some caring for the woman I saw in the mirror in the morning.

I still was having difficulty making a total separation from Dan, but for almost a year, I had stuck to my guns and not let him back in the house, except to pick up the kids. Then, after almost a year of peace of mind, I weakened because he was being so nice and I let him talk me into an overnight date. Everything was beautiful that night. It was like it was when we were dating. The next morning, he asked to move back in, and I knew nothing had changed. When I told him that moving back in was still dependent on his going into therapy, he got really vile and called me all the names I hadn't been hearing for nearly a year. He even talked about hitting me, but I told him that if he did, he would have his next visit with the kids in the county jail!

I got all upset and brought it up in my group that week. The group, especially Ellen, who by that time had become almost as good a friend as Bridget, was not at all sympathetic to me. "Hey, it's your life. If you want somebody walking all over it, that's on you!" Ellen could still cut right through all the bullshit, and now I can say that without flinching! Maybe having a foul mouth is better than having a foul life? That night, I went home from group feeling like a piece of cut-up meat. I must have cried for an hour before I could fall asleep, but I felt as if I was closer to making the decision about Dan which now appeared inevitable. I still hate that word—divorce—it is like saying defeat.

I did very little for the few weeks following that confrontation. I told Robert that I felt ready to leave therapy, but he suggested that I stay for four more weeks. I didn't understand what four weeks was going to do until two weeks later in group. I wasn't planning to talk that night and was still procrastinating on any decision. Robert began the session by telling the group that I was planning to leave in a couple more weeks. It was a shock to hear it coming from him, and for a moment, I felt as though he was kicking me out.

"I have to talk tonight." Usually, when I did speak, it was only when someone else asked me to, or the last five minutes of group when there was no time to really confront me with anything.

"I have to make a decision about di— . . . divorcing Dan. I know inside of me that I can't let him back into my life, but I just sit and still hope that some miracle will get him to change. His whole life says that he is changing—for the worse. He drinks more and is more irresponsible than ever. Something in me keeps saying, 'He's going to change.'"

"Is that a belief, or a wish?" Robert gave me one of his knowing smiles. It hit me like a brick. He had set this up. By telling *my* group that I was leaving, it forced me to deal with my biggest issue *now*! He knew that I wasn't about to leave this group holding the bag for me on the biggest thing I had to deal with. You know, sometimes I think I want to switch careers and be a therapist, just like Robert. Who knows, life is funny.

Robert and I had gone over this in our individual session. I repeated what I had learned like a good student! "A belief has something to back it up and a wish is just something you'd like to happen. For instance, when I was a kid, I always wanted my mom and dad to show me love and caring and it never happened. I did everything to get it from them. I was the perfect kid. Yes, and tried to be the perfect wife, too. I guess I just wish Dan would change, because I certainly don't have anything to back it up.

"I was just thinking how I sat here in group for months and wouldn't talk about anything important and now it's like——you know——'The Sphinx' is going to speak! It does feel good to be able to talk about the real things in my life. I hid the family secrets so long."

Ellen added, "Yeah, me too. I took beatings for years and kept my mouth shut. But it's over now. Nobody better lay a hand on me——ever!" The group all added their agreement to this statement. "Does what's his name still threaten you?"

"He still gets angry, but now he won't hit me. He really hasn't changed though——he's still not working. He still drinks and does drugs. I'm starting to believe that he really doesn't want to change." I knew that he really didn't want to change, but, like mom, I couldn't bring myself to do anything about it. "Every time I think about telling Dan that it's over, I just want to cry. I still love my husband, but I don't like him and I can't live with him. He chooses to be the way he is and I'm worth better treatment than what I got from him."

Pat, who rarely spoke——unless something extremely important needed to be said, commented, "Mare, you don't have to stop loving him, you just have to get on with your life. They're separate things."

At that point, Robert interjected, "Marianne, why did you get married?"

"This is another of those questions isn't it?" I knew when Robert would ask the most innocent questions, it usually meant that he knew you were ready to deal with the real question, not the simple one. "God, Robert. How do you do it? I remember when you said that I already have all the questions and all the answers I need. It's just that I have some of the answers after the wrong questions. This is . . . I see. The simple answers would be 'I loved him', or, 'I was . . . uh, pregnant.'" I looked away for a moment to gather my thoughts.

"I always wanted to be loved for myself, not for my looks, or whatever. I always wanted someone to listen to me. I remember so many times just needing mom or dad to notice me. 'Mom, dad . . . it's me, your daughter.'" I began crying and for one of the rare times in my life, I didn't mind. I continued speaking through my tears. "I'm really here. Look at me. Look at me . . . It never happened. It still doesn't. But Dan, in the beginning, he did listen and he respected me. It changed after we got married. He became just like his dad——hard and mean, and like my dad——drunk and violent.

"It's like . . . a merry-go-round. You just pass the same place over and over, until . . . until you decide to get off."

Robert smiled, "See, you did have the question and the answer inside yourself. Let me ask another one, okay? What do you need?"

Ellen looked at Robert and then at me. "Hey! Gettin' what you need is for later. Right now, you need a shopping list before you go out and get a grocery cart!"

Robert and the group burst out laughing. Robert said, "Ellen, I'm supposed to say things like that. If you steal all my best lines, I'll have nothing at all to do around here." I really loved it when the group had these moments of laughter. I remember hardly any at all in either of my homes. "Anyway . . . you're right Ellen. Now is just a time for Marianne to look at her real needs, not to go out and meet them."

"You know, I love this group. You're like a family to me. Like a family I never had." It struck me fully at that moment. "A family. That's it. That's what I always look for. That's what I need. So, I go around in circles looking for the same thing I already had, and damn it, I keep getting back exactly what I already had—a sick family. What do I need? I need . . . respect from others. I need . . . tenderness. I need someone to tell me that it's okay to be me. I need . . . everything that Dan hasn't given me for the last five years."

"Yeah, me too. In here nobody ever puts me down or tries to hurt me. And when I mess up, somebody cares enough to get all over my case." Yolanda, the senior member of the group, added this very important part for me. A family can criticize with love and respect, and then, you can listen.

Robert then asked me to talk to the group about why I had to leave Dan. I had difficulty sharing details, but I felt I could trust everyone in the room now, and I needed to tell it to other women.

"This isn't easy to talk about. Maybe I have to tell it again and again to get it out of me. The last night we were together, Dan hit me and hit me. I felt as if I wasn't there. I literally blanked it out. When you've spent so much of your life getting hit, you start to believe that it is just something that has to happen." I began shaking with rage.

"I don't remember exactly what happened next. I know that I thought that I was dead—well at least my feelings were dead. It was like I was standing outside myself watching Dan beat on me and for one crazy moment, I was rooting for him to finish the job. 'Yeah,' I said to myself. 'I was born to be killed like this. My parents raised me for this and I'm finally going to do something that pleases them. I am going to become what they meant for me to be—a genuine victim!'

"Something inside of me changed that night. I began to discover that I didn't need to be in an abusive relationship to feel 'normal'. After all those years with mom and dad, Dan had seemed normal to me. After all, everybody fights, every man hits women sometimes, don't they? Our job is to persevere. That's what mom always taught me. Boy, did I have a lot to learn!

"Dan always had a million excuses for being abusive. The floor was dirty, the toys weren't picked up. The dinner he didn't come home for was cold.

"I have to do something—now. It's just like the night I moved out of my parent's house. I was scared, but I did it. I have to do it—now."

After that session, it was as if all the parts of me realigned. I was the same person, but different. I knew that the next time I saw Dan would be the last as his legal wife. We would always be attached by the fact that we had two children, and a part of me would always love the man I wanted him to be, but I would never again live with the Dan that was.

I went to see a lawyer and filed for divorce the same day I expected Dan to come pick up the children for the weekend. I had a locksmith change the lock on the door, so I could feel that the house was really mine. That evening, I was studying for finals and heard a fumbling at the door, followed by loud curses. I took a deep breath— even though I made a decision, it wasn't easy. Reluctantly, I let Dan in. I felt somewhat more in control than I had earlier.

"I see I've been locked out of my own house now." Dan threw his now useless key across the room and stood, swaying slightly. "What's the matter? You afraid I'm gonna sneak into your bedroom in the middle of the night and rape you or something?"

"Last week you did barge in when I was asleep and try to get into bed with me when you were stinking drunk. Dan, you don't live here any more, and I filed for a

Marianne

163

divorce today." The last part came out in a jumble. I was working at not crying—or changing my mind.

"But Mare, I love you." He looked like a little child who had lost his mommy! I had heard it too many times for it to touch me anymore.

"Dan, it won't work anymore. One minute you're throwing things and the next minute you want to carry me off to the bedroom for fun and games. If you loved me, you wouldn't try to hurt me. If you loved me, you wouldn't try to threaten me." I could feel my real anger begin to emerge. "If you loved me, *me*, Marianne, you would respect my rights as a person. Dan, you don't know how to love anyone because you don't love yourself."

"Boy, is that therapist twisting your mind! I bet you and him are . . ."

"Don't you dare say it! You can't twist my life anymore. You can't make me feel guilty because you feel lousy and need someone to take it out on." At that moment, Dan looked as if he was going to hit me. " . . . and if you dare to raise a hand to me in *my house*, MY HOUSE, Dan, I will have you arrested, do you hear me? You had your chance to get help. God knows, much as I need therapy it is still embarrassing to have to share my most private thoughts and feelings with a stranger. Dan, I still love you and I always will. I haven't forgotten the good times and the caring, but I haven't forgotten the abuse and the beatings and all the foul things you called me. I love you Dan, but I don't need you any more. To love you meant I had to give away myself. To make you feel like you were worth something meant I had to feel like I was worth nothing. No more Dan, no more. I can let you go now. I see somebody in the mirror now who is becoming more important every day—me, Marianne.

"Dan, you came to pick up the children. They are upstairs."

Stop the Merry-Go-Round

164

He started to ask me if I had packed their clothes. I always did. I was the good wife until—almost the end. "You know where their clothes are. Take what you need for the weekend. I have studying to do. I have finals next week. Have them back before bedtime."

It was over. I was free. I don't know where life will lead, but I will never again be anyone's victim. Of that I can be certain. I was ready to move on from Robert and the group. I stayed in touch with Robert—and still do—once in a while. Ellen and I meet for coffee every month or so and it is like having a healthy younger sister. We never tell each other how to live—we don't have to. I never did become a therapist, but I help my friends by offering them what Bridget offered me when I needed it. I haven't gotten into a new relationship to replace Dan. I date occasionally, and even have sex once in a while—if the man is special—and I want to express and share my healthy feelings with him in this particular way.

I see my parents more often than I did for years. They have mellowed and seem to be trying to make up for the past although we never will be able to talk about it. I feel sorry for them because I realize how much they missed out on. They treat their grandchildren like china dolls. I have to admit, sometimes I am jealous, but Jeff and Kris will never have to know the pain my parents brought into my life. To them, these two handsome people are simply a loving mom-mom and pop-pop. Dad doesn't drink any more. He had a massive coronary when he was forty-seven that scared him sober. He also stopped being a prison commandant. I guess standing that close to death does something to you. Not drinking seems to do even more —at least for dad and mom. Mom is happier and rarely drinks. Most of the kids are out of the house and her life is now really what it always appeared to be. She is Mrs. Organization President—big time.

Marianne

165

Last week, mom told me how proud she was of me and asked me if I needed anything. I held her and we both had a good cry.

ELLEN

What do you want to know?

Tell Me What
You Cannot Tell Me

Being Therapeutic

No matter how many women share their stories of abuse with me, I will never be able to harden myself to the cold facts and prevent myself from wanting to take action on their behalf—though I know that is neither possible nor really desirable. Ellen is unique, but typical. She is so expressive and articulate that her story literally begs to be told.

Ellen used drugs and alcohol as painkillers to escape from an environment which was abusive in the extreme. She was abused by her parents and by her older brothers. The abuse was physical and verbal. It left her so emotionally scarred that she believed she couldn't go on living even though she had gotten out of the abusive environment. The abuse had become self-abuse by the time I met her.

Perhaps it would help at this point to share with you some of the principles I use as a therapist, as well as some of the general implications which I draw from the situations I encounter. Abuse is never pretty and the woman who has been a victim is left with feelings of pain, rage, impotence, and guilt which must first be brought to awareness and then given an open channel for sharing. The title of this chapter comes from this principle. Many, if not most, abused people are well-trained to keep the family secret. This theme recurs throughout the book, and in each life presented, growth begins only after the victim shares her secret truths.

The true horror of being a victim is that, eventually, there is often no more need for a perpetrator. The victim becomes the perpetrator of the harm to herself. This was especially true for Ellen.

Much of my therapy enables the client to learn to express impressions and feelings about himself or herself to consciousness with relative ease. Much of what hurts women who become addicts, as Ellen did, involves the imposition of certain "Rules of Life" established in the family setting: prohibitions, statements about one's worth, and unrealistic expectations. Most of these women began their addictions because they did not like themselves. Often, they came from homes whose environment made it difficult for them to relate in a healthy manner to the world outside. In the case of those addicted women who grew up in homes with drug addicted or alcoholic parents, the pattern of their lives left them so scarred, that they found it impossible to relate to the world comfortably. Their own self-concepts were so distorted, it was impossible for them to feel wanted, or of value. A false sense of self-image and self-worth left them vulnerable to developing adult attitudes and values which made them especially susceptible to eating disorders, promiscuity, and addiction. Ellen came from just such a family.

A particularly odious rule of family life is the one which states that children have no right to question the judgment of parents. Children are expected to love, honor and obey parents. Many parents govern the family so absolutely that it is impossible for a child to question their pronouncements and rules. Furthermore, parents often set these rules capriciously, to make life more pleasant for themselves.

The maturing woman enters a less structured world than that of her family. She enters this world with only the concepts she was taught at home. In order to recover and grow, the woman who is a victim of abuse or addicted to drugs must begin to challenge these lifelong values. Her first recovery task is to begin to believe that her parents were not always right, and then, to open for examination, the family secrets. This is not easy for a person who was inculcated from first breath with the belief that one is supposed to keep the family secrets secret. These family secrets need to be shared in order to expose the underlying value system from which they evolved. And, they need to be shared appropriately.

Her second task is to question each value to determine if it facilitates or hinders the development of a healthy pattern of living. Because of the prohibitions against questioning family values, a therapist must often use techniques which enable the client to free herself, to open up her values for a more comprehensive examination. I often use the tools of metaphor and paradox to open pathways into heretofore defended realms of the client's life. The title of this chapter is one such paradox. A paradox asks the person to do the impossible. In this case, "Tell me what you cannot tell me," is an injunction which reverses the lifelong parental mandate which says to the child, "Keep quiet about what you most need to talk about!"

Ellen entered therapy to deal with a singular, but profound, issue: to learn to accept her feelings as real and valid, and to deal with them, or die in her addiction. Allow me to share her story with you. The time sequences described are condensed, but represent continuity in the process.

Every therapist has a few magic moments. During such moments, two people, who exist in a relationship only within the confines of an office, lose their individuality for a brief time, and operate in a realm which cannot be described in words. It is during these moments that a therapist ceases *doing* therapy and enters the realm of *being* therapeutic. My sessions with Ellen provided such moments.

Queen of the High School Prom

When I first saw Ellen, it was difficult to imagine that she could have a worry in the world. She looked like the girl most likely to be chosen queen of the high school prom. Looks can be deceiving. Despite the appearance of schoolgirl innocence, Ellen was no child. She had never had a childhood. If a textbook is ever written about the most pathological alcoholic family in existence, Ellen's family will stand a good chance of being chosen. Her family is a classic, especially because most of the havoc in which its members engage is kept within the confines of the home. In the community, the father holds a prestigious position, and the family maintains a front of respectability. However, at home, the father drank from the moment he came home from work until late at night when he would fall asleep——or pass out. The dinner table was like a Mad Hatter's tea party. There were constant arguments over trivia. Everyone picked on Ellen. She was the family scapegoat, but of course they convinced her that whatever abuse they heaped upon her was either for her own good or because she deserved it.

Ellen pulled no punches in her presentation of herself and her family.

"I was scared about coming here, but I know that if I don't get help right now, I'm going to die. I was sober for almost two years, then picked up drugs for one day and was back to where I was at my worst.

"Now, I've been sober for six months. Every day I want to run away, or kill myself. I don't feel that I'm worthy of living, but I know that I don't want to die. I feel terrible all of the time. I hate myself. I know that it is wrong and maybe if I get help I can stop hating myself."

Ellen had the most disconcerting ability to look deeply into a person. I returned her look and saw the most remarkable thing happening. As she spoke, her eyes changed colors—first grey, then green, then blue-green. "The barometers of her soul," I thought.

I asked Ellen to tell me something about herself.

"What do you want to know?" she asked, her suspicion aroused.

"Whatever you think is important for me to know."

At this early juncture in therapy, Ellen's need to tell far exceeded my need to know. I knew that she would select those things she felt were important at that moment. Wherever she chose to begin, it would serve two purposes. Most important, it would further our therapeutic relationship. The ability to actively listen, the ability to accept Ellen's interpretations of events, the quality of caring and concern far outweighed any need on my part for a factual

Ellen

173

presentation of Ellen's history. Second, what she chose to share would give me insight into what she felt was important. Further, what Ellen chose not to share would allow me to conjecture about possible areas which were so painful they could not be discussed at that point in the treatment process. Later in the process, I often ask a client to talk about something that she cannot talk about. This paradoxical request, which I mentioned above, will often break a barrier that a client was unable to penetrate earlier.

I looked at Ellen closely. There was an anguish and fear in her eyes which told me that she was not exaggerating her feelings or her desperation. She sat straight in her chair, and, like a schoolgirl, had her hands folded primly in her lap.

"I come from an alcoholic family," she began. "I have ten brothers and sisters and all of them are alcoholics and drug addicts. My parents are both alcoholics, but I guess you could call them functioning alcoholics, because dad never misses a day of work, and mom is active in the community, and works, too.

"When I was growing up I got everything I wanted. I had the best clothes, went to the best schools, travelled——" She paused and I watched her eyes changing colors rapidly. Her eyes were the only sign that she was involved in her own story. She had spoken thus far in a monotone, choosing each word carefully and pronouncing each syllable with a caution befitting an excursion through a minefield, which was Ellen's emotional reality. Was her presentation of the juxtaposition of what her family *had* with what her family *was* an attempt to justify their existence, or was it simply an example of the disparity between two coexisting levels of reality in her life? Ellen's lack of emotion, I thought, might be a sign of ambivalence or denial. It is difficult to accept that the people you most need in the world are behaving in a way which could destroy you.

Ellen stared into space for a few moments. "Living in my house was like living in a crazy house. There was fighting all of the time. My brothers used to beat me up. It reached a point where I didn't care anymore. I wouldn't give them the satisfaction of seeing me cry. It made me tough enough to take care of myself. If I complained about it to my parents, they would beat me for lying.

"I started running away when I was fourteen. I couldn't take it. I used drugs and drank to escape, and I never could get enough. That's why I have to stop. I don't take drugs to get high. I take them to obliterate myself and no matter how much I take, it never works. I was not a social user—ever! I just wanted to go off into a corner somewhere and get away from everything.

"I used to run away to New York. I'd buy drugs and just go off somewhere and pass out. Sometimes, that could get me in real trouble because of the characters that were there, but I didn't care."

"What are you feeling right at this moment?" I asked.

Her reply came almost too quickly. "Nothing."

"If you did feel something about what you've just told me, what would it be?" I hoped that she would be able to break through her repressed and suppressed feelings via this intellectual back door. "Tell me what you are not allowed to tell me."

Ellen

"I would feel anger—no—rage, but what's the use—it doesn't do any good—it doesn't change anything!" For the first time, there was a hint of emotion in her voice.

I asked her again, "What are you feeling now?"

"A little anger, but what good will it do to feel angry?"

"It does help to get anger out, especially when you were not allowed to show your anger for a long time. I'd be angry, too, if I was robbed of my childhood!"

Ellen paused, and began nodding her head up and down. Her eyes clouded over with a pain she chose not to speak of.

"It's all right," I said, soothingly. I felt, more than saw, her sink down into the chair. I felt a lifting of an invisible barrier between us. A real therapeutic relationship began as Ellen gave a faint sign of trust, accepting a genuine and unconditional caring—perhaps for the first time in her life.

"I feel such resentment," Ellen said. "I hate all of them. But I need them and I still want my dad's approval, and my mom's love. I know that it's sick to keep going back to be abused, but I keep hoping things will change. I know deep inside me that they never will, though." Ellen almost cried, but held tears back by looking away and changing the subject. "I'm feeling a little better now."

"You have a lot of pain to deal with, and I hate to be the bearer of bad news, but if you want to grow into a whole and healthy person, you need to accept that dealing with it will not be as painful as it will be if you choose to continue to live with the pain stuffed inside of you. To choose not to deal with it is to choose to return ultimately to drugs and drinking. That's what happened before. You survived sober until the pain was so intense that even dying from drugs seemed a better alternative than living with unbearable pain." We sat silently for a few minutes before our first session ended with Ellen's acknowledgment of her need for help.

What Did I Ever Do to Them?

Ellen spent the first part of her second session talking about her present situation. She was living with John, a man nearly twice her age, and, though the relationship was often stormy, she felt that there was genuine caring and love between them. Nonetheless, she stated that she was insecure in the relationship and feared that John might return to his ex-wife. At an intellectual level, she realized that this was not reality. She said he was as insecure as she, and believed she would not want to stay with him for long. They had been living together for about a half a year.

One significant fact I learned from Ellen in this session was that she moved in with John just after she had used drugs and was as close to being suicidal as she had ever been. I thought that perhaps she never would have picked him if she had not been so vulnerable. This bit of information led me to conjecture that John needed a woman who was extremely vulnerable and in a weakened position. Why else would a reasonably healthy man select a woman half his age and one day past a drunken, drugged stupor to share his home and his life.

Ellen

"John was the first man who ever treated me with any respect," Ellen admitted. "When I was in my addiction, my relations with men were pretty sick. Sometimes, I'd just be off in a corner by myself and everybody knew better than to try to get near me. Other times, I'd get all over them. I talked them out of money or drugs and gave nothing. And sometimes," she added painfully, "I was so wasted, I didn't know or care what was happening to me. See this?" She pointed to the tattoo of a cross on her ankle. "I hate this! The bastards I was with did this to me when I was unconscious. I sometimes think all men stink!" Ellen's mouth twisted in rage at this permanent symbol of the fact that someone had used her. "How can I ever get a good job with this . . . thing on me. Everyone will know!"

At that moment, there was nothing I could say which would be more than a weak clichè . I remained silent, but felt my own impotent rage for what had been done to Ellen. At least it appeared that her anger was beginning to surface. She has a long way to go to get to the core of that anger, but this was a start."

In her addiction, Ellen used, and was used by, men and she remained distrustful and bitter. "After what I went through, no wonder I'm not about to trust anybody. But, I know I have to find out who I am and make it on my own. I can't depend on any man to take care of me. I have to take care of myself."

"Tell me about you," I said suddenly. "I know a little about your family and your boyfriend, but you are still a mystery woman."

"What do you want to know?" she hedged. She wanted to keep the focus on what she *did* rather than who she *was*.

"Why don't you tell me what kind of a person you are?"

Looking annoyed she said, "I don't know, I guess I'm okay."

"What does 'okay' mean?"

"You know. That I'm basically a good person," she said, trying desperately to close this avenue of conversation.

I spoke softly to reassure her and to move ahead. "I know how painful this must be, but you will have to trust that anything I do is to help you to look at yourself more realistically and that I wouldn't push you toward anything that would be dangerous to your stability or sobriety. Let's try a different direction, okay? If your father were talking about you, what would he say you are like?"

Ellen sat and stared at me for a moment. Her eyes became almost black. In the coldest voice I ever heard she replied, "He would say that I'm ugly, fat, stupid and a slut."

For a moment, my mind could not register what she had said. Therapists are supposed to remain in a state of safe neutrality. In this instance, all I could do was sit and silently cry and try to regain my composure. I had violated a primary rule of my own method and now Ellen would pay an emotional price for it. I always vowed never to ask an important question of a client to which I did not already know the answer. I had forgotten just how sick her father was and what devastation his sickness could reap.

After I regained my composure, I asked Ellen how old she was when her father said that to her. She appeared to be more disturbed by my reaction than her own.

"I didn't know that therapists could cry. I thought you must have heard everything by now."

"It doesn't matter how many times you hear that a beautiful, innocent child was devastated by sick parents, it never stops hurting." I sat quietly looking at Ellen. For the first time, she returned my look.

"No one ever cried for me before," she said, her voice quivering.

"Do you feel okay to talk about it?"

"It started when I was about 11 or 12 and was an almost every day occurrence. You know, when he said it the first time I was still a virgin. I didn't even know what a slut was. I just knew that it was something very dirty." Ellen stared, hollow-eyed, and devoid of expression.

"It must be difficult building a positive self-image hearing that kind of negative comment all the time —especially when it is not only untrue, but the exact opposite of the truth. Ellen, you are beautiful, anything but fat, very intelligent, and despite your addiction, refreshingly innocent." I could see that my words were assaulting her like weapons. Ellen was not ready to hear compliments.

"Sometimes I know that what you said is true, but I can't really believe it," she answered. "I usually feel like a piece of shit! I don't want to go on feeling worthless. I want to like myself. You know," Ellen said, in a revelation, "it was after he started that stuff that I began having trouble in school. I was never a great student, but I did okay. After that, I started flunking everything and getting kicked out of school. And, I started taking all the drugs." She sat silently for a few minutes and I watched her without comment.

Ellen's eyes were cloudy, but no tears came. Ellen had learned from her family that tears were a sign of weakness and surrender. This proud young woman was not about to surrender another inch of herself to these pathetic people who called themselves her family.

"Y' know, even after everything my dad said to make me feel lousy, when I go home I'm still looking for him to say something nice. I want him to say I'm doing good, or my dress is nice, or he's glad I'm sober. It never happens and I guess it is never going to happen. Why? What did I ever do to them?" Ellen cried briefly, but brought herself quickly under control. "And my mom, she just sits there— agreeing with everything he says or does."

Ellen's quandary was that even though she knew that "it was unlikely that her parents would change," she continued to live with the hope that they might someday give her the love and caring that she needed and deserved. There was nothing therapy could do to change this deep and real need. It was premature to suggest to her that she cut her losses. Ellen was barely nineteen. She was not ready to accept a difficult reality and at the same time give up her dream.

I Am Worthy of Giving and Receiving Love.

Sometimes words are like magic. Prayer has long been a balm to mankind. In therapy, we know that words can trigger internal movement and change. I decided to create a set of words just for Ellen which she could focus upon, to replace her father's devastating words and actions. I decided upon a simple, yet profound statement which would enable her to challenge many of her basic concepts of self. The statement I created for Ellen was not original, but it was uniquely designed to meet her present need for a focusing point from which to build her self-image. After I was privileged to share Ellen's reaction to this statement, which I will describe in a moment, I used it with others with remarkable success.

"Ellen," I began. "I want to try something new with you. Do you know how sayings like the "Serenity Prayer" help people to find a way to get through a difficult situation? Well, I devised a simple statement for you to practice repeating to yourself. It will help you to feel better about yourself. Would you be willing to try it out? If you don't want to, just say so, but if you are willing, I want you to agree to do exactly what I ask without knowing in advance what it is. Do you trust me enough to do that?"

"Yes, I've reached the point where I'm willing to try anything."

"Okay," I said, "I want you to repeat a very short statement which I am going to give to you. 'I am worthy of giving and receiving love.' Say it."

"I am worthy of giving and receiving love." She said it quickly and in a monotone.

"Now, say it like you mean it."

"I . . . am . . . worthy . . . of . . . giving . . . and . . . receiving . . . love," she said, as if it would explode if she tried to be too casual about it.

"How does it feel to say it?"

"I still don't believe it, but I'll keep trying," she said, tentatively.

"One more thing we can do with it that might help you is to break it down into smaller pieces. It may be too much to take all at once. Try just the first two words. See how they feel."

Ellen looked at me quizzically and said, "Well . . . okay. I am. I am. I AM! I am."

I could see her eyes shifting colors. "What are you feeling?"

"I am!" she exclaimed, as though she had discovered something new and worthwhile.

"Yes, Ellen, you ARE, you exist, you have validity, you have . . . *worth*. It is your saying now and you can use it anytime you have need to remind yourself who you are and what you are." I found myself once again crying and feeling that I had just been privileged to be a part of something very private and very profound. "Accept your new gift a little at a time; it is not something that can be absorbed all at once. Add on each idea as you become ready for it."

"I really feel better than I have in a long while," she said, as we prepared to end the session.

"Hopefully, this is just the beginning, although it won't be easy. There's a lot of hard work to do to get you to where you need to go." I stood up, and reached out to return the hug she was offering. This was a behavior Ellen was learning in the women's group which I will describe in the next section. Sometimes growth can be measured in just such small changes as reaching out for needed support in a healthy manner. Also, *I* am worthy of giving and receiving hugs—when appropriate, and requested!

Ellen

An Empty Chair

Several women whom I see in individual therapy also attend a group once a week. These women had each suffered some form of abuse in her life—emotional, physical or sexual. Ellen reluctantly joined the group. She feared revealing herself to others, but accepted that a significant facet of her growth involved doing necessary but uncomfortable things. One of the most important aspects of the group is that it is seen as a place where women can share feelings with other women. Much of the recovery fellowships are male dominated, both in actual representations as well as in style. In our group, it is both allowable and commendable for the women to share their soft, feminine sides as well as to test their ability to deal with personal empowerment. It is proper to touch, to hug, and to comfort each other. Making decisions in one's own best interest is also promoted.

When Ellen began therapy, she was unconnected. Her boyfriend provided security, but it was more at a surface level than adding any actual enhancement to her life. Ellen had the security of having a relationship even though the quality of that relationship did not bring her real satisfaction. However, to the person who has wandered forever in the desert, a drop of water seems a deluge. Ellen did not believe that she could ever sustain a healthy relationship, nor did she have any idea of what one looked like.

During her first few sessions, Ellen sat quietly and entered the conversation only when addressed directly. The group made attempts to draw her out of herself, and by about her fourth session, she spoke about herself. She told the group the story of her family and living situation so that they would know that she belonged in the group. She spoke in the same disconnected manner she used in individual therapy.

In the session after Ellen and I had developed her saying about self-worth, I asked her to share it with the group. "Ellen, why don't you share with the group what we did in your individual session? Maybe somebody else will get something from it."

She agreed, and spoke hesitantly, "I am worthy of giving and receiving love."

"Repeat that," responded Michelle, another member of the group. "I couldn't hear you."

Ellen looked uncomfortable, perhaps frightened. She took a deep breath and said, "I am worthy of giving and receiving love."

"How do you feel about that?" I asked.

Ellen burst into tears and sobbed deeply for several minutes. Carolyn, another member of the group, moved over to her and tried to hold her. Ellen remained passive, but did not resist.

"Sometimes I feel like a piece of meat," she said.

"I feel the same as you most of the time," Pat added. "My family are all alcoholics, too. I know just how you feel. My father molested me and also made me feel lousy by what he said. You have to get over expecting any better from any of them. They don't have any more to give. I just wish sometimes that I could take my own advice!"

The group laughed at the break in the tension.

"I feel very good that Ellen was able to get out some of her feelings and share them with us," I said.

Ellen

185

"I was so scared that somebody would laugh at me. Am I crazy, or what?" said Ellen.

Pat sympathized with her. "The first time I talked in group, I thought everybody would faint! I didn't say anything for two months. I still don't like to talk in public."

Others took the opportunity to praise Ellen for the difficult risk she had taken. They assured her that the first time they had spoken in the group about something difficult, they had reacted the same way as she—or worse.

Kathy said, "The first time I came to group, I brought along a pound of cookies to share with everybody. I guess I felt I needed a bribe. Anyway, I was so nervous, I sat there and ate the whole pound of chocolate-chip cookies by myself, and never thought to offer anybody any. And, I didn't say a word!"

Jennifer added, "Yeah, and the first time I came to group, I had my chair outside the door with only my feet in the room."

"Well at least the healthiest part of you was in there with us that night," chimed in Carolyn, her best friend.

The senior member of the group, Yolanda, added, "I felt like running out of the room when somebody asked me my name. For a minute, I forgot it!"

Even Ellen laughed!

Pat added, "I still have a difficult time sharing feelings and I've been in the group for several months. It's good to see you doing it—maybe it will give me the strength to do it, too."

The following week, I decided to conduct a structured activity to enhance the possibility that the members of the group would be able to live through some of their feelings. We used techniques from psychodrama in which the individual says to an empty chair something she cannot say to an individual to whom she needs to make the statement. An addition to the technique which enables the women to express their feelings is that an alter ego, another group member, stands behind the subject and strengthens the statements and eliminates the possibility of censorship of feelings.

After Yolanda had volunteered to talk to the empty chair and obtained a positive reaction to the experience of talking to the brother who had molested her as a child, Pat volunteered to be the subject, and without hesitation, Ellen volunteered to be the alter ego. I knew that she was doing this for herself as well as for Pat, because her issues were so similar. She, too, had a father who had nearly destroyed her life.

Pat, after a brief moment of discomfort, began talking to her father. She spoke in a monotone with no feelings. Ellen encouraged her to let her feelings out. Pat began telling her father how disappointed she was that he never could be a real father to her. "I never got over being abused by you. I know you had sex with everybody in the family and everybody is fucked up over you. I don't accept that your drinking caused it, either. Even now, you had nothing to say when I told you about my new job. All you could do was comment how nice my ass was. You will never change." Ellen interrupted Pat. For a few moments, she stood still. She began shaking violently.

"Here, let me," Ellen blurted in a choked voice. "HOW DARE YOU! HOW DARE YOU! How could you do this to me? You ruined my life! You are a no good jerk off! I hate you, I hate you! What did I ever do to you to deserve this? I wish you were dead!"

Ellen

187

Ellen cried for all of the pain she had endured. Pat and Ellen, two women who had been completely closed off from feelings, held each other and cried together. They stood together rocking gently for several minutes. Each helped the other attach to someone. Each shared the pain of the other. For a brief moment, each was no longer alone.

When Pat and Ellen felt a little better, I said, "How about trying something else? I'd like you to act toward each other as a *healthy* father might have done toward a daughter whom he loved and respected. Are you both okay to do that?"

"Yeah," said Ellen, now much more animated, "I think I'm ready to hear some good stuff about me!" The group laughed in surprise, enjoying this new facet in Ellen's personality.

Ellen began, "Pat, I'm so proud to have you for a daughter. I was so afraid when you were in your addiction. I thought I was going to lose you. I am proud of how you are raising your son and how well you are doing in your new job.

"I can't really feel it when good things are said to me," Pat responded.

It was Pat's turn next, to be Ellen's good father.

"Ellen," Pat began, "I want to tell you how much I love you. You're so special to me. I'm so proud of your recovery and how well your life is working out."

Ellen began crying again. "I can't, I can't! I'm not ready to hear good things about me. I want to hear them, but it hurts so much!"

"I'm not either," said Pat, "but the only way I'm ever going to get well is to keep trying to do the things that are difficult for me. I've been straight almost three years, and believe me, it's still hard for me to accept compliments. I'm beginning to believe I am worth feeling good about, but I still have a long way to go."

Ellen looked at Pat and said nothing. She appeared to be overwhelmed by her feelings and at that moment, her silence was an eloquent testimony to her pain and to the release of feelings she had undergone.

The sessions always end with a group hug. Pat and Ellen were both able to use this moment to draw strength from the group. For both, this two hours was an affirmation of their humanity which had received little validation in the past.

Her Schedule, Not Mine

Ellen appeared more relaxed than I had ever seen her. She began the session by saying, "The experience I had in group was like the science fiction film where somebody gave birth to a slimy creature through her chest. I felt like something awful and ugly pushed its way out of my body. It feels good to have it out, but there is so much more. I want the pain to end. I can't live with this much pain much longer."

"I know how you feel, Ellen, but you have to allow yourself to grow through this experience. The only way to stop the pain is either to anesthetize it like you used to do or to experience it in a way that allows it to pass through you. I wish I could offer you a shortcut, but there is none.

Ellen

In the meantime, you can begin to do things which bring you good feelings. Think of how well your life is beginning to go now. Think of how you are becoming self-sufficient. Begin to believe that all of the compliments you're receiving are earned. Begin to learn how to separate the past from the present." I paused, looked at Ellen and smiled. I thought to myself that I was telling her that there were no shortcuts, but in the same breath, I had diagrammed a year of therapy in three sentences. "Okay," I said to myself, "now that I have *done* all that therapy, it is time to go back to *being* therapeutic. Ellen will attain wholeness on her schedule, not mine."

A therapist needs to remember that teaching is not learning. Teaching is the presentation of subjective and objective material by one person to another person or group. Learning is the incorporation, organization and integration of external information into an individual's knowledge and value systems. At best, we can only speculate about what another person hears when we speak. In therapy, we need to accept that learning is sequential and, if it is to be effective, it must be presented only when a client demonstrates readiness to use it. "Doing therapy" is presenting a package which fails to recognize individual differences. "Being therapeutic" is engaging with the client in a process of change and growth. The latter is slower and often less dramatic, but the changes engendered are far more stable and permanent.

Ellen was beginning to learn to say those things which she could not say. As her values become more aligned with her emerging life purpose, she will become freer of the devastating effects of her past. Therapy and an association with a recovery fellowship will help Ellen believe that she is allowed to feel good about herself—no, great about herself!

Her Own Music

It is now a year and a half since Ellen began therapy. She is no longer involved in individual therapy, and comes to the group only occasionally. Her life has a sense of order and direction. She completed a course in word processing so that she would be able to earn a better salary. After she completed the course, she found a new position which paid her almost double the salary she was earning previously. She is seriously contemplating college next fall. Ellen no longer lives with her boyfriend but now lives alone comfortably. Each of these major changes would have been impossible for her to contemplate a year and a half earlier. At the time she entered therapy, she was too frightened to live alone. She feared school because she had met with failure during her addiction and lack of praise for her success prior to her addiction. She held on to her meaningless, low-paying job because she didn't believe that anyone else would hire her.

Ellen has become much more outgoing and reaches out to other recovering people with powerful nurturance. Just slightly more than a year ago, she trusted no one and opened to no one. She continues to feel that the women's group is her only family, and this is realistic. This is where she was truly born and grew up. However, as an adult, she no longer needs the immediacy of living with family.

Simply knowing that she has one to return to is sufficient to allow her to move out into the world with assurance.

Ellen now accepts her birth family with less anger and knows that there is little likelihood that they will ever have any desire to change. They have yet to compliment this special woman, or even acknowledge that she exists, other than to attempt to make her feel guilty because she has escaped the family influence. She has made a healthy detachment from them. When I see her, I call her, "the woman with the razzle-dazzle eyes." They are now truly the barometers of her beautiful soul. She lives with relative peace, joy and hope and is becoming the full embodiment of her enormous potential.

Ellen learned that therapy is a tool a person can use to open issues buried because family loyalty dictated, "You don't wash your dirty linens in public." The children of dysfunctional families pay the price for this philosophy long after they have physically escaped the family environs. The almost magic paradox, "Tell me what you cannot tell me," invokes a deeper sense of self which says, "No more, NO MORE!" I have expanded that simple, almost poetic dictum and it now reads like this:

Tell me what you cannot tell me,
So that tomorrow you may dream
The dreams you dared not dream.

Sometimes therapy is almost poetry, or music. Ellen turned it into her own symphony. In the playing and replaying of her life she has found the music which was always in her soul.

Ellen now knows that she is worthy to give and receive love. She permits no one to abuse her. She is able to make life choices because she has self-respect. She demands nothing from others except that they respect her rights. She believes that she has the right to dictate her destiny insofar as with whom she will associate, what job she will have, and where she will live. She accepts that she can't control the world, but she can avoid those people whose intent it is to bring misery into her world.

It is painful to see how a beautiful human being's life can be twisted because another person who is responsible for providing her well-being delivers nothing but anguish into her life. The positive aspect of what happened to Ellen is that she has choices as an adult that were unavailable to her as a child. Though change is often difficult and always frightening, it is possible, under the proper circumstances, to alter your life course and create new means of meeting your needs in an often-confusing world.

The world is especially chaotic to someone who grew up in a dysfunctional home. Values in such a home are often distorted because what is learned there does not work outside that home. Too often, the adult child of a dysfunctional or abusive home will end up repeating history, and in doing so, may make it even worse than the nightmare of the original experience. In the next story, Jaime, you will meet a woman who did that—and lived to change it.

JAIME

Every time I tell him it's over,
he gets straight and convinces me he'll be different.
And, every time, I believe him.
Why do I fall for guys like that?
Tell me.

What She Meant By "Love"

Sometimes abuse is dramatic and easy to discern, such as in the cases of Ellen, Marianne, Caitlin or Leslie. However, there are other forms of abuse which are more subtle, but no less harmful. Many families do not beat or sexually abuse their children, but nonetheless leave scars upon their children's self images which negatively affect their lives. Jaime's story is about this latter kind of abuse in which there was never physical harm to her, neither in her parents' home, nor in the adult world. Yet, her home contained so many dysfunctions that she was not prepared to enter the adult world and function effectively in it.

I think it is important for you to understand that the subtle abuse to which Jaime was exposed is probably more prevalent than the dramatic, highly publicized physical and sexual abuse. Nonetheless, Jaime was no less hurt, and, initially, no better able to cope with the vicissitudes and pressures of adult life. That is what life is about—coping. As adults, we are called upon to make critical decisions from moment to moment—especially in the areas of choosing and sustaining relationships. The portrait which we paint of ourselves dictates the directions we will choose. This is not to say that a dysfunctional home always produces dysfunctional children. Nor is it to say that every criticism to which a child is exposed is guaranteed to leave permanent scars which will result in a lifetime of inappropriate choices. Perhaps, however, we do need to address the issue of self-worth as a crucial issue in developing the ability to make healthy life choices, especially healthy choices regarding careers, life-partners, and life styles.

Jaime's story is not as urgent as Ellen's, Marianne's, Caitlin's or Leslie's. Her very life was not in immediate danger, but her pain was as great—and certainly as important as anyone else's pain. Jaime, like Marianne, never drank to excess or used drugs. Unlike Marianne, she was never hit by her parents, or by any of her boyfriends —except for one episode with a recent man in her life. It took only one violent encounter for her to tell him he was no longer welcome in her life. The fact that she was not subjected to physical abuse as a child gave her the ability to refuse to tolerate it as an adult. Yes, very often, we are what we learn.

Jaime had one important characteristic in common with all of the women represented in this book—she had kept the family secrets. She came into therapy with all of the same denial and self-deprecation the others had. Maybe it is sometimes correct to say that more damage can be done with words than with other weapons. However, I'm getting ahead of myself. This is her story as it evolved.

Therapy is About Change

"Why do I always get myself into these kinds of situations?" she began, her head tilted to one side.

Jaime was a study in contrasts. Bright and colorful, yet sad, frightened and lonely. Her hair, dress and makeup showed care, yet there was something about her that was incomplete—something missing. She looked as if she had worked too hard to create an attractive image. Her hair was frosted and teased, and she wore a great deal of facial and eye makeup. She appeared to have skin that needed very little help to be attractive, and her hair was overdone, compared to the more popular casual look. Jaime looked as if she knew she was attractive, yet, at the same time, didn't really believe it. It was as if she were getting her messages from two different realities.

"I'm crazy, that's all there is to it. I've got to be crazy."

For a brief moment, I felt as though I had been parachuted into the middle of a play and I was the only one who didn't know the lines. The litany of therapy is different with each person. Some people like to begin in an orderly fashion with a presentation of who they are, where they work, or what specific problem brings them into therapy. Others begin with questions about therapy or about the therapist. Jaime began with an expression of what she was feeling at that moment.

She appeared to be extremely tense. She was sitting on the edge of the chair, leaning forward, and looking like she was ready to run out of the room. The tenseness showed in her face and body, and her speech was clipped and pressured. She was petite, and her wide blue eyes and high voice gave her a deceptively youthful appearance. At first glance, she could have been mistaken for someone in her early teens. At the same time, her movements, her choice of words, and her adult mannerisms indicated a woman in her early to mid-twenties, which proved to be the reality. I wondered if her 'little girl' appearance was in any way related to her problems. I filed this question for later reference. "Tell me why you're here."

"My boyfriend is driving me crazy. I don't know why I put up with him, maybe I'm the one who's crazy. George, that's my boyfriend, he uses cocaine, and he lies about everything. He disappears for days at a time. I have to chase all over the place to find him. Sometimes, he's good to me. He really is a good person, if he would just stop using drugs.

Jaime

199

"George keeps promising that he'll shape up and I keep believing him. He goes on messing up and good old Jaime keeps forgiving him. I don't understand it. I know he's lying and I know he'll just do it again, but I keep taking him back. I *am* crazy. I must be. Nobody would put up with this kind of behavior."

"What does he do to hurt you?"

"He just makes a mess of my life. He never hit me or anything like that, but he says that he'll meet me and then he comes six hours late, or not at all. He always criticizes what I wear, or how I do my hair. I do everything I can to please him. I know he loves me, though. Just when I think he is going to really do something terrible, he'll turn around and buy me something nice, or tell me he loves me and needs me.

"George takes advantage of everybody. He works for his brother and has a good job, but he stole money from him. He uses everybody—me, his family. He has no friends left. Sometimes, he can be so nice, though."

I thought to myself, "What is it I'm hearing?" I listened to the contrasts in what she was saying. It was almost like watching a tennis match. Everything was back and forth. "He loves me. He's irresponsible. Nobody would put up with his behavior. I keep taking him back." I thought that I have to look for an opportunity to ask her what she believes she deserves in a relationship with a man, but it was too early in our relationship for a question like this to be relevant.

I wondered what she meant by "love?" What internal messages led her to behave in a manner which brought pain to her life? What changes would Jaime have to make to develop healthy patterns of living?

Life provides us with two clear choices when we are in a painful situation. We can accept an unchangeable reality, or change an unacceptable one. The difficulties lie in determining what within a given situation can be changed and then, accept the consequences of the choices we have made. In Jaime's case, she is involved in a relationship with a person who is in an addiction. The relationship is causing her enough pain so that she has sought professional help. Yet, it is not enough for her to know that she can make a choice between keeping George and letting him go. The fact that she would choose him in the first place says that Jaime probably has beliefs about herself and the world which made this choice necessary for her. Therefore, the choice of the person with whom she will have an intimate relationship was not a coincidence, but rather the end product of what she has learned about herself and her world. At this beginning point in her treatment, I could merely guess at what it might be.

Part of Jaime's need was to be allowed to tell her story to someone who would listen without giving advice. I was certain that she had already heard all the advice she needed to hear. In situations like Jaime's it is the easiest thing in the world to give advice, but it is not always so easy to use it.

"Tell me something about you," I said, changing the direction of the session. "You've made me curious. You told me a little about your relationship with George, and something about George, himself, but so far, not a word about you, except that you think you're crazy. And, I don't think you're crazy. At least not any crazier than I am. So, talk a little about Jaime."

"What do you want me to say?"

"What do I want you to say?" I thought to myself. "I *want* you to say you love yourself, you no longer need the Georges of the world to fill your life, and you are able to deal effectively with any and all of the vicissitudes of life." Then, I responded to her question: "What *I* want you to say really isn't important, Jaime. What would you like to tell me about yourself?"

"I don't know what to say. Should I talk about my childhood?"

"I'd like to know about your childhood, sure."

"Where to begin? I'm twenty-three, but sometimes I feel like I'm sixty. Nothing much happened to me as a kid. I have three older sisters—two of them are twins. I graduated from high school—I never really liked school. And, I work—I manage a store."

I felt as well as heard the emptiness which Jaime felt. Of course, when she is presented with specific questions, additional detail will emerge, but at that moment, I almost felt that what she had said was: "I was born, I grew old quickly, and . . ." Again, it is sometimes possible to learn more about someone from what he or she doesn't say, than from what is actually said. Jamie left out two very important characters in her life drama—her parents.

"You left out mentioning some of your family, didn't you? You didn't mention your parents. Are they still alive?"

"My parents!" she exclaimed, becoming agitated and animated for the first time, "I could talk about them all night! But, it wouldn't change anything." Jaime paused and then stared out of the window. When she began talking again, her voice was softer, lower and more distant. "My parents. That's a story in itself!

"My mom and dad are the two most exasperating people in the world. They are irresponsible and . . ."

We sat in silence for a few moments. Tears clouded her eyes, but she tried to hold them back.

"Don't be afraid to let out your feelings, Jaime. That's part of what you came here for. It's being able to share your hurt that is important. Tell me about your family."

"My dad gambles. He's always in debt. I get calls all the time asking *me* when is he going to pay his bills. I'm so tired of it. I tell them that I'm just his daughter. I'm not his bookkeeper. I could probably handle all of that if he would just notice me once in a while. He never looks up from his cards or racing form long enough to even see I'm there. It was always like that," she added, as if anticipating the question I had not asked.

"I always worked for what I have. Always! They never gave me anything. Anything nice I have, I earned. I have to take care of them, and I'm tired of it."

"How about your mom?"

"We fight all the time. She notices me alright, but it is always to criticize or to put me down. She's as irresponsible as he is. I live with them, but it's like living alone. They're never there. I always tell them that they ought to have an extension phone at the Casinos—they spend so much time there."

"How do you *feel* about your parents, Jaime?"

"I love them," she answered, almost too quickly, "but I don't like them very much, and I don't respect them. Maybe that isn't such a nice thing to say."

"More important than 'is it nice,' is— 'is it true?' In this room, remember, anything we say can't hurt anybody out there because they won't hear it unless one of us tells, and I sure won't. Therapy is about being able to share your inner truths, not about being polite. If you leave here feeling better about yourself, then you will be better able to deal with all the problems out there.

"You know, I just thought of something. You were talking about how you love your parents, but don't like or respect them. Is that anything like your feelings for George?"

Jaime

"Well, yes, sort of—except I don't think I really love George," she said, thoughtfully. "You think it could have anything to do with my family?"

"If what could?" I hoped she would draw her own conclusion, rather than accepting mine as her own.

"You know, why I pick men like George to help me ruin my life. Hey, I really don't need help. I'm doing a good job all by myself." The pain showed through her attempt at humor.

It is often difficult for a therapist to know when to divert a session. Jaime was beginning to pick at a wound which we could not re-close in the time left in the session. When a session is nearly over, it is time to seal off what has been opened unless it is meant to be dealt with during the time between sessions. But new material brought up just before the end of a session is better acknowledged and left for another time.

"Jaime, some therapists wouldn't react personally to what you are feeling. They would just allow you to feel it. I need to let you know that when I hear you put yourself down, it hurts me because I see so many positive qualities in you that you will someday see for yourself. At this point, let me say simply that if you really believed that you were worthless, you would not have come into therapy. Therapy is about change, and if you didn't believe that you were capable of change and worthy of something better than your life includes today, you wouldn't be here.

"Change is based on faith because even though you know that you want to get from 'here' to 'there,' you don't know what 'there' looks like, and you don't know where the path is that leads 'there'."

"I don't know what we did tonight, but I feel a little better. How do you do that?"

"I didn't do anything. *We* met, *we* talked, *we* are learning about each other, and if *you* learn that there are some people in the world who do care and who can be trusted, *we* will both grow in this experience." I looked at her and for the first time, she smiled, and relaxed—a little.

"Can I come back to see you again?" She sounded as if she was expecting me to say no.

"If you feel comfortable with me as your therapist."

Jaime looked at me with her head tilted to one side, smiled nervously and said, "I never could trust anybody before now, but I'll tell you what, I'll give you another chance to let me down like everybody else does."

"I'll really try hard not to let you down, as long as you don't expect more than one miracle a week!"

"One a week should be almost enough, but I'm going to be a difficult one because I am crazy, you know."

"In that case, we should really get along well," I said as we moved toward the door. "See you next week, Jaime."

Jaime had to test this new relationship. All of the important people in her world had let her down, at least as she viewed her world. In attempting to develop a positive relationship with Jaime, I would have to face this problem openly. Often, when people have negative beliefs about the world, such as the belief that everyone will let them down, they unwittingly create a situation which makes it more likely that the prophesy will be fulfilled. For instance, a person who believes that she is going to be rejected will often do one of two things to ensure the rejection. Either she will uncannily pick rejecting people with whom to relate, or will behave in such a manner that even the most nonrejecting individual will have to reject her.

Jaime insulated herself from pain with self-deprecating humor, and warded off her fears of insanity with jokes about being insane. The 'insanity' issue would be the easier one with which to deal. She was sane—too sane.

Jaime

She was fully aware of the defects in her world, and lived with the constant pain they caused. One of my tasks would be to help her to understand some of the reasons she acted as she did; this would help alleviate her fear that her behavior was irrational. Her behavior made complete sense when you looked at the values she had learned as a child, values which helped her to survive emotionally in her parents' home.

Adult children of dysfunctional parents resemble Alice escaped from Wonderland. These children grew up in an environment which was a constant Mad Hatter's tea party. The rules established for survival and relationships only worked at their dinner tables, but not in the world outside. Yet, the children of the Mad Hatter do grow up and eventually they are required to deal with the real world. The rules they learned about relationships—people whom you love and who love you, lie; you can't count on anybody; you mustn't tell the family secrets; parents are selfish and irresponsible—or in some cases dangerous— required that they develop protective behaviors which allowed them to survive in sick environments. These behaviors create new problems for the adult child. He or she continues to act as if the rules of living are the same as in the familiar home of the parents, and this creates situations which perpetuate all of the negative results which occurred in the family home—rejection, fighting, irresponsibility, and addiction.

In Jaime's case, George had apparently managed to re-play all of the negative roles in her life. The same people who take care of you also reject you. The people who claim to love you the most also hurt you the most. The people responsible for your well-being are also responsible for your insecurity. If you are writing a play, and one person plays all of the roles, it is a beautiful cost-saving device, but in life, (which is often more of a play than is a play), the intensity of so many negatives in a single relationship can be destructive beyond measure. Jaime's apparent lack of self-esteem comes not only from the damage done in a dysfunctional home, but also from the added damage done in an intense, all-consuming adult relationship. George professed to love Jaime, but he acted irresponsibly toward her. George professed to care about Jaime's well-being, but attempted to control every detail of her life to meet his own needs. George bought Jaime beautiful gifts, and then stole them to buy cocaine! Every negative which Jaime had learned about relationships in a lifetime with her family was being repeated in her relationship with George. As Marianne said, "Life is a merry-go-round until you realize you can get off!"

Old Rules, New Reality

"Should I sit in the same place as last time? No, I think not. I feel different, so I'll sit in another chair, if that's okay with you, Robert?"

Jaime looked at the four unmatched chairs and picked the one facing the back wall of the office. One chair faces a window, one faces a door, another faces a close wall and a fourth chair faces a far wall. Each chair is angled so that any two occupied chairs face each other as well. When a new client comes in, I invite her to sit where she would be most comfortable. This offer has led to more than a few humorous situations such as the frightened client who said, "I'd be most comfortable back home under my bed covers!"

"I hate being so small!" Jaime continued.

"I always seem to enter in the middle of the performance," I retorted. "Did I miss something?"

"Oh! I always do that. I started thinking about what I was going to say before I got here. I was so anxious I started without you! I guess I should go back and start over, do you think?" She looked at me disconcertingly, with her head tilted to one side. I couldn't help but smile.

"No, just go on. I'll catch up. You seem so much more comfortable than you were last week. I'm glad," I added parenthetically.

"I just hate it. I was always teased in school and people still make fun of me. 'Yo, shrimp, yo, short stuff!' I couldn't take it. Just yesterday, this big old lady comes into the store and says to me, 'my, you are so tiny!' I mean . . . she was big as a house! That's why I always wear high heels. Well, that's me. I guess it's my destiny to have to look up to everybody." She looked at her hands which she held in her lap, as we sat silently for a few moments.

I think it was significant that Jaime had chosen to use her physical size as a means of describing her feelings of powerlessness and frustration with a world which had given her 'short measure' in so many areas far surpassing her height in importance. Like so many people who were 'taught' not to like themselves as children, Jaime picked a physical quality which would not have been seen by others as a negative, and used that quality which she perceived to be negative to build the rationale for a negative self-image. In fact, she was graced with exceptional beauty—a beauty, which by itself, would not assure her a valued place in the world, but which could attract positive attention if utilized and prized appropriately.

It is not uncommon for a woman who has a dislike for herself to turn an asset into a liability. Self-image often begins with physical appearance and can be terribly distorted by negative feelings about oneself. In order to sustain self-hatred or self-doubt, a woman may need to produce appropriate negative evidence to justify her opinion. It is difficult on the one hand to talk about the existence of generous endowments of intelligence, likeability, industriousness, responsibility, attractiveness and sociability, and in the next breath, state that you are not a very worthy person. Therefore, she must overlook or minimize positive attributes to defend her negative position.

Dysfunctional, especially addicted parents, are masters at creating an environment which keeps their children feeling badly about themselves. By doing so, it takes the spotlight off the parents who are not functioning appropriately. If they can further make the child feel responsible for their own inadequacies, it gives the parents additional weapons with which to keep the child from rebelling, or worse yet, telling. These parents will often berate and belittle their children in order to balance their own self-hatred and self-doubt. When they are not castigating their children, they are ignoring them totally. The only thing worse than being screamed at for getting 'only' a 'B' on a report card is to get an 'A' and be ignored.

This type of response accounts, at least in part, for the numerous rebellions by children of dysfunctional parents. Unconsciously, and sometimes consciously, the child feels that infamy is preferable to ignominy. More often than not, the only 'victim' of this rebellion is also the perpetrator. Or worse, the result may be an adult who has a high level of accomplishment and can never feel any sense of fulfillment from it. In Jaime's case, she was her only victim. Her only rebellion was to pick losing situations, such as her relationship with George, because of her inability to see anything positive about her life. She appeared to be doing well in other areas of her life, at least as someone else might judge her.

Jaime

"What do you like about yourself?" I asked in an attempt to help Jaime to develop a more balanced picture of herself.

"Not very much."

"Let me put it another way, then, what are some of your good qualities as other people would see them?"

"Well, I'm a nice person. I am really responsible. I'm not like my parents that way. I work hard and pay my bills. I'm friendly, but I have a bad temper." She shrugged her shoulders indicating that there wasn't any more.

"Do you have any talents or special interests?"

"No, nothing I can think of. Wait a minute. I used to like to write, if that's what you mean." For the first time, Jaime became very excited, as though she had just discovered something." I used to write poems and stories."

"What kind of stories?"

"I liked to write . . . like children's stories!" her enthusiasm growing.

"Tell me about some of your stories," my own enthusiasm building with hers.

"My favorite is the one about the princess who got locked in the cookie factory for the weekend. I wrote that one for a school paper and my teacher really liked it. I never really liked school that much, but that was special, it really was." Jaime looked wistful for just a moment.

"Sometime, I hope you'll share some of your writing with me."

"Oh! Sure. You couldn't like my stuff. I mean——you've read all those real books," she responded glumly, gesturing toward my large, overflowing bookcase.

"Jaime, you are you and I am me. This isn't a contest. I enjoy listening to you and I bet I would enjoy reading your work. You have a way with words and ideas which I couldn't duplicate, and I'd love to see how that off-the-wall sense of the absurd which you have, is presented in fiction. Maybe all you ever needed was someone to appreciate what you could do, and you never had that— *yet*.

"What did your parents expect you to accomplish in life?"

"Nothing, I guess. I was supposed to get out of school, find a job and marry a rich guy who would take care of me. Fat chance!" Jaime struggled with her feelings. "Yeah, just like my sisters. They all married losers and I sure don't want to follow in their footsteps."

"Is that what you want for yourself?"

"If I do, I sure have a funny way of getting there, don't I? Yeah, someday I'd like to get married, I guess. But, if all there is out there are guys like George, no—no I don't."

"That's strange," I said, pausing. "You keep saying you love him and you keep taking George back, but you also sound like you're saying you don't want to marry him."

"Marry him? You gotta be kidding! I'd never marry George!"

"How long have you been with him?"

"Three years."

"If you wouldn't marry him, why are you going with him after three years?"

Jaime looked at me and smiled. "I told you I must be crazy."

"Maybe crazy like a fox. Going with somebody you would never marry is one way to avoid a lifetime of problems if you know you can't pick someone worth marrying—or don't believe there's anybody out there who is worthwhile." I sat back and she remained silent, contemplating.

"You know, I never looked at it that way. You have a way of turning the most negative things into positives. I wish I could do that."

Jaime

"Maybe it's something you can learn to do while you're here. Anyway, what's your priority right now?" I asked, changing the subject.

"I have to get George out of my life and I don't think I can do it. Every time I tell him it's over, he gets straight and convinces me he'll be different. And, every time, I believe him." Jaime clenched her jaw in anger. "I'm such a fool. How can I keep believing that asshole? I know he's never—NEVER—going to change. He's . . ." She stopped and looked at me. "Why? Why do I fall for guys like that? Why? Tell me."

I knew she didn't expect an answer. Nor, was it possible for her to reach any reasonable answer so quickly. "Jaime, I hate to put you off, but some things take time, and learning about yourself is one of them."

"How do I get rid of him once and for all?" Jaime seemed sincere in asking this question.

"Are you asking me for a formula, or is it one of those things where you really aren't ready, but just want a way to go when you decide to go?"

"No, I have to get rid of him. I can't live like this anymore. I'm always crying, always wondering where he is. I'm just so afraid to be alone." Jaime began crying.

"Tell me what it's like being with George." I already knew the answer.

"It's . . . like . . . being alone! He's never there when I need him—only when he needs me—like when he is crashing and sick and broke. The last three New Year's Eves—he was gone. At night when he is supposed to stay over—he can't wait till I fall asleep so he can go out and do coke. And . . . I never told anybody this. I got pregnant and decided to have an abortion. When it was time to go to the hospital, there was no sign of George anywhere. And then . . ." Jaime began to cry. She regained control and continued: "After—the next time we broke up, he threatened to tell my parents about the abortion if I didn't take him back. And, like a fool, I did!

"He'll disappear for days at a time and I go crazy and call everyplace, and chase after him to all his sick friends' places—places I wouldn't be caught dead in!

"He always comes back when he's so sick he can't move and I nurse him back so he can go out and do it all over. Why is he like that? What am I doing wrong?"

"Jaime, he's the one whose life is all screwed up and you're sitting there asking what you're doing wrong? Doesn't that tell you something?"

"Yeah," she said, with a deprecating smile. "It tells me I *am* crazy!"

"It tells me you were taught to believe some things that help sick people stay sick. Who taught you?" I looked at her and she seemed very calm.

"Who? My parents? How? What?" She seemed confused.

"What did they teach you about taking care of them?" I asked.

"Oh!" she exclaimed. "I see! Yeah. It's my duty to help my family. Except my family gets into trouble and I have to bail them out. My dad can't pay the mortgage payment and I have to lend him money. He asks me for twenty bucks when he's broke."

"And, what's the connection?" I smiled to encourage the direction she was taking.

"Maybe I'm used to taking care of irresponsible people. Is that it?"

"Well, it isn't that simple, but maybe that's part of it."

"I'm tired of taking care of all of them. I really am!" she said, angrily, but with little conviction. "But, I'm not ready to leave my parents. One thing at a time."

"Are you saying that you are ready to break off your relationship with George?"

"I'm ready to try, but I'm not ready to guarantee results," she answered, trying to make a joke of it.

"How do you plan to do it?" I put the responsibility for the plan as well as the decision on her—where it belonged.

"Next time I talk to him, I'm telling him we're through. I did that fifty times—that part's easy. It's sticking to the decision that's gonna be tough.

"I know what's going to happen. I'll be fine for a few hours or a few days, but then I'm gonna get lonely. That's what happens every time. Robert, I don't even think it's really George. I just need somebody. I'm so afraid to be alone. That's when I'll be vulnerable and beg him to come back. And then I'll feel really rotten. I can't win, can I?"

"Not the way you've been playing. Maybe you just have to change all the rules. Maybe you have to consider taking some time off from relationships. Have you ever done that?"

"No, I always had to have a boyfriend. Before George, there was Doug. That was another story. He was a real head case. He was so paranoid. He was always accusing me of cheating on him. At the time, he was my first and only. We were always breaking up and making up. He'd scream at me and I'd tell him to get out and fifteen minutes later, I'd be begging him to come back. I met George before I broke up with Doug, but I didn't go out with him until after Doug and I broke up. If it hadn't been for George, I might've gone back to Doug."

"It sounds like you've never really had any space to call your own."

"You're right." Jaime nodded her head in assent. "I met Doug when I was seventeen and I was with him for three years, and now George for three more. What am I so afraid of?"

"Yeah," I said. "What *are* you so afraid of? Not having anybody to ruin your life?"

"It wasn't always bad. There were some good times," Jaime added defensively.

"Of course there were. Isn't that what makes bad relationships so appealing? You know, the bad times might have been bad, but the good times were great—or seemed great because they were such a relief from the bad times?"

"What you're saying—suggesting—is I give up men altogether?" she asked sounding very frightened.

"Well, don't give up, Jaime," I said, trying to calm her fears. "Just take a little time off to work on yourself so that the next one you pick will be healthier and really able to appreciate you. And, you can't have one like that until you learn to respect, love and appreciate yourself."

"And I'm a long, long way from that. I don't think I can ever really like myself. There's nothing to like." She stared at me as if to challenge me to contradict her.

"That's because you're only able to see yourself the way you were taught to see yourself. Maybe some of what you were taught was wrong—yeah *wrong*. See? I'm allowed to call your parents wrong. Are you?" I returned her challenge.

"I don't know, Robert. I really don't know if I can. Maybe they taught me too good. Maybe that's it."

"And maybe they taught you that you weren't allowed to question what they said. You know: rule number one—we are always right. Rule number two—when in doubt, refer to rule number one!"

"That sounds about like it was. How do I go about changing that? I can't just go up to my parents and tell them they were wrong."

"Jaime, that's the beautiful part of changing yourself. You don't have to even let them know you're doing it.

Jaime

215

You only have to talk to the voices of your parents you've carried inside your head since you were a kid. I bet today, they would be the first to say you should cut George loose, wouldn't they?

"From the day I met him," Jaime said, smiling.

"Maybe this would be a good time to call it a night," I said. "You have a lot to work on."

"See you next week?" she asked. "No, I'll see you next week. See, I did learn something!"

"Yeah, Jaime, you sure did learn something."

Becoming Ready

"Damn him," Jaime began. "It's like he has radar. He knows I'm planning to dump him so he calls and tells me he knows he's sick and he's checking himself into a rehab. He asks me to please not ditch him while he's in treatment. He needs his mind clear to get well."

"Sometimes sick people can be very manipulative. Maybe they have to be to survive. But Jaime, the issue still comes down to what do you want to do with your life?" I paused. "By the way, how are you otherwise?"

"You know, I was doing real good. I was really thinking about what we were talking about last week and I'm seeing some of the things about how I'm repeating what happened to me as a kid. And then, George has to spoil it by pulling this shit. I'm really angry." Jaime began laughing. "You know what's funny? It just hit me that I really look forward to coming here every week because this is the only sane place in the whole world. I feel so good when I leave here and then I have to go out there and, I don't know, it's so . . . frustrating. Maybe I can bring a blanket and move in here."

"I know how you feel. Maybe we have to look at what went wrong. Was it you? Were you ready to do what you said you wanted to do?"

"Yeah. I was ready to blow his boat out of the water and he runs up a white flag! It's not fair."

"Let's look at all the parts of this thing. What does it mean when George *says* he is going into treatment?"

"Not a damned thing. He's said it a hundred times and done it a few but nothing ever changes."

"So . . . what do you want to do?"

"I want him out of my life. I can't put up with any more."

"And . . . ?" I left my question hanging.

"And I guess I was just reacting like I always did. I let him push my buttons again."

"Which does what?" I asked.

"Which leaves me holding the bag—like always—and I'm tired of it." Jaime began crying, but quickly stopped. "I still have to do what I have to do, don't I? But how can I tell him we're through if he's in a rehab?"

"Is George in a rehab?"

"He's supposed to be going in this week."

"But you're not sure he is really going into one, are you?"

"You mean . . . he might be sayin' it so I won't break up with him? But, how could he know I was gonna break up with him?" Jaime looked confused.

"What does he think you went into therapy for?" I asked.

A look of recognition came over her. "I see. From the day I said I was going to call you, he's been giving me flak. Sure. He knows I'm not coming here to learn how to knit. He just beat me to it."

Jaime

217

"Sometimes the simplest explanations are the best ones, Jaime."

"Okay," she replied, "I know what I have to do. Now what do we talk about?"

"What are you here for?" I asked.

"To learn about me, I guess. But what do I need to work on?"

"What do you want to work on?"

"I want to feel better about myself and I don't know how." Jaime looked at me, almost pleading. "I really want to be able to like myself."

"What's stopping you?"

"What's there to like? I see all my friends. They went to college. They have good jobs. They meet nice guys. They have interesting things to talk about. And look at me. What am I? I have a job in a store. I buy lots of clothes. But, I'm not smart or interesting like they are. I'm going nowhere." She shook her head in frustration.

"Jaime, you need to make a fresh and realistic assessment of yourself . . ." Jaime wasn't ready to hear positive things about herself. I could see her closing off as I began speaking. However, sometimes, therapy is planting seeds for future growth.

In this room, Jaime would be exposed to caring, compliments, unconditional love and respect. It would be her choice as to how and when to incorporate any of what was given to her. Receiving positive feedback was something to which Jaime was unaccustomed. However, she needed nurturing, among other important needs such as empowerment and encouragement toward self-direction. Most important, every word said to her had to speak the truth.

In therapy, it is important to know that readiness is the most important prerequisite for change to take place. You have to start with the belief that change is possible, or it is impossible to change. If, for instance, you believe that the world is flat, it would be useless to give you a map of the globe and tell you to go around it and return to your starting point in a continuous line. Your belief system would not allow the incorporation of the new 'fact'. Likewise, it is not of immediate value to tell a person who has self-hatred that he or she is talented, attractive, or intelligent. Her belief system immediately rejects the possibility that these attributes apply to her.

"Jaime," I said. "I want you to try something different. If you want to, that is."

"I'm ready to try anything. I don't want to feel like this any more. I'm always depressed—except the few times George is doing good. Sometimes, I can't hold food down. I think I'm not worth anything." Jaime stared out the window for a few moments, then looked at me to continue.

"Okay, what I want you to do is ask a few people whom you know but who aren't in your family to tell you what they like about you. Think you can do that?" I asked.

"What if they tell me I'm rotten or miserable?" She replied, fearing that would be a reality.

"Just try it," I encouraged her.

"Okay, but I won't be responsible if I come in here feeling even worse next week!" She smiled and I returned her smile with a reassuring one of my own.

"Sometimes, Jaime, life is about taking chances. You have to decide—which is the greater risk—feeling like you do or risking what people will say about you."

"When you put it like that, it doesn't seem half bad. I'll ask the people I work with. I'm their boss. If they say anything really bad, I can always fire them. I'm just kidding, of course!"

"See you next week, Jaime."

"Where's my miracle this week? I didn't get one."

Jaime

219

"Talk to the people at work before you decide that. Maybe you have it and just don't know it."

Sometimes, it is possible to use reality to contradict the false impressions people have about themselves. Although Jaime was not about to believe me if I told her that she was bright, attractive, interesting and competent, perhaps she would believe others who were not as important in her life. I was facing a paradox—it was the most important people in her life who told Jaime she had very little worth—her parents and the boyfriends whom she chose. Therefore, how could a new important person in her life—her therapist—be believed unless he agreed with them. Jaime had all of the positive qualities I mentioned and more. Perhaps she would believe someone who wasn't important to her. It was a risk worth taking.

If I Had Known What Was Coming

Jaime was frowning when she came in. "I did what you asked me . . ." she said. "What did you do? Tell them all what to say?" Then, she smiled shyly like a child who has been complimented by a stranger. "You're something. You really are. You know I can't stand compliments and that's all I got—including one of the guys who said that I was the cutest girl he ever saw. I guess that's me—cute, huh?" Jaime couldn't keep herself from smiling.

"Yeah, Jaime, cute—as well as a lot of more important positive qualities, and one I want to add—if someone hasn't said it already—unique. You are the most special *you* in the world!"

Jaime sat quietly absorbing what I was saying and began crying. "Yeah, sure. Then why do I have so much trouble seeing it?"

"Because you have been denied the right to hear those truths for so long that you lost faith in yourself." I waited while she blew her nose.

"I must look a wreck. Every time I cry my nose gets all red and my eyes get puffy," she sniffled.

"Jay," I said, gently, "this place isn't about winning beauty contests. It's about finding the real you."

"Nobody calls me Jay any more, she said, shyly. "My favorite sister used to call me Jaybird and it made me feel really good. It was like she and I had something special. It's okay for you to call me Jay." She didn't have to finish that thought.

"Anyway," she continued, "I still don't believe all the good things I heard at work, but I'm gonna try to get used to hearing them——but I'm not going to guarantee it'll change anything!

"You know, every time I come here I feel better and now it seems to last longer. Like the first time, I felt better for a day, and now it lasts almost all week. Is that what's supposed to happen?"

"Each person reacts differently to therapy, but maybe what you're saying is that you don't have as many things making you feel bad as you did before. Maybe it's time to talk about what's changing, okay?"

"It's hard to see any difference, but, you're right. I must feel better about myself. I don't wake up so depressed every morning, and I haven't seen George in almost two weeks. He calls fifty times a day, but I don't answer the phone and I really don't miss him. Before, I'd be calling him and he'd say he'd be over and then he wouldn't show up and I'd be crazy for a week.

Jaime

221

"I still can't tell him I don't want to see him any more, but I'm avoiding him. Maybe he'll take the hint and just go away."

"It usually doesn't happen that easily, Jaime," I said.

"Yeah, yeah, I know, but I'm such a coward, y'know?" She smiled and looked coyly at me.

"Would it make you feel better if he was the bad guy?" I asked.

"Yeah, because then I could cry and it'd all be over, but if I do it, there's always the chance I'll change my mind. I guess I want it both ways, huh?"

"Let's talk about you for a change instead of George, okay? What else is happening in your life?"

"I have to get out of my parents house, but I don't have enough money," said Jaime.

"You could always get a roommate," I responded.

"You know how hard it is to find somebody decent."

"Difficult, but not impossible, if that's the only reason."

"What's the matter? Aren't you going to call me Jay any more?" She looked at me in mock anger.

"You're changing the subject—Jaime," I said, with just a hint of sarcasm.

"Nothing gets by you, does it?" We both laughed. Jaime paused for a few moments. "I'm afraid to leave home. There it is. My parents treat me like I don't exist and I can't leave. Why is that?"

"I don't know, Jay. Maybe you need to look at some of your other feelings, besides the anger."

"Like why I'm so insecure, you mean?" She shook her head in anger at herself.

"Well, why are you so insecure?"

"'Cause I'm afraid I won't make it on my own. I never had to take care of myself." She looked frightened and confused.

"What can't you do?"

Stop the Merry-Go-Round

"I don't know," she whined.

"Well, then, what can you do to take care of yourself? Can you cook? Can you take care of your possessions? Can you keep a place clean? Can you write a check and pay a bill?" I saw that she was nodding in agreement as I listed all the basic things it takes to be self-sufficient. "I never looked at it like that. Maybe I'm just afraid to be alone. I feel that way so much. That's why I can't let go of George. But . . ." Jaime paused and sat contemplating.

"But . . . ?" I encouraged her to continue the thought.

"I'm alone most of the time anyway. My parents are never there. George was hardly ever there, except when he needed me. Whenever I think of being on my own I get scared," she said.

"Maybe you still need the abuse you get from the people close to you." I sat back and waited for her response.

"How can you say that? You mean I like to be abused? I can't buy that!" She looked at me with anger and disappointment.

"I didn't say you *liked* it. I said that something inside you needs it, and that is the part of you we are working to defeat. Maybe when all you know is abuse, you don't believe it can ever be different, so you may as well stick with what you have."

"That makes sense," she said. "So how do I change it?"

"By no longer believing that you need to be abused or to live unhappily ever after." I smiled and she did also.

"How do I do that?"

"You already began by coming here and starting to question your old values. You still have some things you need to learn, but you've made a wonderful start. It just doesn't happen all at once."

Jaime was beginning to allow herself to see a healthier portrayal of her qualities. After years of subtle verbal abuse and the learning which takes place simply living in a dysfunctional family, Jaime developed a set of values which included: I am powerless to change anything; relationships between men and women are filled with pain, lies, anger, distrust, and disappointment; I am not worth anything; whatever I attempt will end in failure; children are meant to be exploited, and are the targets of the pain of their parents; you owe an obligation to the people who love you; and, love is pain, disappointment and obligation. With this set of beliefs, Jaime was destined to repeat as an adult what she learned as a child—until she challenged the learning of a lifetime.

Several days after the previous session Jaime called late in the evening.

"Help me," she cried, through hysterical sobs. "I'm falling apart."

"What is it? Come on, Jaime—try to talk to me" I said, trying to calm her down.

"It's George. He stole everything I own. All my clothes. He robbed my house. We called the police but they can't do anything because we can't prove it was him." She burst into tears and continued crying for several minutes.

"Listen Jaime. Get in your car and get over here right now. There's got to be something that you can do and you and I are going to figure it out. C'mon," I said, encouraging her to begin working on herself immediately.

"I can't do that to you. It's late. I don't have anything to wear. I'm a mess," she said in a mad jumble of words.

"Jaime, when you hurt this much," I said, gently, "it's okay to reach out to someone and accept real help. Now, you must have something to wear. Whatever you had on when he was robbing your house'll do. I'm not going to take you to a formal dinner after we talk!"

Jaime burst out laughing. "You have a way of turning the worst situation into something I can handle. I'll be right over——if you're sure it's okay. You have a life, too, you know."

"Sometimes, I really have to wonder about that," I thought to myself, "but that's another story."

Jaime arrived within five minutes. She wasn't kidding. She was a mess. Her hair was uncombed, she was wearing an old sweatsuit, her eyes were swollen from crying and she even had a red nose, just as she had described.

"Don't look at me," she said in a tiny voice.

"Jaime, you are very beautiful at this moment, and it has nothing to do with your appearance. You look so fragile and hurt, but at the same time, you are here, and here is a place where you come to grow. Now, come on. Tell me what happened."

Jaime took a few moments absorbing what I was saying and then began: "I finally talked to George last night. He called and I happened to answer. He started screaming and accusing me of avoiding him and I just came out and told him that I wanted to end our relationship. Every other time I ended our relationship, it was after a fight, or after he spent a week doing coke, but this time, I came right out and told him it was over. And let me tell you something——I was really proud of myself. I didn't think I could do it, but I did, and it felt really good.

"Then, he came over and pushed his way right into the house, right past my dad. In my own room he starts accusing me of cheating on him and letting him down just when he is getting his life together. Let me tell you——he's really good. He almost had me convinced that I was crazy or that he was right. But, I told him I wasn't going to change my mind. Anyway, then he started to cry and I felt sorry for him so I let him stay and just talk all night. In the morning, he acted like everything was the way it always was and I told him again that we were through. He started screaming and said he wanted back all the things

Jaime

225

he gave me and I told him, 'No way!' Then he said that he would take it all back whether I gave it to him or not. That's when I told him to get out."

"It took a lot of strength for you to do that."

"If I had known what was coming, maybe I wouldn't've been so strong!" she said, now looking like she was going to cry. She continued: "I went to work today and I was feeling good. I expected I'd be all upset because I broke up with George, but I wasn't. I was feeling like this time I was going to make it and I'd have the strength to move on. I was scared 'cause I don't believe anybody is ever gonna want me, but I didn't care. I was willing to take that chance. That was something new for me. I could never be without somebody before. And for almost six years, I've only had two boyfriends. That's since I was seventeen. I never thought of it that way before.

"As soon as I got home from work, I knew something was wrong. I just knew it inside, you know what I mean? I went up to my room and everything was gone—everything! He took all my clothes and my jewelry and everything. I knew it was him. Nobody else would do anything that mean or stupid.

"When my mom got home, what do you think happened? She blamed me. Me! I guess I should've expected that. She never had a nice thing to say to me—never! My dad surprised me. He just hugged me. I don't remember the last time he hugged me. He called the police and he wanted to go over to George's and kill him.

"That's the story." Jaime looked totally forlorn.

"What now, Jay?" I asked.

"Maybe I should be a bag lady. I would, but I don't have a nice enough wardrobe, thanks to George!"

"What do you think he's trying to accomplish?"

"Who knows with him," she said, angrily. "But I need my clothes. That's all I have in the world. They are my things, and he has no right to take them."

"Jaime, what would you do if the worst happened and you never got any of it back?"

She pondered for a moment and said: "I guess I'd have to go out and buy new things, wouldn't I?"

"That's the worst, right?" I asked her, so she could be certain.

"Yeah, that really is the worst, isn't it? And insurance would probably pay for most of it because they were stolen." She brightened. "And you know me, I like to shop. Good old Jaime, never stops shopping. You know, that's another problem we have to talk about some time."

"Okay," I continued, getting her back on the topic, "the worst that can happen is that you have to buy new clothes. What else might happen?"

"He might give them back," she answered, brightly.

"For the moment," I continued, "let's assume that neither of the answers we came up with will happen. What else?"

"That's the one I don't want to look at. I have to make George give everything back." Jaime looked scared. "I can't, well, I don't think I can. You know, I'm so angry at him, maybe I can. Can I call him right now? That way, you'll be with me if I can't handle it."

"Jaime," I said, "take a minute before you call and let's plan it out. That way, you'll say exactly what you want to, okay?"

"Yeah, good idea," she answered, her mouth a grim line, "cause if I say what I'm thinking right now, I'll never get my stuff back!"

Jaime and I rehearsed what she planned to say as well as how she planned to say it. After a couple of trials, she picked up the phone and called.

Jaime

"Maybe he won't be home," she said hopefully as she dialed.

But, George answered on the first ring. Jaime looked panicked for a second and then began speaking in a controlled, yet angry voice: "George, this is me. I know you're the one who took all my clothes and things and I want them back . . . No, I don't want to talk to you, I just want my things back . . . Then I'll come to your place and get them." She hung up.

"Well, how did I do, boss?" she asked with a smile.

"Sounded great to me! But are you sure you can handle going to his place?"

"I'm so angry right now, that he is the last thing in the world I'm worried about."

"Just take it easy and take care of business. Don't try to get rid of three years worth of anger while you're there. Something that isn't worth fixing isn't worth wasting energy on."

"I'll be okay. I really am through with him, you know?" Jaime sat quietly for a moment. "Since he hasn't been around, I feel so much better and when he took my clothes, that was really the last straw. I mean, I'm not saying my clothes are that important, but they are all I really have. And, nobody has the right to come into my room and take my things."

Jaime took out her compact mirror and examined herself carefully. She put on fresh makeup and prepared to leave. "I'll call you tomorrow to let you know how it worked out, and . . . thanks, Robert."

"Talk to you tomorrow," I answered as she left.

After she had gone I thought, how strange it is that a woman will allow such a sick man to be intimate with her. Jaime may have been almost rid of George, but I knew we had plenty of work yet to do because there are an abun-

Stop the Merry-Go-Round

228

dance of 'Georges' out there. I rubbed my eyes. It had been a long day.

The Thought of Being Alone

The following day Jaime called to let me know that she had accomplished getting back everything George had taken.

"It's getting really ridiculous," Jaime began. "He calls a hundred times a day and I can't stand it!"

"What do you do when he calls?" I asked.

"I keep telling him I don't want to talk to him, but he just keeps calling and calling. It's driving me crazy." Jaime was extremely agitated.

"Would you like a guaranteed method to stop his calls? If you can do one simple thing, they will stop soon."

"What's that?"

"Don't answer the phone for a few days. He will eventually get tired of calling." Jaime looked confused. "Unless," I continued, "you really don't want to break the connection with him, Jaime. Let's look at that possibility. What happens if you break the ties with George completely?"

"But, I want to get rid of him, I really do!" Jaime seemed more concerned with persuading herself than in convincing me that she really wanted George out of her life.

"For a moment," I said, "let's just pretend that it is somebody else's situation, and you were talking to her about the same thing, okay? What advice would you give her?"

"Probably to just not answer the phone, but . . ."

Jaime

"But what, Jaime? When you're in love, you have an exemption from reality?"

"A what?"

"You know, because you are in love, the rules don't apply to you, and, what works for everybody else doesn't apply to your situation?

"For everything we do, there are good reasons and real reasons, Jaime." I paused for the dramatic effect, then continued. "What's your real reason for answering the phone every time George calls?"

"I can't stand the thought of being alone. I'm just afraid. I know, you're going to tell me that's silly." Jaime sniffled and wiped her nose which was now red from crying.

"Jaime, is that what we're about here——telling you that you're silly?"

"Well, you haven't done it yet, but . . ."

"There's always the possibility?"

Jaime looked confused. "No, I don't mean that. It's just that's what always happened to me. My parents always told me I was foolish or stupid. George was always telling me I was wrong. He always criticized me for my clothes and my hair."

"Did you feel you had to believe all of them all the time?"

"I guess I must've. Look at the results! What's wrong with me? Why can't I be normal?"

"Jaime, you're about as normal as a person can be. Maybe a better way to say it would be: Why don't you like yourself enough to trust your own judgment?"

"What's to like?" Jaime asked in the tiniest voice I ever heard. She began crying again.

"I feel better, now," Jaime said a few minutes later. "I guess I really needed to get out my feelings. Living with George, not living *with* him——you know what I mean——was tough. He never, never could be depended on. Sometimes, when he would come back after a few days on cocaine, he'd be so sick and I would take care of him. That made me feel needed. He'd promise that he would never ever do it again and good old Jaime would believe him. And then a few days or a few weeks later—here we go again! And here goes Jaime making a fool out of herself again!"

"Do you still love George?" I asked.

"I don't love George. I never really loved him. Well, I loved him, but I wasn't in love with him. I knew I would never marry him. But he was somebody to be with." Jaime began crying. "Gimme the Kleenex. This is gonna be a two box night."

"That's a valid reason. Nobody wants to be alone all the time. But, and maybe that little word—but—is the most important one for you right now, why does the person you let in your life, so you won't be alone, have to be an undependable person who hurts you and let's you down when you really need him?"

Jaime had no answer for that question. The situation in which Jaime had found herself with George is such a common one for women who come from homes in which they were not given feelings of acceptance, security, and, especially value. Jaime was repeating the pattern she had learned in her parents' home. It was time to end the session.

"How are you planning to handle it if George keeps harassing you?" I asked, as we moved toward the door.

"I'm going to take my own advice. I'm just not going to answer the phone—no matter how much I want to."

"Do you have an answering machine?"

"Yes, I do," Jaime said, brightly. "Why didn't I think of that? I know. You'll say, 'Because I really wanted to hear his voice.' I guess I did—do, but I know it's no good for

Jaime

231

me and the longer I hold on, the tougher it's going to be to let go. See you next week, okay?"

"Yeah, Jaime, it's going to be okay, isn't it?"

"Well . . . maybe," she said in that tiny voice she uses when she is feeling very vulnerable and uncertain.

A New Feeling of Control

"The calls stopped after a couple more days," Jaime began—in the middle of an idea as usual. "But, George wasn't content to leave it alone. He had to come over my house to tell me he's leaving town. He couldn't just go and let me alone."

"What did you do?"

"Like a fool, I let him in and we talked and cried for a few hours. He tried everything to get me to change my mind, but I didn't. A few times there I thought I was going to give in like I always did, but somehow, I didn't let it happen. I was stupid for letting him in, wasn't I?" Jaime asked.

"No, not at all. The way things turned out, maybe it was really for the best. You proved you could handle what you said you wanted to do which was end the relationship. It didn't have to end in anger. As a matter of fact, you handled it very maturely."

"Me?" she smiled. "Yeah, I guess I did, didn't I? I always think that no matter what I do, I'm going to make a mess of it."

"Who told you that, Jaime?"

"My parents, my older sisters, my boyfriends. Everybody let me know that I didn't know what I was doing. You know, they'd say, 'if you would just listen to me, everything will be fine.' Well, it isn't fine, is it? I listened to all of them and look where it got me. Nowhere, that's where. They all told me they loved me and that they were telling me for my own good. And where did it get me?"

I didn't answer her. Jaime was learning that she needed to depend on her own judgment. It would take time and a lot of effort but she was beginning to understand that she needed to get control of her life if she ever wanted to feel good about herself. I felt that the time was right to move on to talk about Jaime. She had spent most of her time and energy in therapy accomplishing the necessary task of ending her relationship with George. She came into therapy already knowing that she was going to accomplish this, so the easiest part of her program was now complete. Jaime next had to learn that as long as she chose unhealthy people with whom to relate, she would have the constant problem of trying to wrest control of her life from them.

Why Men Like George?

"It is getting easier than I thought," Jaime began, in our next session. "You know, I never, ever liked being alone. I don't mean having someone in the room with me, or even in the house. I mean, I like to know I have someone in my life. But now, it's just me and my little dog, Peanut."

""How do you find it having no boyfriend for the first time in—how long?"

"Well, really, since I was about sixteen, there was always somebody. I've only had three relationships. I don't like to just date. I never liked myself enough to have any confidence. I like to be with somebody. It's easier."

"Were the other relationships like the one with George?"

"In some ways they were worse." Jaime leaned forward and rested her chin in her hand and continued: "The one before George was really a mean person. He always put me down and was unbelievably jealous. He would follow me all over the place and if I threatened to break up with him, he would almost get violent, but he only really did once—when I did break up with him. I started seeing George before it was officially over, and he threatened to beat me up. He never did, though.

"My first boyfriend was okay, but he wasn't anything special. I went with him for a year when I was sixteen and I never had sex with him, even. I've only been with three guys in my life."

"Why did you mention that, Jaime?"

"I didn't want you to think I was promiscuous, or anything."

"Is your reputation important to you?"

"Well, of course!" Jaime leaned forward and placed her hands on her hips. "I mean, I'm not like a lot of those bimbos out there who will sleep with just anybody. I have to be in a relationship—except once, and I felt so bad about that, I promised myself it would never happen again."

"Jaime, what is sex to you?"

"I guess it's a way of making a man happy, isn't it?"

"What else?"

"Sometimes, a whole lot of trouble. Like worrying about being pregnant and taking precautions, or . . ." Jaime paused and for a moment, was lost deeply in her own thoughts.

"Or what, Jay?" I asked, very softly.

"I was just thinking. I never told anybody about this—not even my parents, but I feel like I need to talk

Stop the Merry-Go-Round

about it." She paused for a moment and took a deep breath. "A couple of years ago, I got pregnant and had an abortion. It was the most awful experience of my life. George was so totally unsupportive. He never even once asked to marry me. I don't think I would've—but that's not the issue. He never even asked! He just said he would pay for the abortion—of course.

"Anyway, comes the day I had to go to the hospital, George was supposed to take me and he never even showed up. He was out doing cocaine. I had to get myself to the hospital and get myself home afterwards. Somehow, I kept my parents from finding out. I told them I had a D and C."

"You must have felt very alone." As I spoke Jaime burst into tears. It's going to be another two boxes of tissues night, I thought.

"That's it!" exclaimed Jaime, after she had regained her composure. "Very alone. I've always felt very alone. I never got any support from anybody. Everybody was great at telling me what to do and how to run my life but nobody was ever there when I needed them." She paused. "Do you think that has anything to do with why I choose men like George?"

"Jaime, let me change the subject just a little, okay? If you want to find out why you do things, I can probably give you simple answers that would be true, but that wouldn't help you not to do the same things again. Instead, let's talk about you. Let's find out what kind of people you really want in your life and how to get them there."

"There isn't much you don't know. I told you just about everything about me. You even know about the abortion, so you know more about me than anyone." Jaime looked extremely uncomfortable.

Jaime

235

"Well," I said, allowing the suspense to build for a moment, "I know a lot of what you have done in your life, and I have my own opinions about what kind of person you are, but I know absolutely nothing about how you see yourself as a person, or what you want out of life."

"What do you think of me?" Jaime asked.

"Jaime, that isn't as important as what you think and feel about yourself."

"It is to me!"

"Is everyone's opinion of you important?"

"Of course. How else can I know whether I'm doing the right things?" Jaime stared at me as if I were a child and was missing something very obvious.

"Okay, but . . ." I paused intentionally, "what if the person is wrong, or worse, what if the person uses his—or her—opinion of you to control you?"

"Go on," she said, her curiosity aroused.

"Let's find out what you think of yourself and then see how that connects, alright? Jaime, tell me about you. What are you worth? What kind of person are you?"

"Those are hard questions. What am I supposed to think of myself?" she whined.

"There is no 'supposed to' here, Jaime. Tell me what kind of a person you are." Jaime's face tightened in deep thought. No immediate answer came to her.

"Well, I'm a good person," she said, finally.

"What does that mean?"

"You know, I wouldn't hurt anybody. I try to be nice to people. I mean, I have a bad temper sometimes, but I'm usually my sweet, pleasant self."

"That's a start," I said encouragingly. "You are a good person, you sometimes have a bad temper . . . Those are two qualities you possess. What others do you have?"

Jaime sat for some time thinking. "I can't think of any others."

"What about your intelligence." I asked.

"Oh, I don't think I'm very smart. I didn't go to college like most of my friends."

"How did you do in school?" I wanted to keep her focused on this issue.

"I usually got A's, or maybe B's if I wasn't interested in the subject." Jaime said this with a casualness that led me to believe that she didn't connect it with intelligence.

"How did you do in school compared to your friends who went on to college?"

"I got better marks than any of my friends when we were in high school, but obviously, I didn't do anything with them. That wasn't too intelligent, was it?" Jaime was getting angry. "Where is this leading, anyway? I don't get the point of all this.

"Let me put it this way," I said. "Somebody tells you they get the best marks in their group and they speak well and have good common sense in most areas of their life, what would you say about their intelligence?"

"I'd have to say that they're pretty smart."

"You just said all of those things and I guess I'd have to say, you're pretty smart!"

Jaime sat back in her chair and rubbed her cheek, and said nothing.

"Let me think of an example from your life," I said and paused. "One example you used before. You said your parents never praised you. Let's look at what that did to your life."

"That's true. I always looked for them to say something nice. If I brought home B's, they'd say, 'you could've gotten A's if you really tried.' If I brought home A's, my mother would be talking about my sister's pregnancy, or her financial problems. It was always me last. You know, sometimes I felt like if I went home and said, 'Mom, I had an abortion today,' she would've just gone on talking about how it was such a shame that my sister's refrigerator broke down just after she bought all those groceries! And, I keep looking for something from her."

"That must have been very frustrating—and still is, isn't it? So, you really do know that you are intelligent, but it never got you anywhere, so you just stopped thinking about it. Jaime, what are you looking for from your mother and father now?"

"Just a little recognition. Just somebody to say, 'Thanks for bailing us out when we were broke,' or, 'you're a pretty good daughter.' I'm not asking for the world, am I? They aren't too proud to ask me for money when they need it. I was always there for all of them. When my sister needed a new washing machine, I'm the one who gave her the money. She has a husband. What's wrong with him?"

"If it upsets you that much, why do you keep bailing them out every time they are irresponsible?"

"I don't know. Maybe I am crazy, like I keep telling you!" When she said it this time, at least she smiled.

"Or, maybe it is simply that you are spending your life trying to please people who can't be pleased no matter how hard you try. Think about it."

"Yeah," she said, after a brief pause, "like my father. He's more interested in his card-playing buddies than he is in me. But that's not my fault, is it?"

"That's the part you have to learn. Not only isn't it your fault, it really has nothing to do with you—or even how your father feels about you."

"You're right, Robert. I know he loves me. Every once in a while, he even shocks me and notices I'm there. Like after the crazy scene with George and the clothes. It was my father who asked if there was anything he could do to help me. I was surprised. I thought he was going to yell at me for going out with George. Of course, I was the one who had to call the locksmith to get the locks changed!"

"Hey, remember I told you—never expect two miracles on the same day!" Her face broke into a wide smile. She needed to do that more often. Her humor was so often self-deprecating. No, Jaime was not crazy, nor did she lack drive, common sense or intelligence. She lacked only people in her life to tell her they recognized her good qualities.

Maybe I'm Not So Bad

"I've been thinking about what you said," Jaime began. "Sometimes I think, 'maybe I'm not so bad.' But, most of the time, I think I'm not very smart and I don't have a nice personality. And, I can't stand my height. I'd give anything to be taller. Do you know how hard it is to work on my feet for eight or ten hours a day in high heels?"

"Jaime, let's look at your feelings and also, let's look at other views of reality, okay? What are the important characteristics a person can have which make life better for her? Or, put it this way. You manage a store, Right? What qualities would you look for if you were hiring a new employee?"

"First, she has to be tall." Jaime giggled at her own humor. "Seriously, I look for someone who can learn the routines, be pleasant with customers, be honest, be able to handle unexpected things—you know how crazy people are in stores! And, it doesn't hurt if she is fairly attractive because she has to make a decent impression on the public. She has to dress appropriately, and most important—she has to worship me!"

"Jaime," I asked, "how did you first get your job there?"

Jaime

"I got hired by the manager who was there before me. Oh! I see!" she exclaimed. "You mean I had to have all those qualities or I wouldn't have gotten the job? You're pretty tricky tonight, mister!" We both laughed.

"Do you buy that, Jaime? You must have had something special or you wouldn't have been hired, and then you became the manager."

"It's only a little store!

"I know *you* were going to say, but I'm only a little person." Jaime added, pouting.

"What makes you think I'd say something like that?"

"All the kids in school used to call me shrimpboat, and the elf." Jaime looked misty-eyed as she recalled her school days. Who at one time or another hasn't been the victim of peer cruelty?

"Jaime, this isn't school. This is the real world where you're judged for the beauty in your soul, not for the number of inches tall you are. And you are, by all methods of measure, a truly large person. You make a positive impression, you have plenty of important things to say, you have a goodness toward other people. I could go on, but I'm embarrassing you, aren't I?"

Huge tears began streaming down her face. Jaime's parents were too wrapped up in their own problems to take time out to really notice her. She had been such a good child and young adult. She took care of herself. She did well in school. She didn't drink to excess or use drugs. She was in every sense of the word, an ideal daughter. So, her parents didn't have to spend any time keeping her in line. She was left to care for herself—or partially in the care of her older sisters until she grew. She turned out just fine—except she picked potential partners who treated her in the same way her parents did—only with their own sick variations. At least her parents really did love her. And, if they used her at times, it was somewhat reciprocal. At times, they could be nurturing. It was simply not often enough or consistent enough.

So, Jaime grew up to have sufficient skills to get a decent job and develop relationships—albeit—unhealthy ones.

In a New Light

"Why don't I have friends?" Jaime began. I mean, I have some people I go out with, but I don't have any real friends anymore."

"When you say 'anymore,' I take it you used to have friends. What happened to them?"

"Oh, some of them got married, some went to college and have real careers, and I sort of got left behind."

"You have choices, too, Jaime."

"I guess I could have gone to college, but I never thought it was important. I figured I'd get married and just have some kind of job. I never would be dependent on anyone, but I'm making a nice living. I'm making more than a lot of college graduates," Jaime added, somewhat defensively.

"How did your parents feel about college for you?"

"They both thought it was a waste of time. According to them, I was supposed to learn how to find a husband who would take care of me and my most important responsibility in life was to learn how to shop! I'm good at that—even without a husband—but I'm usually very careful. I try not to let myself get in over my head."

"That's really you. You are a very responsible person, Jaime."

Jaime

241

"But, I do like to shop. When I'm depressed, I just go to a mall. Sometimes I buy things I don't really need just to feel better, but the next day—I return them. I keep plenty of them, too! Is that crazy, I ask you?"

"No, Jaime, it's not crazy. Everybody needs something to make her feel better. You don't do drugs. You don't run around with wild and crazy people. You shop. But even then, you do it responsibly—most of the time."

Jaime studied her hands for a moment. "I want to learn to feel good without having to spend six hours wandering around a shopping mall."

"Let's take a look at your life. What do you have in your life today?"

"Nothing."

"You mean, you are living in a cardboard box, you haven't had a meal in three days—or a bath in six?"

"No, silly!" she said, giggling madly. "You have a way of making things seem so—I don't know—but you know, maybe I need to do that, too. Really, my life isn't that bad when you look at it that way. I live in a nice home. I have a new car—that I paid for myself—well, I'm paying for myself. My job is pretty good. Everybody at work respects me. "But some things aren't right. I don't have a social life. I'm lonely."

"Those are things which you can choose to do something about."

"Yeah, sure, I'll just wave a magic wand and Prince Charming will come along and put a glass slipper on my perfect size five foot! Come on!"

"That's not quite what I mean. I didn't say you have control over who you will meet, but you do have control over where you go, who you call, and who you choose to be with of those people who are available.

"What do you like to do socially?"

"I guess more than anything, I love to dance." Jaime became totally animated as she spoke. "You know, when I'm on a dance floor, I can completely forget about myself and really be the life of the party."

"So, why don't you go dancing?"

"That's not a bad idea. Some of the girls who work for me go out every Tuesday to a club. Maybe next week, I'll go with them—if they'll have me." Jaime appeared genuinely excited about this new direction. "Of course they'll have me," she continued, "if they don't I'll simply fire them and get some new ones! Listen to me, here—Miss Ogre."

"Why do you always put yourself down? Of course, the women who work with you will go with you. They may be shocked at first that you asked, but I'll bet they think that you felt that you were too good for them, not the other way round."

"Really?" said Jaime, in a tiny voice.

Jaime was beginning to see her reality in a new light. She was no longer able to make derogatory comments about herself without looking at how another person saw her. She was now able to listen to opinions about herself which differed from her own negative ones. Soon, I hoped, she would be initiating these positive statements about herself.

What Do You Want in a Relationship?

"I met a guy at the dance the other night," she began. "He's really nice and real good looking."

"Yes, but is he the kind of man who is good for you, or is he another George?"

"How can I tell?"

Jaime

"Right now, you can't. Just take things slowly so you don't fall in love and be blinded to his flaws too early in the relationship."

"You don't have to worry about that. I'm not falling in love—well not really falling. I don't want to go through another scene like with George or the one before him. I'm not going to let this guy take over my life."

"Let's talk about what you want in a relationship. Then we can test everybody you meet against some kind of standards, okay? First of all, what qualities are important in a man?"

Jaime thought for a few moments and then said, "He should be kind and gentle. He should have a good sense of humor. He should be responsible and independent. He should really care about me—at least as much as he cares about himself. I'd like it to be more, but I'll be a little realistic."

"And, how many of those qualities did you find in any of the men in your previous relationships?"

"Exactly none."

"Why do you think that was so?"

"Because that wasn't what I was looking for then. I still don't really believe that all those things exist in real people, but I know that not everybody is like George." Jaime curled up in the chair, quite relaxed.

"More important than whether there is anybody with those qualities is: Are you worthy of the best out there?"

"Oh, sure. I'm the best, don't you know? They are falling all over themselves to be in my presence!"

"Jaime, now you're putting yourself down again. Did I ever tell you it hurts me when I hear you do that? I think you have everything a woman needs to be successful in every area of life, and that includes competing socially.

"You look like you're disagreeing with me. Okay, tell me what is wrong with you."

Jaime looked perplexed for a moment as though I should simply take her word that she was unworthy. "Well," she began, coquettishly, "I guess I can be pretty cute sometimes—when I really want to be."

"More than cute. Cute is a little girl mannerism which you use. You can be a lot of other things, too. What are some of them?"

"I'm short—that's what's wrong with me."

"How much has being short handicapped you in life —other than not being able to reach the top shelf at the supermarket!"

Jaime thought for a moment and said, "I guess really not much. I got a decent job. A lot of guys seem to pay attention to me, so I guess it can't be that bad. I just wish I was taller."

"And what would you do if you were taller?

"I don't know." Jaime pondered, and smiled. "I guess nothing, really."

"Then, it's just that you hated being teased by the other children when you were younger?"

"I suppose so, but it still bothers me."

"There's an old saying that time heals all wounds. Sometimes, it doesn't work that easily. You have to do more than just let time pass. You have to let out the feelings and also learn that it is not likely to happen to you now. Some of the things that hurt us as children wouldn't hurt as much if they happened to us for the first time as adults. Some things like this, only children and very immature people would tease anyone about. Tell me, does anyone tease you about your height now?"

"Sometimes people I know kid me about it, but no, nobody looks down on me now." Jaime tilted her head to one side and waited for a reaction.

I smiled and shook my head. It was a sign of real growth that Jaime could make herself the butt of her own joke and not mean it in a negative way. "Soon," I thought, "there are going to be two people in this room who think you are a very special person!"

The Same Four Feet Eleven-and-a-Half

"Look!" exclaimed Jaime in a later session.

"I'm looking," I responded, somewhat confused as to what she was referring.

"My shoes, silly!" she said, with the biggest smile I had ever seen on her.

"Sneakers!" I exclaimed. "No more high heels. That IS saying something."

"I decided I have to be myself. No matter how many times I complain, I'm still going to be the same four feet eleven-and-a-half inches tall."

"Jaime, how are you feeling about yourself now?"

She didn't hesitate as she had done earlier. "I'm starting to like myself a little. I get a lot of compliments—from people I work with, from customers in the store—and I'm hearing them now. I guess they always said nice things, but I was always out of it because of what was going on in my life."

"Tell me some of the things people say about you."

"Aw, I'm embarrassed!" Jaime said and blushed beet red. "Well, okay, they say I'm cute, and my boss says I am doing a terrific job managing the store—he gave me a fifty dollar raise this week. Somebody told me I had the prettiest smile he's ever seen. I said, 'Yeah, sure, but don't plan your Saturday night on my account, yet!' Lots of nice things are happening.

"And, that guy I told you about, I decided not to see him anymore. He was becoming so possessive—just like George. I don't need to be owned. And, I like to be alone—sometimes. I don't feel so lonely anymore. Sometimes, it's nice just to be in my room. I've been going out with friends and having a good time.

"Y'know, I've been thinking. Maybe I should go back to school. I mean, I like my job, but it's not going anywhere. I am as far as I can go and all of a sudden, it's not enough. I don't want to do it now, but maybe next fall."

Gaining Self-Confidence

Sometimes feeling better about yourself begins with the simple process of allowing yourself to share your pain with one trusted person who does not deny you your right to that pain, or attempt to minimize what you are feeling. Then, by making choices to remove the negative forces from your life, you create room for the introduction of new people and ideas. So it was with Jamie.

"I think I'm in love. You know, I think you'd like him. His name is Allan and he's a lawyer—that's not why you'd like him. He is kind and has a great sense of humor. He likes himself and really shows a lot of care for me without getting 'mooshy' about it. He's not the same as any of the others. In most ways, he's the opposite. I don't know what he sees in me."

"Jaime, don't go back to that kind of negative thinking. He sees in you the same things that all of the others who throw compliments your way see in you. You are attractive, bright, lovable, and you make people around you feel good with your caring and special sense of humor."

Jaime

247

"You know, a few weeks ago, I would have gotten angry at you for saying those things. Now, I'm thinking—don't stop! Aren't I terrible?"

"No, Jaime," I said, "just the opposite. You are about as well as you need to get—here."

"Hey, guy!" Jaime said with mock indignation, "Are you kicking me out of here?"

"No dear Jaime, I am preparing you for graduation. You and I have shared something very special and very important here, but part of growing for you is having to do it on your own. It's about time to fly solo."

"But what if I need you? I'm scared I'm not quite ready. I'm making excuses, aren't I?" Tears were streaming down her face, but they were tears of joy.

"Jaime," I said, "if you need me, pick up a phone and call.

"I'm really graduating," she said, excitedly. "I can't believe it. It's like . . . I'm finishing something that's really important to me. If it wasn't for you . . ."

"No, Jaime. If it wasn't for you. You did all the work. You took all of the risks.

"But you were there, giving me guidance and encouragement—and boy did I ever need it. And I know I'm going to be okay now. I don't know where my new relationship will lead, but I know that I can have a healthy relationship and I'll never settle for less.

"I even get along better with my parents. I don't expect anything from them, so I can't be disappointed.

"You know what I'm going to get you? A case of Kleenex. I must have used a million of them while I was here. There're going to have to grow a whole forest just to replace the paper I used getting my life together."

Jaime learned that there was nothing wrong with her that developing a new self-confidence would not remedy. She developed her negative self-image through benign neglect and through the vicissitudes of simply growing up. Her parents were not bad people. They wanted what was best for their daughter. They simply were wrapped up in their own problems and didn't leave themselves the emotional reservoir necessary for the task of raising children. As a matter of fact, they must have had some influence upon the development of her healthy values as well as the problems which she developed. These values came from somewhere. The fact that she was diligent, trustworthy, loving, and ambitious were traits which had to have been stimulated at some time.

Jaime did remain in contact with me. At this juncture, she is still in a committed relationship with Allan, she has enrolled in college, she has decided to seek a career in teaching, and she continues to live at home with her parents. We talk about how pleasant life can be—when you are open to good things happening. Her sense of humor is still outrageous, but that is one of the things that makes her unique. When I first told Jaime that she was special, she didn't understand that I was not putting her above anyone else. Specialness is simply your own unique means of meeting the world and allowing the world to meet you. Once Jaime understood that, she was able to begin appreciating her own specialness, and her sense of humor is what others see and appreciate first.

Jaime is unusual. Most women facing the kinds of problems which faced Jaime do not seek help. She was not the victim of violence. Her life was not threatened. Yet, she was being robbed—robbed of her right to a relationship in which there was trust and caring, not deceit and selfishness. Many women like Jaime drift from one negative relationship to another, or worse yet, remain in the perpetual bondage of a relationship with a soul-sick man who needs a caretaker, not a life-partner. Because she feels badly about herself, she has come to believe that

Jaime

the relationship she has is the best she can have. Jaime didn't know where the exit was to her situation, but she knew there had to be one.

Sometimes, I pose the following paradox to my clients: "If you are in a room that has no windows and no doors and is solid top, bottom and sides, how do you get out?" The simple answer is: "The same way you got in!"

SOLUTIONS

*Some values are burned into the psyche
at such a vulnerable time
that they are difficult to purge
regardless of how certain you are
that they are untrue.*

It Only Stops
When You Get Off!

Five women. Each different. Each the same. Each came to therapy with a sense of frustration at the direction her life had taken to that point. Each came with a need to express those feelings which circumstances had prevented her from expressing. Each had been a victim——of parents or parent-substitutes who, because of their own shortcomings, were incapable of meeting the needs of the precious child to whom they had given life——of the men and women whom she allowed into her life as an adult, unaware that she had the right to exercise choices and the ability to select friends and lovers who could have brought comfort, acceptance and joy rather than rejection, fear and pain.

Each woman became the adult version of what she was taught to be. The values learned as a child translated into behaviors used as an adult to relate to the world. We treat the world as we believe it to be, and each of us creates a world in our own image. Our beliefs about the nature of relationships leads us to choose relationships which confirm this image. The adult children of dysfunctional parents have an image of the world which leads many of them to choose to repeat the uncertainty, violence, addiction or chaos of the family into which they were born. The most unfortunate aspect of their adult lives is that the entire world is not a duplication of the parental home. There are healthy people in the world as well as dysfunctional ones with whom a person can choose to relate.

Change is difficult and can only take place when the individual begins to believe that the principles by which she lived were wrong. For instance, as Leslie said when she entered treatment, "I hate men and I don't trust women." This all-encompassing negative view of the world came out of her personal experiences. Her mother, who professed love for her, also beat her unmercifully and capriciously. Her father wasn't there to protect her, although he, too, professed his love—occasionally. Leslie even married a man for whom she had no love—as did her mother. Leslie subjected herself to a variety of abuses because she felt she had no worth. She could love only a man who had no love for her—at least then, she couldn't be 'hurt.' The really deep hurt was already built into her life's equation. With the generalized negative belief about all men and women so deeply established, how, I ask, is it possible to choose positive people to take part in your life? Any time you generalize, you eliminate the possibility of the existence of exceptions to the rule.

Marianne believed that husbands abuse wives, and women get abused, so she chose a husband who abused her. She believed that men are dangerous, so she was attracted to dangerous men.

Jaime believed that men are unreliable—her father certainly was—and she picked one who spent his evenings snorting cocaine rather than developing a relationship with her. However, she would never allow a man to physically abuse her, because physical abuse was not part of her learning experience.

Ellen was taught that she was worthless, so she dropped out of school, allowed men to use her sexually, lived a pattern of emptiness and self-destruction, and was without friends.

Abuse, abandonment and rejection were an integral part of Caitlin's early life. Her adult life was a continuation of the same pattern. She remained in an incestuous relationship with her father, her husband beat her and slept with all of her friends—sometimes in her presence. She rejected men and women before they had a chance to reject her.

All of these negative patterns created situations in which the women remained victims. The only significant difference was that they no longer needed perpetrators, rather, they unconsciously set up the situations in which they were victimized because they came to believe that they were destined to live out their lives as they had begun them!

All of the women entered therapy with a belief that nothing of significance could change. They came to therapy either out of desperation, or with a belief that therapy could invoke some kind of magic which could change their circumstances, or the people around them. None of the women had been introduced to the possibility that she could change from within. As each learned that what she knew of the world was not necessarily true—at least not to the degree that she believed it to be true—she was able to modify her self-concepts and begin to make realistic, positive demands on persons around her. She learned that not all men abuse women. Not all women are untrustworthy. Not all life is painful.

All of the women discovered that they had real needs which they had a right to fulfill. They had a need for respect and affection. They had a need for self-respect and accomplishment. They had a need for intimacy. They came to realize that the stereotypes they held about men and women were just that—stereotypes. They learned that each person and situation must be judged on its own merits. And, most important, they learned how to make more accurate judgments about the people who came into their lives.

How did Ellen, Marianne, Caitlin, Jaime and Leslie learn that they were special? What was it that enabled them to reverse the fictions which supported their old values? It would be too simple to say that therapy was responsible. Sometimes, when clients try to thank me for helping them, I respond, "All I do is sell road maps to minefields. You are the one who has to negotiate the terrain."

The form of therapy which I practice does not attempt to deal extensively with the reasons people do what they do. Knowing why a partner is abusive may only excuse the inexcusable. Knowing why you allow yourself to be abused does not stop the abuse. There is a need to know that nothing this serious is coincidental. An established pattern of dysfunctional living in the past was essential to the continuation of such situations. Anyone can be abused—once. However, when there is a pattern, the adult victim finds it necessary to cooperate with the abuser. The cooperation is not a conscious decision to be abused. It is, rather, a belief that it is not possible to change anything. It is an acceptance of negative attention as love—the same as it existed in the victim's parental home.

Such issues as a determination of rights and needs, and the appropriate expression of them, are the focus of a program of change which I recommend. People need to develop skills for differentiating between sick and healthy needs. We need to evolve healthy, mutually rewarding contracts with the significant others in our lives. We need to have healthy responses to statements of unhealthy values such as, "If a woman is bad, a man has a right to hit her." We need to begin with a response like, "Who said so?" Usually, the person that said so first in the life of the abused woman was the man who abused her—or, the man who abused her mother!

Sometimes, it is necessary to use several techniques to help people trapped in the role of victim to accept that their rules for conducting relationships need to be changed. You do have a right to your feelings. You do have the right to express pain and rage. And, most important, you do have a right to have your healthy needs met. You do need to understand that a victim is not responsible for the consequences of the actions of the perpetrator. Often, a woman with whom I engage in a therapeutic relationship has been exposed to teachings which have left her unable to express her feelings to the degree that she will deny the existence of the feelings, or even support the right of the abusive person to continue the harm he or she is perpetrating.

No human being should accept victimization. Why, then, would an otherwise intelligent adult accept physical, verbal, emotional and sexual abuse from a family member, spouse, friend or lover? As Marianne, Ellen, Leslie, Jaime and Caitlin learned—the past is repeated because you come to believe that what you learned as a child is true throughout the world. If you believe that abuse, whether physical, emotional or sexual, is a natural though repugnant state of being in a family, you accept that it may be unpleasant but inevitable. Violence, addictions, or the existence of other major dysfunctions within the family are always accompanied by chaos, whether it be the chaos of constant fighting, threats of violence, or the simple uncertainty of one's position in the family.

Someone who is raised in chaos is often unable to tolerate the peace of a quiet home, interpreting the absence of conflict as boring. Unconsciously, you recreate the atmosphere of the home in which you grew up, until you understand that is what you are doing. The real problem is that what you create is often worse than the original situation. At least in the family home, there was some semblance of love—even if it was not a healthy love. There is some bonding which occurs even from the most defective parent to her child, and at the same time, the child forms a total bond before she or he realizes that the home is dysfunctional. An infant can only record what it sees and hears; it cannot make value judgments about them. Someone who has tasted only lemons and vinegar has no conception of what 'sweet' is!

Marianne, Ellen, Leslie, Jaime and Caitlin were all born with the gifts of intellect, common sense and sensitivity, but these inborn capacities did not allow them to see beyond their early experiences. Their value systems were developed in homes that taught them they were stupid, dependent, unattractive, subject to the whims of their parents, targets for their parents' frustrations, and sexual objects rather than choice makers. They were taught to be inferior, subservient, grateful for the crumbs which were tossed to them, and they were taught that the world was a capricious and dangerous place. Worst of all, they were taught that they needed to become dependent upon a man to protect them. As it turned out, the man in whom they placed trust to protect them was the only one from whom they needed protection!

Each of the women whom you have met in this book came a different background; each of their lives evolved somewhat dissimilarly, but when they found themselves desperately reaching out for help, they all had one thing in common—the pain they had been enduring became so overpowering that they had to change the way they were living or risk extreme consequences. Ellen wasn't exaggerating when she said that her choice was to let go of her rage or die. Marianne was a reflex away from suicide the night her husband almost killed her. Her existence had stopped mattering to her. Leslie had escaped into her own world, and used drugs, alcohol and men to keep from feeling the desolation and desperation which abstinence forced her to confront. After three years of drug-free living, Caitlin had gone back to drugs to relieve the emotional pain which she actively continued to deny for some time. Jaime allowed a sick relationship to keep her life from having any meaning or direction. Her jealous, possessive, insecure boyfriend picked her clothes, dictated her makeup and hair style, and controlled the choices of the people she would engage in her social life.

Are You in an Abusive Situation?

How does a woman determine if she has a problem, and what are her choices for a solution? Seeking help through therapy is one choice for a large number of people. Therapy is not, however, a magic cure-all. In fact, for some people it does not provide solutions to problems or respite from them. Because I am a therapist, I write about people who have made positive use of therapy, but I am not recommending it as a universal panacea for all of the ills of the world.

Therapy is the proper answer when the individual cannot attain a workable solution simply by taking suggestions, or even by knowing an appropriate answer. Therapy is also appropriate when the individual desires to engage with a professional to seek a deeper self-understanding than could be obtained by any other means. There are numerous self-help groups as well, many of which have outstanding records of providing nurturance, identification and practical answers to individuals who face the kinds of life problems faced by the heroines in this book.

There is much of a positive nature to be learned from the examples of these five women. First, there is always hope. Second, there is no need to accept that you must remain in negative situations or relationships. Third, change, though always possible, is never accomplished without sacrifice. Moving to a new pattern of living required each woman to change her beliefs about herself and about the world around her. For example, Leslie began her process of change by developing a conditional trust in her therapist—the first person in her world who didn't victimize her, or get rejected by her because he didn't victimize her. The trust came slowly, but after a long period of testing and even setting up situations in which she could have been rejected, she began to generalize that if there was one trustworthy person in the world, perhaps there were others. It may be that Leslie needed a longer period of time to change her negative beliefs because she was somewhat older than the other women. An additional ten to fifteen years of negative living did much to harden Leslie and to cement her distrust, resignation and bitterness.

An important focus for writing this book is the hope that some of you will be able to gain an awareness that you are confronted with problems in relationships that can be solved. Once you recognize the nature of the problem, it is a much simpler task to find a means of developing a solution. The route you take toward that solution may not be the same as that taken by Marianne and the others about whom I have written. Perhaps, however, if there are some similarities between your situation and theirs, you may find benefit in the knowledge gained and conclusions reached by these women.

When you have beliefs which are negative, and your beliefs cause you to choose negative people, it is not apparent to you that what you are doing is not accidental. Some time ago, I met a woman who was complaining because she had been married four times—each time to an alcoholic who abused her. You couldn't produce those results by accident if you tried. I asked her to describe her father and she said, "He was an alcoholic—but don't get me wrong—he was a great guy." I won't go into detail, but needless to say, her father did beat her mother. So, she married four 'great guys' just like dear old dad!

How do you determine if you are in a situation which is abusive to you? There are several key questions which you may wish to ask so that you avoid a stereotyped answer such as, "But, I love him!" This problem has nothing to do with love. Every child starts off life loving his or her mother and father. In truth, there is almost nothing for which a child will not ultimately forgive a parent.

The crucial questions are:

- What do I want out of the relationships in my life?
- What are my personal goals and how many of them am I meeting?
- What is preventing me from attaining satisfactions in my life?
- If someone else were in my situation, what would be my advice to him or her?
- How do I feel about myself?
- How do the people closest to me treat me?
- To what lengths would I go to gain the acceptance of others?
- What am I worth as a human being?

If you feel that your life lacks some of the positive rewards you think you should be receiving, I would like you to try a little experiment. Find yourself a private space where you will not be disturbed for the next half hour or so. Then, write answers for each of the above questions in great detail. Leave enough space so that you can go back to them and add on to your answers. When you have finished, put your answers aside. We will return to them later in this chapter.

We have discussed abuse as a problem which prevents the victims from developing healthy relationships, even long after the abuse has stopped. When the abuse has been severe enough to leave the recipient with negative beliefs about herself and the world about her, she is likely to repeat the pattern or create an even worse situation. Perhaps it might be wise to spend some time discussing the elements of healthy relationships. To say simply that people shouldn't enter into unhealthy relationships does not define what it is that they might need to avoid in an unhealthy relationship, nor what constitutes a healthy one.

Achieving Genuine Intimacy

The ultimate goals of healthy persons would include the development of intimate relationships. The inability to do so can often be attributed to the inability of parents to demonstrate a capacity for intimacy to or around their children. What is intimacy? Some people think that it is sex. Yes, sex is an intimate act. It is intimate to share ones body with another person, but in many instances, your body is all that is shared through sex.

It is easy to understand how some women presented in this book came to confuse sex with love or intimacy. We all cry out for genuine intimacy—even when we are unable to define it. The need for connectedness to other human beings is so strong that when we are forced to live without it, we often seek inappropriate substitutes just to feel some sense of belonging to or with another person. Remember how Leslie wanted a man to whom she could cling. She wanted to absorb him. Leslie was never able to develop the trust in her childhood that is required to attain genuine intimacy, so she used constant sex to ward off her feelings of loneliness and emptiness. However, this was not true intimacy. The more she was drawn toward unfulfilling relationships, the more empty she became. The beginning of her journey to recovery did not occur until she let go of all her unsatisfying relationships and learned to trust others. In this way she could accept love and caring from people she allowed into her life instead of settling for sex and games with men who wanted only casual relationships.

Intimacy begins with a belief that the person whom you are permitting to enter into your life will not hurt you, and a willingness to reject from your life anyone who does attempt to hurt you, degrade you, belittle you, or lead you to believe that he or she is more important than you. The abused woman often does just the opposite. She will allow a man into her life only if he has the potential to hurt her in some manner, and she excludes from her life anyone who threatens to bring peace and joy. The 'wild one' is the familiar man. He is the image of her father (or mother). He is a swaggering, bullying, raging hulk (sometimes, not so much a physical hulk as an emotional portrait of one) or he is the smoldering mystery man. This one keeps his feelings hidden which allows the woman to fantasize what he 'must' feel for her. Through this fantasy, she is able to imagine that he is constantly offering protestations of eternal devotion.

In many cases, the man selected by the abused woman as a lover was probably himself abused as a child, which leads her to believe that she has an ally. In the beginning of the relationship, he appears to be the tower of strength for which she was looking all of her life. He is attentive to her, he tells her what she wants to hear; he is possessive of her, he knows 'simply everything;' and he tells her he loves her and will take care of her forever. This is what she dreamed of hearing all of her life. She had always felt so alone——so uncared for. Like all fairy tales, it is only after they decide to live happily ever after that the problems begin. Just when he should begin to feel that his dreams are all coming true, the tapes of his family scene begin replaying. "Men beat women when they don't 'obey' and I'm a man!" he reasons, unreasonably. Or, the abuse may be verbal rather than physical. "You stupid bitch, who the fuck do you think you are, talkin' back to me?" She is used to a family in which everybody screams at everybody, "Doesn't every family do that?" The merry-go-round goes round. Another cycle of abuse begins.

What would be the healthy alternative? Anybody can meet one abusive individual by accident, but a healthy person would not tolerate continued abuse from anyone. A healthy person values herself too highly. The scenario above would conclude quite differently. "If you don't behave yourself, I'm gonna punch your lights out," would be swiftly answered by, "If you ever raise your hand to me, you're going to jail and if you can't treat me with the respect I deserve, you are going to be alone." Yes, healthy people have disputes——even arguments. However, they do not have screaming matches; they do not raise their hands to each other; and they do not engage in name calling!

Intimacy is a two-sided process. It involves giving and receiving at the deepest levels. It necessitates the existence of trust so that you can be open to giving and receiving. The basic components of intimacy are mutual love and acceptance, with the emphasis upon 'mutual.' The need to give and receive love and acceptance is deep, and most probably inborn. Think of an infant giving unconditional love to its parents and hopefully receiving the same in return. Think of the level of disappointment when nothing is given. Young children initially care little if a stranger doesn't like them. They will have tantrums in restaurants——who cares what 'they' think about 'us?' But children do their darndest to please mom and dad—even to the extent that they will fulfill the parents' most negative prophesies about them. "Take my word for it, Harold, Jimmy is going to come to no good in this world!" Little Jimmy, wanting only to please his mother, comes to no good in this world!

Sometimes, children learn only one side of intimacy—usually that side is the giving side. Think of Marianne or Jaime, both of whom appeared normal and healthy. Neither used drugs or alcohol to feel better and they each accepted what the world offered without complaint. They were able to give full measure of love to a man. However, each picked a man who could not return their healthy feelings. Each picked a man who needed her to fill vast voids in his life. She was not allowed to be herself, but rather a symbol which fulfilled his needs. When you are given a role to play rather than being accepted for who you are, you are not in a relationship—you are a hostage. You are required to play a game in which the rules change constantly and the outcome is meant to satisfy another person, often at your expense. To ascertain whether your situation resembles this example, it is necessary to determine the needs which are being met in the situation, and the needs which are being denied.

The first steps in the development of intimacy can be accomplished while you are alone in a room and not involved in a relationship, because in order to attain intimacy, you must feel that you are worthy of intimacy, and that intimacy exists in this world. Remember how Ellen, beginning with the simple, yet profound two words, "I am!" came to believe that she was special and had a right to create a healthy life for herself? She needed to begin at the most basic level—her right to exist. Before you are ready to seek intimate relationships, you need to know who you are and what you are worth as a human

Solutions

being. So, you begin with yourself. You need to begin by developing some ground rules which you will use to evaluate yourself. In order to begin to build a foundation for developing intimate relationships, you may want to take the following steps to form an appraisal of your stand in relation to the development of intimacy:

Begin with an honest self-appraisal. Assess your own strengths, talents, interests and abilities. If you are having difficulty finding answers, ask someone who knows you to give you his or her honest appraisal. You might be pleasantly surprised to learn how many positive answers you can come up with if you really work at this task.

Pursue your interests rather than sitting and waiting for something to happen. It is through self-fulfillment that you begin to become aware of your potential. Reawaken the dreams of your youth. Try something you always wanted to do but put off. We are all guilty of that. Doing something pleasant makes us feel better about ourselves and serves as a needed reward for all of the difficult things we have to do to survive.

Become comfortable with yourself. Be your own best friend. Accept the fact that having no relationship in your life is better than a sick relationship. Remember that negative relationships always take more from you than they give to you. All of the women you met in this book had to remove themselves from relationships for a period of time so that they would simply not continue the negative pattern to which they were accustomed.

Accept that you have little control over whom you meet. Don't prejudge people or set artificial goals about meeting someone at a particular time and place. Instead, go to places where the kind of people whom you would like to meet are likely to be. For instance, if you use a bar as the place where you will meet people, what kind of people are you most likely to meet? The answer is obvious—you will meet people who find drinking more important than people do at many other places you might choose. The majority of people who marry alcoholics met them in a bar. That is not to say that everyone in the bar is an alcoholic, but the odds are much greater than at a museum, or a meeting of some activist organization.

In assessing others for potential relationships, give the highest priority to qualities which are necessary to the development of intimacy. Eye color, height, weight, and charm may be stimulants to the game of sex but they produce nothing in the development of enduring intimacy. If your goal is to develop a relationship that will meet your deepest needs for attachment, you will find that a relationship that focuses exclusively upon physical attraction will wear thin very quickly. Caitlin always looked for the 'macho' guy who would take care of her. She was attracted by his physicality, but was later repulsed by his behavior.

Success in developing intimacy depends upon an ability to communicate effectively and compromise fairly. The highest level of intimacy is a relationship in which both parties accept each other and admire each other for their special qualities, rather than attempting to change the other person into a desired image. When Marianne gained a real sense of herself, she was able to tell Dan that there was no place in her life for him despite the fact that she loved him. She knew that her needs would never be important to him and that he would always see the world with himself at the center.

Solutions

Success in maintaining a positive sense of self is a continued belief about your own worth. Define your worth yourself. Do not become dependent upon another person to define it for you. Jaime allowed her sick boyfriend to determine how much she was worth at any given time. He doled out her 'worth' to meet his own needs. When he felt secure in his relationship with her, he allowed her to have little worth so that she would always be subservient to him. However, when his behavior became so irresponsible that she was ready to walk away from him, he would profess his eternal love, need and admiration for her. This was just enough to keep her coming back for more!

Life is based upon a set of rules which are constantly being revised by reality. We learn through experience. Perhaps it would not be an exaggeration to call children little scientists. Like scientists, they observe everything around them and eventually draw conclusions from their observations. These conclusions become 'shoulds,' and 'supposed to's.' For instance, Marianne was taught that a wife is 'supposed to' respect and love her husband. As a child, she was 'supposed to' keep the family secrets. These rules allowed her dysfunctional family to maintain its major dysfunctions—alcoholism and violence. She was taught that she should obey her parents, even when their decisions were arbitrary and capricious.

The assumptions made by the women in this book created gaps in their ability to function as adults in a difficult world. Where flexibility was needed, they had rigidity. Where they needed to be able to make relative judgments, they knew only absolutes. The world isn't either/or. There is a broad spectrum of choices, each of which has some positives and some negatives. Until you learn to evaluate all of the qualities of a person or situation, you are likely to attain flawed results.

In order to function effectively, especially in the difficult realm of relationships, it is necessary to possess a set of rules which are effective. In order to develop rational rules, it is necessary to begin with a statement of healthy needs. At the most basic level of existence, everyone needs to give and receive unconditional love and acceptance. Whether those needs can be fully realized in an imperfect world is questionable, so perhaps the first rule of healthy living might be:

I will seek to maximize my opportunities to give and receive unconditional love and acceptance.

There are conditions which I will place upon my willingness to enter into or remain in any relationship. I do this not only for my protection, but for the real benefit of the other person. I accept the following as principles by which I will live:

- I would rather be alone than be in a relationship which undermines my good feelings about myself.

- I will not give love to someone who cannot or will not give love to me.

- I will not make excuses for anyone, or accept excuses from anyone for his or her inconsiderateness of my real needs.

- I will not give love to someone who has no love for himself or herself.

- I accept, with no exceptions, that I am worthy to give and receive love, respect and acceptance.

Solutions

269

- I believe that my needs are genuine and reasonable.

- I have love and respect for myself regardless of what anyone says about me.

- I would enjoy and appreciate the love, acceptance and respect of every person, but I do not need it to have self-love and self-respect.

- I have feelings and accept that both the positive and negative feelings are real and need honest, healthy expression.

- I am responsible in the expression of my feelings.

- I trust my feelings and have the ability to act upon them in an adult manner.

- I will not enter into relationships which do not meet my healthy needs.

- I will not expect others to be aware of my needs. It is my responsibility to communicate my needs to others.

- I have a trust in the worthiness of others. I will not prejudge anyone.

- I am willing to accept the consequences of my actions. I will not lay blame for my own short-comings upon another person.

- I can accept that my feelings may be one-sided and I am willing to accept that you have the right to reject me for your own reasons.

- I am willing to listen to your opinion of me, but I will not allow a lifetime of effort to build myself into a healthy, worthwhile person to be invalidated by your opinion.

The maxims which I have listed do not by themselves offset a lifetime of abuse. When you are belittled regularly, you come to believe that there must be truth in what was said. Ellen's father began calling her a slut when she was twelve. By the time she was fourteen, she was living down to his estimation of her. He also called her fat, ugly and stupid. Though she was a perfectly proportioned, brilliant and astonishingly beautiful twenty year old, she continued to see herself as fat, ugly and stupid. No matter what was said, she was unable to invalidate her father's messages—until she was allowed to invalidate her father's right to make value judgments upon her.

When she changed her belief from "My dad said it. Parents are always right," to, "How dare he!" Ellen began to see her own value. She learned that she was intelligent. School validated that. She learned that she possessed worth to others. Her group validated that. She learned that she had virtue. The confidence to say no to men validated that.

She can't seem to shake the belief that she is fat. Some values are burned into the psyche at such a vulnerable time that they are difficult to purge regardless of how certain you are that they are untrue. Perhaps at the age of twelve, which is a particularly sensitive age for a girl, Ellen was going through puberty and was frightened by her changing proportions. Her parents never taught her about the facts of life. She was left to learn these things on the streets, and at twenty, was ignorant of her own reproductive physiology.

Solutions

Why her father did such terrible things to his precious child will never be fully known. His motives are not really important unless he is the one desirous of change. All Ellen needs to know is that father doesn't know best, and that she needs to use a new frame of reference to judge her worth in the world.

Why is it so difficult to change values, even when you realize that the values which you have are ineffective? Values are developed over a long period of time, and the roots of the values date back into childhood to a time when our memories are most vague. They were taught not as verbal rules, but through examples. Therefore, we truly do not know where our values originated. It is possible to trace the origin of values through a process such as therapy, but it is not a simple task, and many of the conclusions are really suppositions because it is not possible to remember everything which went into creating the value.

Values are the rules which underlie attitudes. Attitudes allow us to make generalizations about people and situations. Caitlin's values included a belief that all men were violent and used women sexually. Her attitude resulted in rejection of all men who didn't fulfill her stereotype. This was not really rejection to her. These non-violent, gentle and caring men could not exist, therefore they were not to be trusted. The sullen, sarcastic, angry man was flying his true colors and at least she knew how to handle him! If he ended up hurting her, well, that was what she expected from him.

What are some of the specific effects of abuse? With what negative feelings do abused children need to deal as adults? What are some of the gaps in their learning which do not allow them to make healthy choices as adults?

Probably the most prevalent belief which prevents a victim from getting out of the trap in which she finds herself is a generalized distrust. This distrust is reinforced through her continuing pattern of developing negative relationships. When a woman meets with enough defeat, eventually she comes to believe that there is no hope. Caitlin, for instance, could pick only the most unhealthy men because her early experiences provided her with absolute certainty that there was no other kind of man in the world.

The early experiences of all of the women in this book taught them that they had little worth. The way in which their parents treated them created a feeling in themselves that they were worthless and helpless. Therefore, there was little sense in attempting to accomplish anything in life because it would only end up being taken away. Leslie was an honors graduate from college, yet she had never worked in her field. She chose to be dependent upon family and the men she was invoved with rather than take control of her life. It was not that she didn't have the ability. She didn't believe that she did. Even after a year away from drugs and alcohol, she worked only part-time at a far smaller salary than she could have commanded had she tried to assert herself.

A person who feels badly about herself has no fear of failure, but rather has a fear of success. Failure is something with which she has lived all of her life. She is intimate with failure. It is a fear of success which throws her into a panic. Since she does not believe that she is worthy of success, moving up even slightly in any area of life will only result in further disappointment.

The fear of rejection was another major roadblock to change for all of the women. They had suffered the most extreme kinds of rejection early in life. They had been abused, neglected, abandoned, molested, and most important, their very right to be themselves was totally denigrated. Marianne was never praised for her many accomplishments, but she faced unrelenting punishment for the most minor transgression—the worst of which was being there when her parents were drunk and angry. When you possess an unrealistic fear of rejection, you conduct your life in such a manner that you can never suffer real rejection. This is accomplished in two ways—both blockades to the development of real intimacy.

The first way of avoiding rejection is to do the rejecting before anyone can reject you. Leslie's method of conducting her life was to reject any man who fell in love with her. Of course, she created the situations which assured that men would fall in love with her. As soon as they did, she would reject them harshly. The second means of preventing rejection is never to allow yourself to have a relationship with anyone who shows evidence of caring for you. In that way, you get only rejection. There is no difference between being in a relationship to being out of one. Leslie would fall in love only with men who did not love her. In this manner, the rejection which she expected in any case was an integral part of the relationship itself and reconfirmed the belief that she would always be rejected. To make the game complete, she would always be the one to terminate a relationship, thereby convincing herself that she was never rejected.

Another feeling common to most victims is unrealistic guilt. Each of the women was made to feel that everything that went wrong in the family was her fault. Marianne was made responsible for her parents' anger and pain. She learned through this early training and the beatings which accompanied it that she was 'responsible' for the beatings which were administered by her husband. This belief almost led to her death. It was only when she denied the right of anyone to blame her for their own problems that she was able to let go of her guilt and the destructive relationship in which the guilt was being perpetuated.

Accompanying the guilt which is imposed upon the victim is a corresponding responsibility to keep the family secrets. Loyalty to the family is placed above all else because if the secrets were to be revealed, the family would be placed in a negative light by the community. So, Leslie put up with years of beatings, as did Ellen, Marianne and Caitlin. Caitlin put up with conditions of involuntary servitude, neglect, and sexual abuse as well. Jaime's family was always in a state of financial chaos. She never knew if there would be furniture in the house, or heat. As a teen, she was often the only source of money for food for the family. She was the one who had to deal with the bill collectors while her father and mother were gambling it away. Her irresponsible sisters also leaned on her for help even though she was the youngest. These women never told. Even after they entered therapy, they apologized for being hurt by their families.

It is most difficult to develop intimate relationships when you have never seen one. None of the women saw intimacy between her parents. Each learned that couples fight, belittle each other, and behave in ways that bring pain to their partners. Sex is used to make up after fights and to gain advantages. Children are supposed to behave perfectly, perform tasks, and if there are any rewards, they are as capricious as punishments. Is it any wonder, then, that when the women in the stories grew up, they chose partners who offered them the same instability as they experienced in their parental homes?

If you don't like your life where it is, you need to begin with a belief that change is possible, regardless of the circumstances you have endured in your life. Change is more than a word. Simply saying, "I'm going to change," leads only to frustration. In order to change, it is first necessary to know two things: first, you need to know from what you need to change, and second you need to know to what you desire to change. That is why it is so important to understand what it is that keeps you from being who you want to be. Knowing you shouldn't allow yourself to be abused, doesn't stop the abuse unless you believe that ending the abuse is more important than financial security, love or anything else which may be used as an excuse for perpetuating the abuse.

Most excuses cover the real reasons which underlie them. Marianne 'loved' Dan. She didn't want to 'break up' her family. Dan helped her when she needed him, and it was her obligation to help him because he was sick, not bad. The real reason was something much deeper. She believed that violence was a fact of family life and it was her duty to stand by her husband no matter what. After all, that is what her mother did through decades of physical abuse. How many times had she heard her father say to her mother, "If you didn't make me so angry, I wouldn't have to hit you?"

Once you accept that change is possible, the next step is the most difficult. In order to develop new behaviors which are more effective, you must first let go of the sick values, attitudes and behaviors which are contributing to your pain. Much of what needs to be changed can be determined from the outside in. Look at the behavior. If it is not producing positive results, you work backward toward, "What do I believe so that this behavior persists?"

Assume that nothing is accidental. We generally receive from life about what we think we are worth. This is not to say that you get exactly what you want all of the time, but our major accomplishments are a reflection of our estimation of our own self-estimation. Whom we choose as a partner, what kind of work we do, how we value our health, even what styles we wear are dictated by our internal image of who we are. Do we dress for comfort? Do we choose our mate because he will impress our crowd? Do we choose a career because we feel that it is the best we can accomplish?

This might be a good time to return to the questions which I asked you to answer earlier in this chapter. Now that we have discussed in greater detail some of the reasons why women who were abused as children have such difficulties attaining satisfactions in major areas of existence later in life, perhaps you will want to add to or change some of your answers. Some of the questions are much more complex than their initial appearance would lead you to believe. They ask you to express your inner self. They do not ask what you have accomplished, or your social status. They ask you to evaluate the true measure of your humanity. They ask not that you measure yourself in comparison to others, but rather that you allow yourself to express your longings—to be complete, to be worthy of the caring of others, and to be of value to others. Every child is born perfect. It is only the battering that life may give us that leads us to the belief that we are flawed. It is our capacity to have feelings and the right to express those feelings that makes us human.

If the road you are travelling is not the road which you would choose, it may be necessary to accept that the road for which you are looking is not even pictured on your map. You cannot be expected to know what you were neither taught nor exposed to. However, true wisdom is not the knowledge of everything. It is simply the knowledge that there are things you do not know. True strength is the willingness to turn to someone more knowledgeable than yourself to obtain new information. A flaw common to people who really have no desire for change is to seek advice only from those who have less knowledge than they do. In this manner, it is possible never to learn anything! Until Marianne was ready to hear something new, she had to reject her friend Bridget.

Marianne went through three stages before she succeeded in opening herself to new beliefs. First, she denied that there was a problem. Second, she allowed herself to complain about the problem. Even then, she was unable to accept the possibility that she could change her situation because her beliefs did not allow it. It was only in the third stage, when she let go of the old beliefs and said, "No more!" that she was able to hear what her friend said. Only then did she begin listening to other voices which helped her change her beliefs. These new beliefs were effective in helping her move her life forward.

Letting go allows you to open to the possibility of moving on. Accepting that you have the right to change and developing new beliefs about your worth is simply the groundwork preceding change. The most difficult task lies ahead. In order to truly have a belief in yourself, the belief must be put into practice. If you are worthy of love and respect, a new contract must be established with those persons who are bringing pain into your life. The new contract calls for changes in how you will be treated and establishes the consequences that will result should your demands be rejected.

You are not asking for anything unreasonable. It is not unreasonable to expect that you will never be hit. It is not unreasonable to expect that you will not be the target of verbal abuse. It is not unreasonable to expect that if you have a partner in life, responsibilities will be shared. Of course, the same expectations which you place on your partner hold true for you as well. You need to accept that part of the responsibility for the chaos in your life is upon you. Because you believed that life was supposed to be chaotic, you contributed to the chaos. It takes two to have an argument, though it often takes only one to be violent. In many instances, however, even the violence was two-sided.

I have a philosophy which has helped me to keep my own priorities ordered and, hopefully positive: "I am responsible for myself, but at the same time, I am responsible to everyone with whom I have contact." I take this to mean that I will do nothing to hurt myself or allow anyone to hurt me, but at the same time, I am also responsible not only to not hurt others, but to act in such a way that what I do benefits others as well as myself. This philosophy is simply an ideal toward which I can strive. It is not a set of rules which can be followed to consummation. However, positive philosophies are necessary for positive outcomes. If I believe in my own worthiness as well as the worthiness of others, I am more likely to attain positive outcomes in many of my experiences and at the same time, avoid producing negatives in the lives of others. It lends a balance. It is sensible and selfless at the same time.

If you have read this book because you are not content with your life, perhaps the time has arrived when you should consider how much you need to do in order to attain the change you desire? Too often, people will read books and expect that change will occur simply by attaining the knowledge contained therein. I wish it were that simple. Even the best information obtainable can do little more than point out that there are specific areas which you can change if you choose to do so.

Solutions

If you have come to believe that it is necessary for you to change, I hope that some of the revelations discovered by Caitlin, Jaime, Marianne, Ellen and Leslie enabled you to identify both with the events and their process of discovery. However, knowledge is only the first step in change. As I pointed out to Leslie, "Being hurt is like swallowing fish hooks. They hurt going in, they hurt remaining in, and they can hurt like hell coming out. However, you can't feel better until you get them out." Sometimes, the first stage of healing is sharing your tears with another person who is in a position to help you. Complaining about pain doesn't lead to change. It simply provides a little space for a new 'fish hook' to be inserted! As Marianne said, "The cycle of abuse is like a merry-go-round. It only stops when you get off!"

The cycle continues. The names change. Marianne, Ellen, Caitlin, Jaime and Leslie have moved on. Their lives are ordered and their growth continues. Their lives are far from perfect. Life can still be a struggle for each of them. Marianne is now raising two pre-teens and that is hard work for the best parent. Caitlin is learning how to relate to the healthiest man she has ever known, but both of them come from dysfunctional families and sometimes, their old tapes play in spite of their continued vigilance and deep devotion to each other. Leslie is trying to make her career and her children her first priorities. Ellen is going to college and supporting herself. Sometimes, it is lonely. She feels that it will be a long time before she is ready for a committed relationship, but she is not yet twenty-one and has all the time in the world. And Jaime is in a healthy relationship with a man who cherishes her and has a positive sense of his own worth. She is in college and has decided that she wants to be a teacher. She called the other day to tell me that she received—I told her earned—straight A's in her first semester at college.

Now, there is Lisa. She is twenty-one and looks like fourteen—except for the terrible toll that cocaine has taken upon her frail body. She is the child of an alcoholic father who beat her mother. She has a sister who shoots heroin and her best friend recently died of an overdose of drugs at age twenty-two. She wants to change and doesn't know how. Under all the drugs is a powerful intellect and a wellspring of deep feelings yearning for expression. She joined the women's group which I conduct. Last week, one of the women in the group held her and rocked her like a baby when she was expressing her pain. "I can't stay here," she said. "I don't want to let you all down, and I don't think I can stop takin' drugs yet. I want to, but I'm not strong like you all are."

"You listen," said Cindy, who just four months earlier had been drinking herself into oblivion, and who had at that time said she would never accept help—she had to do it herself—"Don't you give up. You hear? You are beautiful and special and, and I love you, Lisa." They held each other and cried for the pain of the past and present, and the hope of the future.

Sometimes, I hear voices . . .